ANABAPTIST PREACHING

Published in association with the
Preaching Institute of Eastern Mennonite Seminary

ANABAPTIST PREACHING

A Conversation Between
Pulpit,
Pew,

Bible

Edited by
David B. Greiser and Michael A. King

Foreword by Brian McLaren

Cascadia
Publishing House
the new name of Pandora Press U.S.
Telford, Pennsylvania

copublished with
Herald Press
Scottdale, Pennsylvania

Cascadia Publishing House orders, information, reprint permissions:
contact@CascadiaPublishingHouse.com
1-215-723-9125
126 Klingerman Road, Telford PA 18969
www.CascadiaPublishingHouse.com

Library of Congress Cataloguing-in-Publication Data
Anabaptist preaching : a conversation between pulpit, pew, and Bible / [Edited
by] David B. Greiser and Michael A King.
    p. cm.
Includes bibliographical references and index.
ISBN 1-931038-19-8 (alk. paper)
    1. Preaching. I. Greiser, David B., 1955- II. King, Michael A. 1954-

BV4211.3.A53 2003
251'.0088'243--dc21
                                                              2003051674

12 11 10 09 08 07 06 05   12 11 10 9 8 7 6 5 4 3

CONTENTS

Foreword

*A*lthough I did not grow up Anabaptist, I am a confessed sympathizer. When I was a boy, I did want to be a Baptist, but not Ana- (mostly because I had never met one). My desire was to become a Baptist of the Southern variety. I had no idea what being a Southern Baptist meant, other than this: my Baptist friend attended a church that had "ice cream socials." Meanwhile my church (of a non-denomination that will remain nameless) did nothing of the sort, not because it had anything against ice cream, but because (I imagine) ice cream socials might lead to "the social gospel," which, being (in)tense fundamentalists, we wanted no part of. That gives you an idea of my own background (and my ongoing need for counseling).

Anyway, it also suggests the kinds of problems all movements or denominations face over time, including Anabaptists: The original conditions in which the movement arose change to new conditions, the original problems to which the movement addressed itself either are solved or are eclipsed by greater problems, the original errors against which the movement reacted give way or disappear, leaving the movement pushing against something which no longer exists. As a result, the movement becomes known for odd distinctives, superficial uniquenesses, or esoteric (but firmly held) positions on the burning issues of yesteryear. In short, a once-august movement is seen by others (and maybe itself) as being about ice cream socials (or lack thereof).

One might conclude from this analysis that these entities formerly known as movements and now known as denominations should just go away or shut down or shut up. But that is not the case, in my opinion. Because most if not all of these entities have either accidentally or on purpose or by the grace of God or surely all three developed wonderful treasures too . . . spiritual treasures of insights and practices and forms of community and perspectives on mission which, were they to go extinct, would be a loss no less tragic than any biological extinction.

I truly believe this: that each heritage, including and especially the Anabaptist heritage, has precious treasures that it is often unaware of. While it is proud of distinctives X, Y, and Z; and while it is zealously defending positions Q, R, and S; its real treasures turn out to be F, G, and H, characteristics it hardly knows about itself.

So here I am, a friendly outsider who would now much rather be Ana- than Southern Baptist any day (with or without ice cream, no offense to Southern Baptists intended). Perhaps I am (accidentally but surely by the grace of God) well placed to encourage my Anabaptist friends to figure out what F, G, and H are, especially in light of the peculiar times we are in and the peculiar history of the Anabaptist tribe. As well, because I have been so kindly treated by my Anabaptist sisters and brothers, and because they have helped me see their treasures, perhaps I am well-placed to invite other non-Anabaptists to enjoy the same hospitality I have enjoyed in the house of the Radical Reformation, and to savor, with me, the unique treasures found there.

This book presents many of these treasures, surprising treasures to people who have only an "ice cream social" understanding of Anabaptists.

For example, a lot of people will be surprised to find Anabaptists reflecting on Gadamer and Ricouer. But they shouldn't be too surprised. True, the Radical Reformation has all along been united by a gospel ethic rather than a systematic theology, which has helped keep them less visible in intellectual and theological circles than, say, Presbyterians. But their emphasis on gospel ethic often produces in them a largeness of heart and a stability of mind which make them less nervous in the presence of new ideas than many other Protestants (especially folk of a fundamentalist turn). So, Gadamer and Ricouer fit after all.

Similarly, the Anabaptist emphasis on a gospel ethic naturally leads to a special sensitivity regarding the power issues inherent in preaching. This sensitivity creates a natural but to some, surprising, synergy between Anabaptists and, say, feminists thinkers or postcolonial theologians (who pick up themes earlier addressed as part of liberation theology). It also inspires a special concern for integrity regarding rhetorical coercion or manipulation. This rhetorical nonviolence would revolutionize many combative Christian communities (how's that for an oxymoron) that sanctify verbal pugilism. The house of the Radical Reformation is a natural place for these sensitivities to season and find solid expression.

For these reasons and more, I'm honored to encourage both not-yet-Anabaptists and Anabaptists to value this book because Anabaptists know things that all of us need as we slide or run or crawl or are dragged into the postmodern world. While virtually all the rest of the Protestant traditions in the United States, for example, have been baptized with either Republican or Democratic waters, Anabaptists have understood that Jesus' not-of-this-world kingdom is active and alive in this world. This is why they have understood following Jesus as a way of life that looks on nationalism and its politics from a higher perspective. In our post-world (postmodern, post-Christendom, post-9/11, and so forth, and so forth), this higher perspective must become contagious, or we're all in a lot of trouble.

So I hope and pray that this book will succeed and Anabaptist preaching will continue to improve. I hope this will happen so that Anabaptists will be strengthened in their mission and so that the rest of the Christian community will hear more and more about what Anabaptists are thinking and saying—about discipleship, about community, about the land, about peace, about mission, about the gospel. May God give the Anabaptists grace to speak wisely and well, and may God give all of us ears to listen.

—*Brian McLaren, Laurel, Maryland, is a pastor and speaker as well as author of* A New Kind of Christian, Finding Faith, The Church on the Other Side, *and more.*

Editors' Preface

*T*he chapters that follow signal a new day for preaching in an Anabaptist (and Mennonite) context. Thirty years ago we would have been hard pressed to find two, let alone fourteen, Anabaptists interested in shaping a volume on the preaching ministry from a scholarly perspective. As editors we are pleased to present the thoughtful reflection of this collection of scholars, most of whom have not previously published on the topic.

Our hope is that this book may serve several purposes. First, we envision its use as a text in preaching classes at Anabaptist-related as well as Mennonite colleges, seminaries, and conference-based or regional training programs. When used alongside the more standard "Introduction to Preaching" volumes, this collection can enable students to reflect on issues especially crucial in preaching to Anabaptist congregations—such as the place of the Old Testament, the role of the congregation in preaching, preaching within the worship context, preaching doctrine, and so forth. Second, we hope the book will help seasoned preachers to think through some perennial preaching issues and approach their task more reflectively and intentionally. Third, the book can offer a window into the Anabaptist homiletical world to homileticians and others who are interested in preaching and rhetoric in general.

We do want to recognize the complexities of speaking of *Anabaptist* preaching at a time of increasing awareness not only that Anabaptism can be seen as having multiple roots but also that today various denominations see themselves as Anabaptist. To some extent this book represents that diversity, given that authors from a variety of Anabaptist denominational streams are included, but (amid awareness of our own Mennonite bias) we do not claim that the book comprehensively incorporates either all Anabaptist groups or the many preaching topics that could be addressed from an Anabaptist perspective.

It is fitting that a book on Anabaptist preaching, like the preaching event itself, should be a communal undertaking. We thank the community of persons who made this project possible, starting with the Preaching Institute of Eastern Mennonite Seminary. As a member of the Preaching Institute advisory council, Michael participated in discussions of Institute vision and needs, including brainstorming how to find or generate Anabaptist-related preaching resources to be used in Institute training as well as more broadly. Also significant was the fact that David and Michael, both pastoring congregations in Franconia Conference, a regional denominational body based in southeastern Pennsylvania, became aware of each other's preaching visions through taking in preaching seminars led by the other. Thus we are grateful to James M. Lapp, conference pastor in Franconia Conference who invited us to offer preaching seminars as well as to Ervin Stutzman and Mark Wenger, Preaching Institute leaders who, along with advisory council members, helped shape the vision for this book as well as generate funds for it.

On a more personal level, our thanks go, most notably, to our spouses, Anita (married to Dave) and Joan (married to Michael). We are grateful to our adult and nearly adult children, Hope and Aaron on Dave's side and Kristy, Katie, and Rachael on Michael's side. By tuning into their dads' preaching when they thought it worked and tuning it out other times, they taught their fathers the power of preaching and the power of listeners to keep preachers humble.

We are grateful also to each other, since we brought complementary gifts to this project. Dave, with more specialized training in homiletics, preaching-related teaching assignments at Eastern Baptist Theological Seminary, and colleagues and friends in the community of homileticians, brought particular awareness of current preaching theory. Michael, with more generalized training in rhetoric and communication as well as years of experience as editor and publisher, brought more technical book-developing skills. The teamwork was rewarding.

Finally we must thank the congregations who have sometimes benefited (we hope) from our preaching, have endured our failings, and have provided a training ground for our growth as preachers.

—*David B. Greiser, Telford, Pennsylvania*
  Michael A. King, Telford, Pennsylvania

Eastern Mennonite Seminary Preaching Institute Preface

*T*he Preaching Institute at Eastern Mennonite Seminary is privileged to help sponsor this book on Anabaptist preaching. The Preaching Institute serves preachers who desire to increase their communication skills. We believe that the present volume makes a specific contribution to that end.

The Preaching Institute reaches out from the seminary to help local conferences and congregations. We share in the seminary's overall purpose, which is stated as follows: *Eastern Mennonite Seminary equips men and women to grow as disciples of Jesus Christ, prepared to lead the church in mission with passion and integrity. As a community of disciples, we are humbled by God's call, formed in Christ, transformed by the Holy Spirit, and empowered to serve with knowledge, wisdom and grace.*

The Anabaptist Christian tradition has vitally shaped our purpose, particularly our vision for disciple-making. It has also shaped our vision for preaching, which we have summarized in the following phrases:

Men and women
as servants of the Word

empowered by the Holy Spirit
proclaiming the gospel of Jesus Christ
amid the worshiping community of God's people,
co-creating with listeners the meaning of God's message,
the power and presence of God's reign,
with justice and mercy for all.

The third-to-last line above is echoed in part of the current book title—"a conversation between pulpit, pew and Bible." We believe that listeners as well as preachers help to shape the meaning of God's message for a particular time. This may happen in different ways, as June Alliman Yoder asserts in her chapter for this book.

I highlight June here because her insights sparked particular enthusiasm in Stephanie Bartsch, a student of mine who was wrestling with her call to preach. As part of an assignment in my preaching class, Stephanie read a preview of June's chapter. About the same time, she received an invitation to become a co-pastor with her husband of an urban congregation. Stephanie hopes to form a circle of people in the congregation who can help to create her sermons. The group will study the Bible and draw relevant lessons for Christian living. Stephanie believes this activity will keep her sermons relevant. It will also help group members to grow in Christian discipleship. She hopes to offer different people the opportunity of participation over time, so that she can encourage Christian formation throughout the whole congregation.

Not all preachers will be as enthused as Stephanie about engaging congregational members in the preparation of a sermon. But our hope is that all of the many preachers we expect to study this book will find a chapter or chapters able to generate for their settings the type of enthusiasm Stephanie experienced in applying June's chapter to her context.

Although preachers studying this book alone should find rewards, we also hope many readers will test the book's insights in communal contexts such as we encourage Preaching Institute students to participate in. Nearly all preachers, for example, will benefit from congregational feedback regarding the sermons they've preached. One of the most notable features of the Preaching Institute is our facilitation of Lay Listener Groups as a means of gathering congregational feedback for preachers. While preachers tend to engage in this activity with some trepidation, they commonly cite it as one of their best learning experiences. It represents a lived form of the conversation between pulpit, pew, and Bible this book envisions.

The Advisory Council of the Preaching Institute engages in vigorous conversation about preaching. In one of our more animated discussions, we agreed that good preaching has the following characteristics. It is—

- Expository (grounded in the biblical text)
- Relevant (speaking to contemporary hearers)
- Inspiring (engendering hope through judgment and grace)
- Prophetic (delivering a word from the Lord)
- Communal (co-creating with listeners the meaning of God's message)
- Evangelical (proclaiming God's good news)
- Charismatic (empowered and directed by the Holy Spirit)
- Invitational (calling people to follow Jesus in the world), and
- Captivating (holding people's attention)

We hope *Anabaptist Preaching* can help both preachers and listeners to achieve this kind of preaching in the church today.

—*Ervin Stutzman, Harrisonburg, Virginia*
Director, Eastern Mennonite Seminary Preaching Institute

ANABAPTIST PREACHING

Chapter 1

What Exactly Is Anabaptist-Mennonite Preaching? A Nod to the Ancestors

David B. Greiser

With all of the publishing in the field of homiletics in the last thirty years, it may be necessary to justify a book on preaching with such a specialized focus. Why a separate volume on Anabaptist preaching? Is there anything specific that distinguishes preaching in Anabaptist faith communities from preaching in other faith communities? Is there a uniquely Anabaptist hermeneutic or rhetorical strategy? If so, are these elements significant enough to justify an entire volume?

The authors of the following chapters obviously believe that the answer to the last question, at least, is affirmative. Before considering their claims, let's explore broadly what we know about preaching in Anabaptist history, how it developed and changed, and how it later came to be practiced in North American Mennonite churches.

First, some personal history. I heard two very different kinds of preaching while I was growing up in the 1960s. Until I was fourteen, my main source for sermons was my home church—Grace Mennonite, a General Conference congregation in Lansdale, Pennsylvania. The General Conference churches, in my part of the country, arose in the nine-

teenth century as a modernizing movement among Mennonites.[1] And
the Mennonites, in their various groupings, are themselves one branch
among the various groups tracing their roots back to the sixteenth-cen-
century Anabaptists. Modern styles of dress, church music accompanied
by instruments, and modern modes of pastoral training came to be affirmed in General Conference churches. The pastors of my church were
mostly trained in evangelical Bible institutes and Protestant seminaries
such as Philadelphia College of Bible, Dallas Theological Seminary,
Prairie Bible Institute, Taylor University, and Princeton Seminary. Their
sermons were well-prepared, delivered from notes or a manuscript, and
rather polished, rhetorically speaking. Often rooted in Paul's epistles,
they dealt with themes like justification, personal salvation, prayer, and
verbally sharing one's faith with others. Sometimes there were public invitations to come forward to make a commitment to Christ or to rededi-
cate one's life to Christ. I do not recall sermons on what I later came to
understand were uniquely Anabaptist themes like peace, community, or
simplicity. Of course, as a teenager I was not always listening!

At age fourteen I entered Christopher Dock Mennonite High
School, an "Old" Mennonite school which featured daily chapel services
at which attendance was required. For a while I found chapel a daily exercise in culture shock. On my first day of school the chapel speaker (introduced as a minister at Franconia Mennonite Church) wore what appeared to me to be an odd black nehru-type jacket. He seemed to have
done no advance preparation on his oration. His comments on the Bible
roamed the canon, from Genesis to Revelation. He quoted lengthy passages of poetry and verses of hymns from memory. If there was an outline or an arrangement for his sermon, I could not discern what it was. It
was preaching unlike any I had ever heard before!

In subsequent chapel services, few of the ministers were as animated
as this first man, but most were equally unpolished. Most carried a
strong sense of personal humility into the pulpit.[2] They frequently
spoke about the way of peace and nonresistance (with extra urgency, I
recall, during those Vietnam War years). They talked about simplicity,
about nonconformity to the world in matters of lifestyle, and about
hearing and responding to God's call through the church.

The dissonance created in my mind by my conflicting experiences
of church and school was probably the genesis of my search for an answer to the question "Is there a specifically 'Mennonite' kind of preach-

ing?" I reflected on this question at age twenty-five, when I was a fledgling preacher in search of a personal preaching style. I reflected on it more analytically somewhat later, as a Ph.D. candidate in homiletics and as an aspiring seminary teacher. What I learned became the substance of a dissertation, a part of which I will summarize in the pages that follow.[3]

A qualification: Much of what I write here relates to preaching I experienced and researched in eastern Pennsylvania. My conclusions will not always match what some readers see as the "Mennonite preaching" practiced in their own communities and will be even less generalizable in Anabaptist settings beyond Mennonite. I do have a hunch that much of what I say *will* have a familiar ring to many—but the hunch will need to be tested and and my views broadened by the *Gemeinschaft* (the larger community), as Germanic Mennonites used to put it!

THE EVOLUTION OF EARLY ANABAPTIST PREACHING

There is scant data to be found concerning preaching among the sixteenth-century Anabaptists. This fact stands in marked contrast to the extensive documentation of Lutheran and Reformed proclamation during the same period. Luther, Zwingli, Melanchthon, Calvin, and their successors left behind hundreds of sermon manuscripts and stenographically recorded sermons.

Since much worship in the first Anabaptist communities was furtive, it should be no surprise that few samples of sermons have survived. One of the earliest references to the spoken Word in worship comes to us from the court record of an interrogation of a suspected Anabaptist:

> They [the Anabaptists] have no special gathering places. When there is peace and unity and when none of those who have been baptized are scattered they come together wherever the people are. . . . When they come together they teach one another the divine Word and one asks the others, "How do you understand this saying?" Thus there is among them a diligent living according to the divine Word.[4]

The most notable aspect of this testimony is its inference to what Anabaptist scholars now call the "hermeneutical community."[5] The idea of the hermeneutical community is that, in some manner, preaching and teaching are dialogical activities. When the Word is proclaimed in the faith community, believers are responsible to interpret, test, and apply what is said.

Historically, one way this dialogue has been carried on has been through the practice of *Zeugnis*, or "testimony." Zeugnis was the practice of offering a verbal response to the sermon after it was preached. As the late John Oyer has pointed out, the evidence for Zeugnis after sermons is thin in early Anabaptist sources, but two brief references do provide peeks into early worship. A certain Hans Graci, writing in 1528, complained of the preaching of brother Hans Zuber of the Esslingen (Germany) congregation. Zuber, Graci asserted, was unwilling to submit his rambling attempts at preaching to the scriptural analysis and the approval of the believers who were present. Graci's comment suggests that the usual practice in worship was, in some way, to submit a newly preached sermon to the congregation for its response and testing.[6]

A second and somewhat different illustration of Zeugnis was recorded a generation later in the same geographical vicinity. Esslingen police interrogated twenty-one Anabaptist men whom they surprised at worship in a ravine outside the city. During the investigation, it was revealed that this group was functioning without an ordained leader. Rather than having an officially appointed preacher (who would surely have become the target of arrest and torture), the members of the group simply took turns reading and commenting on Scripture texts, interpreting them to the others who were present.[7]

It is difficult to discern to what extent this "hermeneutical community" functioned out of simple necessity and to what extent it was the product of more intentional theological reflection on the work of the Spirit in the gathered church. Oyer pointed out that early Anabaptism had no means for maintaining a consistent biblical hermeneutic that could be compared to the means found in Catholicism or among the Reformers. Rome controlled its biblical interpretation through the Tradition as interpreted by scholarly councils. Lutherans and Reformed relied on the carefully nuanced wordings of their confessions of faith. The Anabaptists had no comparable system for hermeneutical control. In the absence of such control, Anabaptists may simply have conversed with one another around the Word, trusting in the Spirit for guidance.[8]

Over time, a more institutionalized form of Zeugnis developed which continues to be practiced in some form in many Amish and Mennonite communities today. Anabaptist confidence in the power of the

Spirit to speak through ordinary believers was high. As Arnold Snyder observes, for Anabaptism as a whole the final authority for faith and life was not Scripture alone, but Scripture and the Spirit working together in the church.[9]

One written sample of a sermon survives from the Anabaptist preaching of the sixteenth century.[10] Bearing the date 1527, this untitled and anonymous manuscript is believed to have been composed by Eitelhans Langenmantel, an early convert of the South German itinerant Hans Hut. Based on Jeremiah 7:3-4 ("Amend your ways and your doings, then I will dwell with you in this place; and let no one deceive himself"), the sermon has a strongly ethical content with an emphasis on repentance and obedience to Christ. The opening sentence—"May God be with us and with all who so desire, to teach and to show us the command of Christ which the Father demands that we fulfill, through Jesus Christ"—inaugurates a rambling and mostly hortatory discourse on subjects ranging from the general purity of the church, to the necessity of separation from Catholic practices, to the seductive dangers of material wealth. To what degree this sermon is typical of Anabaptist preaching of the period is difficult to determine. It is interesting, however, that Anabaptist themes of obedience, separation from sin, and discipleship are already dominant.

PREACHING IN THE NEW WORLD

By the time the Mennonite stream of Anabaptism (to focus on the stream I have particularly researched) came to North America in 1683, patterns of worship were more settled and uniform. A 1773 letter from American bishops to counterparts in Holland refers to an early account of Mennonite church life in Pennsylvania written by Jacob Gottschalk, the first bishop at Germantown. Gottschalk reported that in the earliest days of the church he and other ministers read from books of sermons to the congregation. The Germantown community possessed books of sermons from seventeenth-century Dutch and German Mennonite preachers Joost Hendricks, Willem Wynands, and Jacob Denner.[11] Wynands (1630-1658) and Denner (1659-1746) had preached to wealthy congregations in Hamburg-Altona, Germany. Their sermons filtered Anabaptist themes through the florid rhetoric and emotional intensity of seventeenth-century German pietism. Denner's preaching stressed the importance of the "felt Christ" of pietism, indicating a shift in emphasis from earlier sixteenth-century themes of obedience and discipleship. These Pietist emphases later became prominent in the folk art and hymnody of the eighteenth-century American church.[12]

For several hundred years, Mennonite preachers were chosen from within the membership of congregations through the use of the lot. Sermon books such as Denner's were given to fledgling preachers to provide them with models of good sermons. In a few cases where preachers found public speaking to be too difficult a task, the reading of published sermons became a common practice. For the most part, however, it is believed that the sermon collections served as examples for preachers and as devotional reading in homes.[13]

What do we know about how Zeugnis was practiced during this period? There are no accounts of the practice from the eighteenth century, but from the nineteenth century we learn a little more. The practice appears to have been institutionalized into the form of "giving liberty" for other ministers to speak in response to the sermon. For example, in a letter describing his visit to the Skippack, Pennsylvania, congregation, an Ontario minister reviewed the hour-long sermon, after which the bishop rose and extended liberty "for any brother present who wishes to say anything . . . for the benefit of all present."[14]

"Giving liberty" after the sermon continued in some form into the twentieth century and up to the present in many traditional Mennonite church communities. In Franconia Conference, a regional cluster of congregations located largely in southeastern Pennsylvania, many people over sixty years of age can clearly recall the days when a deacon or another minister would get up after the sermon was preached and offer a word of comment on what had just been proclaimed. Most often it took the form of a simple affirmation that the sermon had been a word from the Lord, but occasionally it could take the form of further elaboration on the theme or even a correction of a misstatement.

Though no longer referred to by name, the practice of giving liberty for further comment after the sermon continues in many Mennonite churches today in the form of "sharing time." Many congregations combine an "open mike" time of naming prayer requests with an opportunity for making further comment on the sermon. In other churches a Sunday school elective class discusses the sermon as the focus of its input for the morning. Thus the practice of Zeugnis continues.

THE PROGRESSIVE IMPULSE

While some American Mennonite communities experienced little cultural change in the early nineteenth century, there was a spiritual restlessness in other quarters. In eastern Pennsylvania, the beginnings of the General Conference Mennonite Church came about in part because John Oberholtzer and his sympathizers wanted to hear a greater overall competence from the preachers. Oberholtzer judged that four out of five ministers ordained through the lot were failures in the pulpit. He called for ministers to receive formal training. The "General Conference" eventually opened an institute for preachers in Wadsworth, Ohio. Other signs of modernization included dropping the strict dress requirements for members, the beginning of Sunday schools, the organizing of evangelistic activities and the introduction of musical instruments in worship. Eventually in many places there developed a greater openness to evangelical influences on the faith, including sending young people to schools such as Moody Bible Institute and Philadelphia School of the Bible.

The preaching of Bishop Moses Gottschall (1815-1888) serves as an illustration of the progressive shift in preaching. Gottschall, a pastor for many years at Eden Mennonite Church in Schwenksville, Pennsylvania, preached with a level of pathos unheard of in traditional Mennonite churches. An eyewitness account by one of Gottschall's grandsons is vivid (and humorous) enough to bear quoting at length:

> He spared no one in his fiery zeal for righteousness against iniquity. I well remember. . . . the significant nods and glances that were exchanged between pews after some besetting sins of the day had received the most merciless flaying and excoriation . . . It was a judgment day in miniature. . . . His pulpit manner was intensely dramatic. He repeated conversations between men, mimicking their attitudes and expressions . . . and emphasized the realism of the scene by making use of the Pennsylvania German dialect. . . . His earnestness gained momentum, his eyes flashed fire, his delivery doubled its speed, his voice awakened reverberating echoes throughout the building, and his right hand, raised above his head and trembling ominously like the dreaded lull before the storm, presently came down with terrific force into his left palm, or upon the pulpit or the Bible. Every eye was winking in anticipation of the crash."[15]

Alongside the modernizing influences of the General Conference, Mennonite preaching was shaped by its encounter with the so-called "Third Great Awakening." Articles in the *Herald of Truth* publication, edited by John F. Funk (a convert of an associate of D. L. Moody) fanned the flames of revival across the Mennonite Church. By 1900 Mennonite revival preachers were making appearances in Mennonite pulpits from Goshen, Indiana, to Souderton, Pennsylvania.

This contact with the broader Protestant world continued and deepened in the twentieth century. In most communities the German language was gradually dropped in favor of English, and use of the lot gave way to calling ministers by congregational vote. Graduate seminary education introduced further changes and probably hastened the homogenization of Mennonite preaching. As stated earlier, seminary education was briefly tried at Bluffton College in the late nineteenth century. Through the development of the Biblical Seminary at Goshen College in the 1940s, graduate theological education became firmly established. With it came formal classroom instruction for preachers. By the 1950s, a growing number of Mennonite preachers were being called and prepared in ways not unlike preachers in the Protestant denominations.

This chapter is too brief and impressionistic to attempt a definitive statement about the nature of Anabaptist preaching, and as ever it must be recognized that the Anabaptism particularly in view here is the Mennonite stream. Nevertheless, some characteristics are noteworthy.

(1) Mennonite preaching emerged *from within the congregation.* While this truth can in some way be affirmed in every Christian tradition, there is a sense in which it is even truer for Anabaptists. For several hundred years, preachers were ordinary members of the congregation, set aside for ministry by the lot and by congregational request. Even today, with seminary training a fact of life, it is not uncommon for persons to be identified as having pastoral gifts, to be sent to seminary, and to return as pastors in their home churches and communities.

(2) A great deal of the preaching in Mennonite churches can be said to be done in a *communal voice.* In the practice of Zeugnis, in "sharing times," in the open-mike conferring that typically happens after the sermon in a conference assembly, preaching is one part of a larger, ongoing church conversation.

(3) Preaching is important to Anabaptists. Despite the fact that there has undeniably been much bad preaching in Anabaptist churches,

congregations and individuals have cared enough about it to give it prominence in worship and to struggle to find written and instructional resources for doing it better.

(4) Mennonite preaching has paid little overt attention to what preaching textbooks often call the *delivery* of the sermon. While collections of sermons were used to help new preachers with sermon content, there has been, until recent days, a studied reluctance to discuss the delivery of the sermon. In my dissertation research I listened to many hours of cassette recordings of sermons from the 1950s to the present. One common thread in those sermons was a constant attempt by preachers to establish their humility in the preaching task. Preachers repeatedly qualified their assertions with admissions of limited knowledge and lack of general ability.[16] Only among younger preachers today is there a sense of preparing to deliver the sermon through repeated readings of a manuscript, practicing the sermon in the pulpit, or other measures. For former generations such preparations would no doubt have smacked of "play-acting."

(5) Mennonite preaching historically has been *biblical*. As Mary Schertz describes it later in this book, many sermons in Mennonite churches had the whole Bible for a text. While this did not produce well-organized messages, it did communicate to congregations that the Bible—the *whole* Bible—is foundational to Christian living.

Hopefully this sketchy snapshot is sufficient to suggest that the Anabaptist tradition deserves to be a conversation partner with the thinking and writing in the broader homiletical world. Preaching, for Anabaptists, is not only the result, but a participant in, a conversational hermeneutic. It needs to enrich, and be enriched by, conversation with other Christian preaching traditions.

PREACHING AS VIEWED IN THIS BOOK

In the chapters that follow, other voices contribute to the conversation by exploring various aspects of the preaching task from an Anabaptist perspective.

Michael A. King's chapter examines the effects on preaching of the breakdown of forms of thought, knowledge, and authority that accompanies the decline of modernity. As part of asking how preachers can within postmodernity earn authority, weave enchantment, preach a different script, and value a form of eisegesis in addition to exegesis, King brings insights from Brian McLaren and Walter Brueggeman as well as the German philosopher Hans Gadamer into the discussion. Gadamer's work on the horizons of interpretation offers fruitful insights for preaching in Anabaptist "hermeneutical communities" amid influences within postmodernity making increasingly evident that preaching involves not only interpreting the Bible's meaning but also co-creating it in the act of present-day application.

Nancy Heisey broadens the discussion of hermeneutics in preaching by taking us from the world behind the ancient text, to the text itself, and on to our world in front of the text. Traditional homiletics conceives of preaching as carrying the "freight" of an ancient book across a "bridge" to the contemporary setting. Heisey argues that the preaching task is akin to a dance, in which the preacher interacts with several partners simultaneously: the Bible, the living Christ, the preacher, and the congregation to be addressed. She suggests a practical process for engaging each of these dance partners in the rhythm of the Holy Spirit.

Mary Schertz raises the question which must surely be answered first by any would-be preacher: "What, exactly, is meant by biblical preaching?" Mary recalls the preaching in her childhood church, in which the entire canon of Scripture was preached each Sunday. Rather than dismissing this style of preaching out of hand, Mary demonstrates that the preacher demonstrated the organic connection between the entire Bible, and the congregation's life of discipleship. While she does not encourage weekly "Genesis to Revelation" sermons, she stresses the need for making the entire Bible available for the Anabaptist pulpit. She argues that the Bible is foundational to all *Christian* nurture.

Preaching from the First Testament has always created challenges for Anabaptists. David Stevens makes a strong case for why we should preach the First Testament "on its own terms," and offers suggestions for mining its riches for the pulpit.

Dawn Wilhelm delves specifically into the prophetic writings and, indeed, into the entire prophetic impulse of the Bible. Fruitfully and passionately she explains the ways in which prophetic preaching functions-and must continue to function within the faithful Anabaptist community.

At the heart of an Anabaptist "theology of preaching" is the notion that the sermon is not the work of the preacher alone but actually the project of the community of faith. June Alliman Yoder takes up the matter of whether, and how, sermons may be produced collaboratively. Yoder states that an educational culture which insists on having students "do their own work" has contributed to the notion of sermon preparation as a solitary endeavor. What if the preacher collaborated with others in the church at various stages along the way? Yoder's suggestion may strike preacher-readers as unusual, trained as we are in the solitariness of study. The editors urge you to give her proposal a hearing, and a try!

Since Anabaptists have produced few systematic theologies, they have often been perceived as uninterested in doctrine. Mark Wenger makes the case for preaching the doctrines of the faith in Anabaptist settings, insisting that doctrinal preaching (and indeed, any preaching that addresses the mind) is crucial in a time when the worldview of western culture is shifting. Wenger suggests some concrete ways to approach the preaching of doctrine and making it interesting.

In a multicultural era, preaching must address the reality that in any given congregation more than one culture is likely to be represented. Nate Showalter, himself experienced in pastoral ministry in an international congregation, talks about the dynamics of communicating the Word in situations where cultural differences make it likely that the sermon will be heard through radically diverse filters. Do we know the cultures of our congregations? How does preaching take those cultures into account, so that the message that is intended has the best chance of being the message that is heard?

Directly related to preaching is the question of listening. How do people hear a sermon? Lynn Jost, a student of the homiletical theory of David Buttrick, suggests a method for the construction of sermons based on Buttrick's groundbreaking work, *Homiletic: Moves and Structures*. Jost suggests that by arranging the sermon as a series of "moves" instead of "points," the attention and comprehension of hearers can be maximized and the preacher's intended meaning retained.

In the past three decades, "narrative preaching" has gradually gained a large following among preachers and hearers. Starting with the work of homiletician Fred Craddock, and continuing with the writings of Eugene Lowry, Charles Rice, and others, narrative sermons are now standard fare in many churches. Renée Sauder examines the advantages of the narrative sermon and suggests specific linkages between the narrative sermon and Anabaptist communities of faith.

Rebecca Slough takes up the question of the place of the sermon within the larger worship service. The Anabaptist tradition has been slow in developing a theology of worship. What is the place of the Word in worship? What does it mean to say that preaching is an act of worship? Can preaching and worship each find adequate space in a culture in which the one hour time limit weighs heavily in planning?

Dennis Hollinger addresses some of the ethical issues facing the contemporary preacher. Is the act of preaching an act of persuasion (as in classical rhetoric), revelation (a la Karl Barth), or, as suggested by several authors in this volume, a form of conversation? Hollinger believes that preaching is inescapably a persuasive form of communication. Having said this, Hollinger believes that there are guidelines for pulpit address which keep the persuading ethical. He clusters his suggestions under the heading of "integrity." Preaching which is ethical is preaching in which there is congruence between the preacher's life and words, and an honest love between preacher and people.

I suggested earlier that some early Anabaptist preaching bordered on moralism, with heavy doses of admonition. Is it possible, in discipleship oriented churches, to keep a message of grace central in the preaching of the Word? Ervin Stutzman insists that grace must be kept central in Anabaptist preaching. At least Mennonites among the Anabaptist groups are often "recovering Pharisees," he asserts, and their preachers need to find ways of keeping sermons redemptive in focus. Ervin offers helpful questions to guide the preacher's preparation and some practical suggestions for crafting grace-filled messages.

Following these chapters are questions for discussion related to each author's project along with general questions addressing the entire book. Prepared by Mark Wenger and Ervin Stutzman of the Eastern Mennonite Preaching Institute, the purpose of these questions is to make this entire volume more user friendly for study groups, conference-or district-based (or other grouping, depending on denominational polity) theological education classes, and seminaries. Since Anabaptist preaching is, as I have repeatedly said, a communal endeavor, this text will find its purposes best fulfilled when read and discussed corporately.

NOTES

1. An entertaining and detailed narrative of the division of Franconia Conference is in John L. Ruth, *Maintaining the Right Fellowship: A Narrative Account of Life in the Oldest Mennonite Community in North America* (Scottdale, Pa.: Herald Press, 1984), 232-316.

2. Humility has traditionally been an essential quality of the Mennonite *Diener zum Buch* (servant of the Word). Joseph Liechty has argued that for Mennonites, humility is the internalized manifestation of *Gelassenheit* (yieldedness), the attitude of one who would follow Christ to death if necessary. See Joseph Liechty, "Humility: The Foundation of the Mennonite Religious Outlook in the 1860's," *Mennonite Quarterly Review* 54, no. 1 (1980): 5-31.

3. David Greiser, "The Franconia Conference Pulpit: Evolution of a Mennonite Preaching Tradition" (unpublished Ph.D. dissertation, Louisville, Ky.: Southern Baptist Theological Seminary, 1996).

4. "Interrogation of Ambrosius Spitelmaier, 1527," *in Anabaptism in Outline: Selected Primary Sources*, ed. Walter Klaassen (Scottdale, Pa.: Herald Press, 1981), 124.

5. Much has been written on the topic of the hermeneutical community. A recent and fairly complete treatment is Stuart Murray, *Biblical Interpretation in the Anabaptist Tradition* (Kitchener, Ont.: Pandora Press, 2000).

6. John S. Oyer, "Early Forms of Anabaptist Zeugnis After Sermons," *Mennonite Quarterly Review* 72, no. 3 (1998): 449-454.

7. Ibid.

8. Ibid., 449, 454.

9. C. Arnold Snyder, *Anabaptist History and Theology: An Introduction* (Kitchener, Ontario: Pandora Press, 1995), 161-172.

10. J.C. Wenger, trans., "Two Early Anabaptist Tracts," *Mennonite Quarterly Review* 22, no. 1 (1948): 34-42.

11. D. N. Pannabecker, trans. "A Letter From Pennsylvania Mennonites to Holland in 1773," *Mennonite Quarterly Review* 3 (1929), 225-234.

12. Jacob Denner, *Einfältige und Christliche Betrachtungen über Einige Texte des Alten und Neuen Testaments* (Altona, Hamburg, n. p., 1730). For Pietist influences on Mennonites in the eighteenth century, see Robert Friedmann, *Mennonite Piety Through the Centuries* (Goshen, Ind.: Mennonite Historical Society, 1949).

13. Ruth, *Maintaining the Right Fellowship*, 209.

14. Jacob Krehbiel, "A Few Words About the Mennonites in America in 1841," trans. Harold S. Bender, *Mennonite Quarterly Review* 6 (1932), 114-115.

15. Ruth, 347-348.

16. See Greiser, "Franconia Conference Pulpit," particularly the sections on delivery in chapters four and five.

Chapter 2

Weaving Enchantment:
Preaching and Postmodernity

Michael A. King

A conversation with a congregational member I'll call William seems to me to embody many of the issues affecting preaching amid postmodernity. Whatever else postmodernity includes, it involves the passing, fragmentation, and sometimes breakdown of what once seemed settled forms of life and thought. How postmodernity has affected the authority of the preacher was what became particularly evident in the interchange with William.

It all started when during our congregational Christian education hour I was teaching a series based on Brian D. McLaren's *The Church on the Other Side: Doing Ministry in the Postmodern Matrix*.[1] William, member of what one of my supervising conference ministers once called "the loyal opposition," had been making sure the opposition side of that equation was not lost to view. He had set himself the goal, evidently, of providing a counterpoint to every assertion offered by McLaren, whose views he saw as an egregious example of the breakdown of true Christian values. He had even one morning made the rather striking comment that where McLaren's book belonged, if anywhere, was in the trash.

Before continuing the story, some background. On this particular Sunday a topic of discussion was the weakening of traditional forms of authority in our postmodern milieu. For example, McLaren notes that in contrast to the days when the church burned heretics,

> We have one factor in our favor in the new world: Nobody has that much power anymore. And I think it is power that makes us into Pharisees who see Jesus as a threat. We don't control governments, our denominations aren't monolithic; we have to tolerate diversity in nonessentials so as to enjoy unity in the essentials. (69)

And even as he bemoans that too often the young radicals in the church "ignore the counsel of their experienced elders" (103), McLaren highlights the passing of an era when "the robed priest" could be seen as representing "traditional culture, bound together by the priesthood's divine authority, revealed belief, sanctioned customs, absolute rules, accepted rituals, and meaningful holidays" (160). We live now, contends McLaren, in a time when forms of authority once simply accepted no longer are. This affects the Bible, one prime source of authority for Christians, since often in postmodern settings "biblical authority is either questioned or unheard of rather than assumed" (75).

Now McLaren is addressing large matters. The case he makes for our being in a postmodern era is arguable. We can each weave different stories about and make different sense of the times we are in. A feature of postmodernity is that its very existence is often debated among those sometimes seen as its intellectual or cultural founts. During my graduate school studies of postmodernism I recall discovering, for example, the hesitance of French thinker Michel Foucault to see himself as postmodern, when many of those convinced we live in postmodern times tend to see him as a source or at least interpreter of postmodernity (the state of being in a postmodern time) and postmodernism (a particular form of thought typically committed to postmodern characteristics).[2] And I recall a post-graduation lunch with my dissertation adviser in which I told him my denomination was beginning to enter the debate over postmodernity—and he laughed. Why? Because, he said, it seemed to him that now in academia postmodernism was becoming passé.

But whatever the complexities involved in assessing our times, I am convinced that McLaren is correct in seeing Western culture and the Christians within it as living on "the other side" of something. That something is sometimes called modernity, the era, lasting perhaps particularly from the Enlightenment into the twilight of the twentieth century, in which we humans—at least Western ones—tended to think we could know and control reality and ourselves through the power of our rational minds. Because I share it, I find myself wanting to teach and preach McLaren's conviction with, frankly, some authority.

So there that Sunday stood I, seeking ways to bring home amid the lived experiences of congregational participants the breakdown of modernity and particularly, this morning, traditional forms of authority. The task was made no easier because here we were facing one of the complexities of postmodernity. This is that often what has broken down is not only modernity but also the lingering traces of premodern tradition often interweaved with modernity.

As I grappled with how to make such complexities accessible and meaningful, not only to congregational members but also to my own overtaxed brain, there sat William, visibly unimpressed. Eventually he spoke up. "What is wrong with the church," he offered, "is precisely that our teachers and pastors no longer teach us the time-honored biblical truths and expect us to follow."

I pondered this. I sensed that I could make a small or large move in response. I do love William and wanted to respect him. I also had a suspicion that here was potentially a dramatic moment, in that it might show us all why whatever we think of the times, there is no going back. With William, I am old enough to remember the days of "the bench." Back then, in some of the classic Mennonite congregations I visited as a boy, I would first see a largely black-clad congregation in which women gathered on one side and men on the other. Then at the front would be a row of men sitting behind the pulpit in plain coats. Their very demeanor seemed to radiate an intense authority, a kind of authority strikingly evocative of the type McLaren associates with the "robed priest" (even though these descendants of the Radical Reformation would *never* have seen themselves as priests, whatever else they were).

So with images of the bench dancing—or sitting solemnly—in our heads, and with William wishing for the days when preachers spoke with authority, I decided to risk claiming some authority of my own. "William," I said, "suppose we imagine a Sunday morning much like this one. Suppose someone much like me is teaching a course on McLaren. Suppose someone in the class proposes that McLaren's book should be thrown in the trash."

"But *I* did that!" William broke in.

"Yes," I said, "I know. Now here's the thing: I am now pastor of this congregation. I am now intending to propose, with at least some authority, that we live in a world whose outlines someone like McLaren at least helps us glimpse. You say you want to return to a time when people followed pastors. I'm ready for you to follow me on this. But you say the book I'm using should be thrown in the trash. You're not willing to accept my authority because you disagree with what I'm teaching."

William saw the point. I emphasized that my own goal was not to smash his disagreement. I had said publicly before, and repeated it then, that I saw William as one of our more courageous and helpful participants. I observed that in a congregational milieu where the tendency was to underplay conflict and to settle instead for a lifeless peace, William invited us to vigorous and life-giving interchange.

Still I hoped, I said, that our exchange helped illustrate that the days of traditional authority are no more. William was prepared to honor authority—but only if he granted his assent. This is a classic feature of postmodernity. As McLaren notes, postmoderns say "You can't believe everything you hear. The experts especially should be doubted. . ." (173). This is not to twist William into a postmodern person, a travesty he would hate. It's simply to note that even he now is unprepared to trust the "expert" if the teaching does not match his own beliefs. He too, even as he wishes he lived in a different reality, contributes to what Walter Brueggeman, in a classic article[3] on preaching "in our changed preaching situation," identifies as "a great new reality for preaching," which is "pluralism in the interpreting community of the local congregation" (314). Amid this pluralism, Brueggeman observes, "The old modes of church absolutes are no longer trusted" (313). The paradox for William is that I am his pastor, so according to the old modes he should trust in and follow my authority, but he too is now unready simply to submit to such authority if it does not mesh with his values and beliefs.

Though it may take different forms in different settings, this breakdown of authority, and the pluralism which flows from and helps reinforce that breakdown is, a common feature of postmodernity. What are the implications for preachers of dwelling within such features of postmodernity, of life "on the other side," or whatever label we may choose to give times like these? Among the nearly endless list that could be discussed, perhaps four particularly deserve consideration: earning and not assuming authority, weaving enchantment, preaching a different script, and valuing not only exegesis but also eisegesis.

Earning and not Assuming Authority

Even as I taught that traditional authority can no longer be assumed, I did mean to claim some authority. There is little point, it seems to me, to naming something preaching—as opposed to speaking, chatting, conversing—unless it is done with authority. The preacher means to claim that something beyond mere opinion is being shared in a sermon; in some way, God is speaking through the preacher. But if within postmodernity the authority of the robed leader cannot be claimed, from where does authority come? From the authority of the Bible itself, and its claims to be the Word of God, might be part of the answer. Yet within postmodernity that authority is also in question.

What now? McLaren helps point the way. He notes that "on the other side," Scripture is not so much "the authoritative foundation" as it is "a part of the fabric of the message itself" (75). He also observes that a key characteristic of leaders no longer able to assume the authority of the robe is "personal authenticity" (112). Weave such comments together, and what emerges is something like this: authority continues to matter and to be needed, but it must be earned, not assumed. Both Bible and preacher earn authority through the authenticity of their message as sensed by those experiencing it. I certainly know that judging the effectiveness of my own preaching by explicit responses to it is a dangerous move. It may be pertinent, however, that amid the many times William continues to provide loyal opposition, after a sermon in which I myself knew I had invested extra passion—possibly in fact extra authenticity—William said to me, "That was precious." He meant it, and he was in that moment granting, I believe, his experience of authority in that particular waltz of Bible and preacher.

Now even if authority cannot be assumed in our era, the dynamic involved in earning it is no recent one. In Mark 1:27, part of a story I explore below, those who listen to Jesus and watch him heal are "all amazed, and they kept on asking one another, 'What is this? A new teaching—with authority!" As Don Kraybill observes, "Jesus comes to the people without the traditional trappings of authority. He doesn't have any political clout nor the training of a scribe. . . . His words earn their own authority. The audience certifies his authority, not a board of theological experts in Jerusalem."[4] We preachers aren't Jesus, but we can learn from him here.

If it is granted that increasingly authority must be earned and not assumed, this of course poses challenges. It leaves preachers and congregants to some extent lost in a fog of unclear expectations, often yearning, as William does, for the greater clarity provided by clearer structures and boundaries of authority. It leaves all of us needing to dance more nimbly amid various ways of understanding church, world, and Scripture itself. This dance unfolds amid what Brueggeman calls "an emerging awareness of the polyvalence of the biblical text" (315)—meaning that texts potentially have multiple meanings, thus we can rarely expect to arrive at just one settled conclusion about the meaning of given texts.

Such fragmentations of authority and meaning are one reason, no doubt, that congregations dominated by "William's" do sometimes attempt to retreat into more traditional forms of authority even amid a larger postmodernity. That in fact may well be one valid alternate response to losses of authority; sometimes recreating zones of church life within which something resembling those forms of authority now fading may be an important countercultural way to apply the gospel. However, even congregations or denominations that intend to create zones of internal authority must still more intentionally than in the past work at this. In addition, they must themselves ponder ways to earn authority once they enter the fragmentations of the larger culture and leave behind those settings in which their style of authority prevails.

WEAVING BIBLICAL ENCHANTMENT

Happily there are gains as well as losses in earning instead of merely assuming authority. One gain is that truly the earning and granting of authority becomes a community activity, and in this way the priesthood of believers long affirmed by Anabaptists gains fresh life. [5] And how often as pastor have I heard from congregants from many different denominational roots who nearly gave up on the church because what they heard from pastor or priest was, to be blunt, drivel. What I mean by that is that in fact the Word of God was often accurately quoted but what was done with that word was lifeless. On the preacher would drone, these congregants report, lost in some arcane world back then, back there,

into which he (often) or she (rarely, until recently) expected to be duti-
fully followed. But there was no "there" there, because the biblical world
is dead, buried under the debris of twenty centuries of living since then.

I don't mean to be as shocking as that sounds. The Life to which the
Bible testifies lives on. The very Spirit of the living Jesus, the comforter
he promised to send once he in the flesh departed, dwells among us. The
spiritual world of the Bible is as alive as ever. But its culture is dead, not
in the sense that there was something wrong with it, simply in the sense
that the fabric of cultural arrangements within which the people of the
Bible experienced God was theirs, not ours.

Certainly, because much of what it means to be human transcends
particular cultures or is common to all cultures, much of what we read
about in the Bible still makes sense to us, even without scholarly study.
The gap between then and now is by no means absolute. What I mean to
highlight is just that if all a preacher manages to do is invite hearers to go
back there (as can be particularly tempting to preachers if we can assume
rather than earn our authority to be heard), the question of how the
gospel throbs among us here remains unaddressed. But if we must earn
our authority, this gives preachers the incentive to ponder again and
again what it is about preaching that brings life, what it takes for those
among whom we speak to sense that indeed within our midst the living
God is once more present. There is no failsafe formula for this, as any of
us who grasp that last Sunday or some other it just didn't go too well can
attest. But what we are at least seeking to do when we earn authority by
offering preaching that gives life is this: to weave enchantment.

Recently I discussed the power of enchantment with a participant of
my congregation who, based on her rapt gaze at her lap while I preached,
was experiencing not my sermon but her reading as enchanting. I asked
this young woman, whose lust for books at age eight so reminded me of
my own at that age, what she found so entrancing. "Fairy tales," she said.
"I just love fairy tales. I love going into their world in my mind and living there." To weave enchantment involves something like that: helping
to provide a different world within which our hearers can dwell and
learn and live, not to flee the ordinary realm but to learn from within the
world of enchantment more about what is going on above, beneath, beyond—and often through—the ordinary.

As that young reader intuited, what matters is not just any old enchantment, not the enchantments of money, lust, or power so common

in our culture, but the enchantment of fairy tale. And not just any old fairy tale but in this case a fairy tale which just happens, as J. R. R. Tolkien once memorably exulted,[6] long before the "Lord of the Rings" film series brought him new posthumous fame, to be true.

It is no accident that if weaving enchantment is key to our preaching task in postmodernity, the power of storytelling has gained fresh prominence among those seeking forms of preaching suitable to our age. A generation ago already Fred B. Craddock helped preachers learn about weaving enchantment through his concept of preaching that engages listeners in "overhearing the gospel."[7] This involves inviting hearers to ride into the gospel on the backs of stories[8] rather than being commanded into it. Craddock is inviting "showing" rather than the "telling" so common when traditional authority undergirds the preaching.

Meanwhile today McLaren, no surprise, calls us to "learn a new rhetoric" (ch. 7) in which our words "will depend more on the power of story" (90) and "seek to be servants of mystery, not removers of it as they were in the old world" (89) McLaren too is helping us understand the difference between telling and showing. In the first approach I tell you what the world or the Bible or the church are and what to believe about them. In contrast, in the showing approach I journey with you through mysteries I can't fully comprehend and help you experience with me the not-always-fully glimpsed yet spine-tingling marvels to be found within Bible and faith and life when brought together. So the preacher will "use words," as McLaren puts it, but "will be a weaver of parables, a designer of proverbs, more a sage than a technician" (90).

On a related note, Brueggeman contends that "reality is scripted." By this he means that we do not encounter naked, raw reality (as modernists have sometimes been tempted to think) but reality already embedded within a script, within a story or stories, before we can even begin to think about or experience it. On a day not long after 9-11, U.S. President George W. Bush declared that the nation was at war. The nation was not in a struggle, not in a police action, not in a time of punishment by God, to name a few of the alternate and sometimes competing stories that could have been told. No, the nation had entered a war in which U.S. justice and goodness, not evil, would prevail. On that day he was drawing on and contributing to a script with great power to shape the world. He did enchant the world with this story, he did weave a potent spell. The power of script, story, spell is strikingly clear.

PREACHING A DIFFERENT SCRIPT

A different story could have been told. A tale could have been spun of a great empire, an empire greater even than Babylon, the Whore so often decried in the Bible, an empire which had flung its tentacles so far and wide across the world that some in the world rose up against the Whore. Then reality would have seemed rather different indeed. Now whether America is God's sword used to bring vengeance to evildoers (as might be argued based on Romans 13) or a Babylon in the end to be brought low is not the point I want to debate here, except to say this much: If reality is scripted, then the question of whether there is a true script arises.

In modernist mode, the way to answer that question would likely be to trust in logical reasoning to arrive at an answer. But thinkers like McLaren and Brueggeman are saying, in effect, that this is an "understanding seeking faith" move, whereas what we are left with in postmodernity is "faith seeking understanding." This is why Brueggeman turns away from an Enlightenment-based view of "the individual knower as the decontextualized adjudicator of truth" (315) and toward a view of truth which involves choosing for a particular story, then discerning what truths can be learned from within that story (320-329).

Of course for the Christian preacher, Brueggeman affirms, the story to be entered is the one told in the biblical text, which "is an offer of an alternative script, and preaching this text is the exploration of how the world is if it is imagined through this alternative script" (320). But the task is no so much to logically reason hearers into this story, since logic is itself a tool of the Enlightenment story and "old modes of certainty are no longer trusted" (324). Rather, the quest is simply to present the biblical story, in all its wild magnificence, as large enough and grand enough to deserve and to entice our allegiance. Or as Anabaptists have long put it, with a wisdom often more profound than the stark simplicity of the admonition might suggest, the call is just this: to follow Jesus as encountered through New Testament teachings and as our still-living Lord.[9] Thus as national leaders tell a story of noble warfare, others may tell a tale of a different kind of kingdom whose citizens declare allegiance to God and not to any one human nation.

Of course in postmodernity simply entering the Bible is not the end of the matter, given that indeed the Bible itself can be used to tell strikingly different stories, as evidenced by the fact the Bible can be used to weave both tales of peace and tales of war. This validates Brueggeman's point that texts will often turn out to have or at least support diverse meanings and to remind us that choosing faith that seeks understanding is not the end but only the beginning of a journey that never ends.

VALUING NOT ONLY EXEGESIS BUT ALSO EISEGESIS

Now if our overall task is to weave enchantment on this never-ending voyage, what understanding of hermeneutics do we bring to the task? Among the many issues to be pondered, I suggest that an important one to highlight is the potential resource of what might be seen as a rehabilitated eisegesis. Brueggeman is already beginning to teach something like this when he says that the preacher does not "describe a gospel-governed world but helps the congregation imagine it" (321). But for me the story starts with Hans Georg-Gadamer, the intellectual mentor of my graduate work in hermeneutics. "Not just occasionally but always," believes Gadamer, "the meaning of a text goes beyond its author. That is why understanding is not merely a reproductive but always a productive activity as well." And so "we understand in a *different* way, *if we understand at all*."[10]

Why quote Gadamer? Partly because this German philosopher is a leading commentator on how we understand anything. And partly because his views can make the Bible leap alive.

Take a biblical text. How do we work at understanding it? Well, goes a common response, we try to get our prejudices out of the way and enter the world of that day. We *exegete* the text. In exegesis we set aside our culture, language, ways of seeing the world. We enter the worlds of Isaiah, Matthew, Mark to reproduce their intended meanings.

There is this bad thing, they tell you in seminary, which is the opposite of exegesis. This bad thing, which can get you expelled, is *eisegesis*. Eisegesis means not getting yourself out of the way. Reading the Bible through your pet peeves and loves, you produce new meanings rather than reproducing the Bible's meanings. Then the Bible doesn't speak to you; you use the Bible to speak to yourself.

Gadamer agrees eisegesis can be bad. Gadamer thinks all texts come about as answers to questions. If in the text Jesus commands a rich young ruler to sell all he has, the text may be answering the question, "What must we do to have eternal life?" To understand the rich ruler or any text, we must open ourselves to the question the text is exploring. Eisegesis is bad when it lets us evade the question the text asks. Then it needs the exegesis that helps us clarify and confront the question.

But Gadamer also claims something like eisegesis is the *only* way we understand. We do not understand something by getting outside ourselves but only by applying it to who we are.

Think about it. We wrestle with words that at first are over our head. All gibberish. Nothing registers. We keep working. Something starts to dawn. We think, *Oh, that's like when. . . .* Suddenly it connects with something familiar. It starts to make sense. But it was strange to start out. Whatever made it strange comes into what is familiar and makes us see the familiar in a new and bigger way.

So two things are happening. We are changing what we try to understand by bringing it into our world. But it changes our world by entering it. We and it work together to create what it means for us. As we marry what is strange with what is familiar to us, each of us produces new meaning in each act of understanding.

Back to the Bible. So often the Bible is dead for us—particularly, I am contending, when preached by one who believes that robed authority, rather than living "eisegetical" engagement with a text, is enough to make it throb among listeners' experiences of today. The cause may be our aiming to leave ourselves behind when we enter the Bible. What happens if instead we connect the Bible with our world? Then we value who we are as crucial to understanding the Bible. And we let the Bible change who we are by allowing it to ask us the same questions that brought it into being.

Suppose the question is "How do demons possess me?" as they do so many in first-century Palestine. Again and again in the Gospel of Mark, for example, Jesus is surrounded by the throngs longing for his healing touch, and how often among the needy are those afflicted by demons. Now here exegesis is critical; as a responsible preacher, I need to have a reasonably well-informed understanding of what we know about how demons were viewed in New Testament times.

I claim no expertise in the topic, but after investigating the issue for a recent sermon on Mark 1:23-34, I hope I was at least safe in saying this in my sermon:

> Commentators emphasize that people in Jesus' day believed in
> demons far more than we do; they thought there were millions

of demons in the world and that in all kinds of places you had to look out, or the demons would get into and take you over.

Were and are there such demons? I don't really know. What I'd guess, based on what I know of cultures then and now, is this: there really *are* powers that can take us over. How we understand those powers may differ from culture to culture, but that doesn't mean the powers don't exist. So *something*, whatever it might look like if it happened to one of us today, had really taken over that man in the synagogue, and Jesus really did tell it to come out, and it really did.

That was how I attempted to keep the sermon disciplined by a measure of exegesis. Obviously given the brevity of my focus in that area, conveying exegetical learnings was not my key aim; in a different time and setting and with different sermonic goals, I might in fact keep much of the focus on exegesis—if, and only if, I had concluded that exploring the *then* would truly, in the end, bring life to the *now*. But in this sermon my main concern was to bring Jesus into the now. So quickly I moved to that task:

> What might take us over today is the next question we might want to ask if we try to imagine Jesus into our midst. Even today there are places where missionaries testify to being convinced of the presence of demons, and even in our own culture some try, such as through Ouija boards, to speak to invisible spirits. I am concerned enough about what powers can take us over in ways that may be much like what happened to demon-possessed people in Jesus' day that I said there would be no more of this when some years ago I learned of something that had happened in my own house. I put my foot down when I discovered that a gathering of girls in my basement had consulted a Ouija board, that it did seem to move in scary ways, that the room did seem to take on an ominous feel. Were there demons there? I don't know. I just don't rule out the possibility of there being powers even in our day much like demons and who are therefore not to be dabbled with but cast out.

In this passage I tried to do several things that fit the characteristics of preaching amid postmodernity I have been aiming to sketch: I aimed not to deny that a view of demons much like the one that seems to have prevailed in New Testament times may still be meaningful today. Here I was drawing on exegesis while beginning to move its fruits more fully into the present. I was assuming a worldview as close to the New Testament understandings as I knew to sketch out, and I was looking for comparable manifestations in the present. Note also that I intended to claim authority largely to the extent I earned it. I indicated what I did not know rather than claiming to know more than I do. Whatever may be compelling in the authority I claim here emerges hopefully with my listeners' assent, not against it. Finally I connected my move here with a story fragment (Ouija board).

But there is one move yet to be made, the one we are impelled to take as we revalue (carefully!) eisegesis and learn from Gadamer's view of how we understand: Suppose I don't imagine myself as demon-possessed in first-century Palestine or in a non-Western contemporary culture. Suppose I conclude, as I have, that in my congregation spirit/demon-dabbling remains what it tends to be in much of North America: a fringe practice. Dangerous as dabbling in that fringe I suspect is, and as important as it is to address its issues among those particularly drawn to it, it seemed to me if I stopped there the Bible would have come only marginally alive in my setting. I needed to ask yet what demon possession might mean among reasonably ordinary regular North Americans in the first years of the twenty-first century.

Here I made that leap which is always dangerous and which is why anything resembling eisegesis has to be handled with care yet also can be a great adventure: I aimed imaginatively to draw correlations between what possessed demon-haunted people in the New Testament and what possesses us today, without trying to treat the two forms of demonic power as exactly the same thing. Here my bridging principle was less "What are demons today?" or "How do demons possess us?" and more "What possesses us today?" combined with understandings of the biblical principalities and powers implicitly influenced by John Howard Yoder and Hendrik Berkhof.[11] So I said this:

> Still, I think it would be a shame to focus only on what I might
> call traditional demons, because in our culture, in contrast to
> Jesus' day, such demons are such a narrow slice of what we need
> healing from. Our culture too is full of powers that take control
> of us and from which Jesus can save us.

What might such powers be? Each of us in the end has to name the powers that particularly control us, but to start with one of my own examples, I feel often possessed by the demon of worry. Along with others of you, I've been particularly aware of financial worries in recent months because much of our family income comes from various forms of self-employment quite affected by the shape of the economy. So I spent weeks late last year waking up night after night at about 2:00 a.m. just absolutely terrified of financial ruin. The demon of worry had me in its clutches. I prayed. I asked for healing. It just wouldn't come. Then amid the intense spiritual voltages I was caught up in during the days I was participating in preparing for and officiating at the funeral of a dear friend, I noticed a strange side effect: the worry was losing its grip. It may well come back, but so far I've been free of its tentacles for weeks. I believe that was a way the power of Jesus worked in my recent life to say to the worry demon, "Be silent, and come out of him!"

What other powers are there? The list is probably endless. Craving for food beyond what we need is a huge power in our culture. Such craving is fed by all kinds of forces, including a capitalism that in the 1990s invented super-size everythings as a way to get us to give movie theaters, restaurants, and stores more profits. The result is a power so omnipresent, and so hard to resist, that it truly can feel like a demon has gripped us.

Cravings for popularity, celebrity, money are obvious in today's reality-based TV shows, which often capture the attention of some of my loved ones, though their sin shall remain anonymous. First I poo-poo each show, then someone convinces me to watch once, so to my shame I've taken in quite a few episodes of persons eating great gobs of live larvae or seeing who can win whose favor and gobs of money by being voted the sexiest. In each case, there is the seduction of watching other people grasp for whatever they see as the brass ring that will give them their heart's desire. Because we too always long for more than we have, we feel with them the desires that make these shows tick. But look at what power these shows and cravings have over us, as shown by the fact that millions and millions of us tune in. Are these really the powers we want controlling us?

So what would it look like for Jesus to show up amid any of these cravings and tell them to "Be silent, and come out of them!"? I don't fully know, because I'm me and not Jesus, because I'm part of this culture with all of us and can often feel its powers more easily than the counter-authority of Jesus to cast them out. But I do think the Spirit of Jesus is alive today. The authority of Jesus to cast out powers dwells among us.

How Jesus casts out the powers today seemed to me a huge additional issue, so that became the focus of a second sermon. But I hope in what I have shared there can be caught at least glimpses of how insights indebted to Gadamer can help the Bible spring alive. Because then the Bible and I and you will be in a living, breathing conversation. We will be talking about one of the most important questions in the universe. But we will be helping to construct the answer from the flesh-and-blood of my and your own day-to-day struggles and worries and joys.[12]

When we find the answer, though that will take a lifetime and beyond, it will be the Bible's answer. It will also be *my and our* answer, the answer we helped create, and so the scriptural oxygen will mingle with our blood and flow from head to toe with our every heartbeat. And something new will be born because, as Brueggeman dreams,

> The preacher traffics in a fiction that makes true. But that is why preaching is so urgent and must be done with such art. This world of the gospel is not real, is not available, until this credible utterance authorizes a departure from a failed text [such as that of the Enlightenment] and appropriation of this text [the biblical one]. 321

POSTMODERNITY AS GOLDEN AGE?

There is so much more, of course, that could be said about how postmodernity influences preaching, and so much that could be debated. Is postmodernity good or bad? Should it be fought or embraced? Or both? Is the crumbling of the Enlightenment and the modernity it fed, along with structures of authority it helped sustain, cause for panic or joy? Such matters deserve much debate and careful discernment. There are, I believe, many dangers in postmodernity to ponder, particularly in corrosively postmodern settings in which renewed humility bred by realizing we cannot after all know all truth becomes a rejection of any quest for truth or right living.

But for now, I simply note what is likely obvious, which is that I myself think that, like it or hate it, something other than what was, whatever we may call it, is what we are on the other side of. And there are losses to be mourned. Yet also it is evident, I hope, that I see much to be celebrated in the times we have entered and I believe in the end preaching will be the better for it.

Suppose that we—

- earn our right to be heard through the integrity and the authenticity of our speaking and the life journeying from which it emerges;
- approach the Bible as seekers and conveyors of its own self-authenticating and life-giving integrity, rather than as robed priests assuming and demanding that people accede to its authority whether or not they sense it making any convincing claims on them;
- see our preaching task less as providing logical argumentation and more as inviting listeners to live with us a different script;
- trust that by bringing then into now, now can vibrate with every bit as much power as then.

If we suppose and practice all that, then our times may ultimately come to resemble less a period of collapse and more a golden age. Then postmodernity may come to be named an era open to the fresh reign of God, an epoch in which the very Lord of Hosts, the Holy One of God as the demon names Jesus in Mark 1, comes to dwell among us with power and glory.

Notes

1. Brian D. McLaren, *The Church on the Other Side: Ministry in the Postmodern Matrix* (Grand Rapids, Mich.: Zondervan Publishing House, 2000).

2. This is why I attempt to highlight in some of my own academic works on postmodernity the fact that a truly postmodern reading of postmodernity does not allow for neat, logical assessments of what postmodernity is or whether we live within, since one of the claims of those whose thinking tends toward postmodern is that none of us can reliably see enough from a bird's eye view to claim to visualize the entire landscape below. For more on complexities of postmodernity see Michael A. King, "Valuing the Story of Power and Telling a Grander One: Anabaptism and

Power Postmodernism in Mutually Enlarging Conversation," in Susan Biesecker-Mast and Gerald Biesecker-Mast, *Anabaptists and Postmodernity* (Telford, Pa.: Pandora Press U.S., 2000), 91-105; "Angels, Atheists, and Common Ground: Toward a Separatist and Worldly Postmodernism," *Conrad Grebel Review* 15 (Fall 1997), 251-268.

3. Brueggeman, Walter. "Preaching as Reimagination," *Theology Today* 52, no. 3 (October 1995): 313-329.

4. Donald B. Kraybill, *The Upside-Down Kingdom,* 3rd. ed. (Scottdale, Pa.: Herald Press, 2003), 233.

5. Much more deserves to be said on this significant topic, but I will leave it to others, and in this book perhaps particularly chapters by David Greiser, Mary Schertz, and June Alliman Yoder highlight the key role the community plays in engaging the authority of preacher and Bible as well as contributing to genuinely communal hermeneutic practices, agenda which also has a bearing on my discussion of Gadamer and hermeneutics.

6. J. R. R. Tolkien, "On Fairy Stories," in C. S. Lewis, ed., *Essays Presented to Charles Williams* (Grand Rapids: William B. Eerdmans, 1966), 81-84. I elaborate on the fruitfulness of this concept for preaching in Ronald J. Sider and Michael A. King, *Preaching About Life in a Threatening World* (Philadelphia: Westminster Press, 1987), 24-28.

7. Fred B. Craddock, *Overhearing the Gospel* (Nashville: Abingdon Press, 1978).

8. See Renée Sauder's chapter, later in this book, for much more on narrative preaching.

9. As mentioned in note 4, the role of the church, the gathered people of God, the body of Christ tends to be addressed more implicitly than explicitly in this chapter since other chapters provide the more overt treatment, yet it does bear mention that key to following Jesus, as John Howard Yoder repeatedly affirms, involves starting less with first or foundational principles of logic and reason and more from within the faith language and practices of the Christian community. Yoder's view is that "the life of the community is before all possible methodological distillations," as he puts it in "Walk and Word: The Alternatives to Methodologism" in *Theology Without Foundations: Religious Practice and the Future of Theological Truth*," Stanley Hauerwas et. al., eds (Nashville: Abingdon, 1994), 82.

10. Hans-Georg Gadamer, *Truth and Method,* 2nd ed., trans. Joel Weinsheimer and Donald G. Marshall (New York: Continuum, 1994), 296-297. Parts of my interaction here with Gadamer and biblical hermeneutics were first published in Michael A. King, "Oxygen from the Bible" *Christian Living* (Autumn 1996), 18.

11. As in John Howard Yoder, *The Politics of Jesus* (Grand Rapids: 1972) and Hendrik Berkhof, *Christ and the Powers*, trans. John Howard Yoder (Scottdale, Pa.: Herald Press, 1962).

12. Although I want to be careful not to implicate her in views on exegesis/eisegesis she might or might not fully endorse, I see Nancy Heisey's chapter in this book, particularly her comments on reenvisioning the hermeneutical task as a dance rather than bridge-building, as another helpful and related way of emphasizing the dynamism required of preaching amid postmodernity.

Chapter 3

Premodern Text to Postmodern Ears: Steps Across the Hermeneutical Bridge ... or Joining the Circle Dance

✧

Nancy R. Heisey

INTRODUCTION: WHO IS LISTENING?

The elderly woman whose husband died three years ago sits near the front, always carrying her Bible with her to the service. It is well worn, and the preacher knows she reads it every day. The youth group members clustered in the back rows have each received a Bible as a gift from the congregation. They remember some of the stories from childhood Sunday school. Occasionally when facing a hard question, they flip through the text looking for something. The single mother, who discovered this congregation through other young parents who had befriended her, isn't sure how to look up the biblical references printed in the bulletin. She wonders at times why the preacher tries so hard to connect her remarks to such an ancient book. The middle-aged high school teacher who has spent his life in the church can't stop thinking about the recent article he read discussing new archaeological evidence that contradicts the biblical story he learned as a child. Silently, he asks whether the preacher pays any attention to such information.

Such economic, social, and faith-background diversity in many congregations within the Anabaptist tradition in North America is part of the reality many people now call "postmodernity."[1] Perhaps the most helpful way to think about what this term means is to note characteristics of an earlier way of thinking that used to be but is no longer widely shared. The "modern" view was defined by the understanding that human beings were rational and that society was continually making progress. It was also based on the belief that particular causes led to specific effects.[2] Most people in North American congregations have begun to think of reality as more complex and less mechanical. As biblical scholar Edgar McKnight explains, "Machines are relatively simple mechanical instruments, but conscious beings are very complex and unpredictable. *The world we see is like the human beings we are.*"[3]

Those responsible to proclaim God's Word in the congregation thus face a daunting task. On one hand, a preacher has the Bible, an ancient library which reveals high moments of God's encounter with humanity. On the other hand, he is part of a twenty-first-century community whose world is very distant in time and space from that of biblical characters. As part of the Christian community, he turns to this library as an authority for life, and calls it "the Word of God." Upon reflection, however, that expression does not directly describe how God speaks through the Bible. Instead, it is a metaphor. As biblical scholar Sandra Schneiders notes, "metaphor is perhaps our most powerful use of language, our most effective access to the meaning of reality at its deepest levels. . . . (But it) is not translatable into literal meaning."[4]

While today some preachers and congregations still assume there is no difference between the biblical world and the world they live in, most Westerners have long sensed a gap between their world and the world of the Bible. This has led to the image of interpretation as throwing a bridge across that gap—an "ugly broad ditch," as one scholar called it.[5] A postmodern perspective offers a more hopeful way to bring the Bible into conversation with the life of the church.

Those who study the practice of interpretation have described this approach as an experience in three worlds. First, all people begin to listen or read from where they stand, with their daily lives, varied pasts, and different social and economic situations. Coming to the Bible as they are, they can be helped by thinking about ways this identity shapes what they think. Such reflection can be called entering "the world before the text."[6]

Second, the Bible, like any book, is more than a ream of paper with printing on it. As anyone who has gotten absorbed in a good book knows, reading can lead readers to forget themselves, as characters, word pictures, themes, or plot take on a life of their own. The world of the text is this wealth found in the written material itself. Bible students have always thought this world mattered, but seldom done so while also consciously reflecting on the world before the text.

Third, the settings where the Bible was written and edited, the social and political realities that affected the people of that time, and the author(s) of the texts have an impact on what it means. These realities can be called "the world behind the text."

McKnight suggests that people who study the Bible envision these different worlds as "circles which hang together in an interlocking fashion and form a dynamic unity."[7] To imagine moving through these different worlds, made up of intersecting circles, the idea of a dance may be helpful. As the preacher works with the Bible in the preparation of a sermon, she will step back and forth between circles, sometimes dwelling longer in one or the other, but eventually taking all of them into account. There is not just one place to begin, nor one direction to go. But there is pattern, discipline, and rhythm to the process.

Such an approach to bringing the Scriptures, their authors, and today's people of God into a lively conversation is not only postmodern. Origen, an early Christian biblical scholar from Egypt, described a similar understanding with a different word picture:

> The whole divinely inspired Scripture may be likened . . . to many locked rooms in one house. By each room is placed a key, but not the one that corresponds to it, so that the keys are scattered about beside the rooms, none of them matching the room by which it is placed. It is a difficult task to find the keys and match them to the rooms that they can open.[8]

This dance also draws today's preachers into step with our Anabaptist forebears. The biblical interpreters of the Radical Reformation, suggests McKnight, worked from the conviction that they needed to "try," or test, the mainstream biblical interpretations of their time. They did so not to destroy meaning, but rather to attain new understandings that would strengthen faithful lives.[9] Likewise, a preacher's movement through the three worlds may open new windows of understanding and faithfulness for herself and her hearers.

THE WORLD BEFORE THE TEXT: CALLING OUT FOR SOMETHING NEW

Most preachers take the first steps of interpretation in the worlds where members of their congregations live. While some Christians continue to feel separate from our society, most have been swept into the rhythms of the broader culture. Church communities are marked by marriages and divorces, layoffs and job successes, health crises and healings, births, infertility and adoptions. After the terrible losses suffered in the terrorist attacks on New York and Washington in September 2001, white middle class Christians have also become part of a threatening world long familiar to people of color in the United States and to many citizens of the rest of the world. Learning the steps of faith where violence, injustice, fear, and grief are constant is a new challenge for many.

Living in this world, sometimes the biblical materials stand before a preacher dry and lifeless. At other times he is stunned by words that are painful to hear, let alone proclaim to others.[10] Sometimes he is moved by the excitement of being pulled forward into a new partnership with the Bible. As a dancer in the world before the text, the preacher's role is much like that of other artists. He must be shaped by extended practice and deep study before "performing." Yet his own life should also be changed by ongoing encounters with the text. He both studies and experiences the text; his story is found in its story.[11]

In the twenty-first century, a new challenge for preachers in the world before the text may be to rediscover a practice that shaped our Anabaptist forebears.[12] That practice was based on the confidence that everyone in the community could be a partner in the dance of interpretation. Even when a preacher finds her own life touched by the biblical material, she cannot merely recount that personal experience. Hearers want to be drawn in as well. This process may be partly the task of other elements of worship, such as prayer, litanies, dramatic readings, hymns, and visual arts.

But what of the sermon itself? Some preachers enjoy joining sermon talk-back groups. Others work hard to respond to office or e-mail conversations in the days following a sermon. A few have invited congregation members to a dialogue within the sermon itself; possibilities such as call and response, movement, and role play are only beginning to be explored. Such participation is not designed to manipulate everyone into agreement but rather to build a common experience of God's call that will affect the lives of all in the community when they leave the sanctuary and return to homes and places of work.[13] Another important question from the world before the text is how to converse with the Bible when it offers a picture that seems unjust or ungodly. Recognizing that the congregation is part of a historical community that has always struggled with such questions, the dance in the world before the text may take the shape of an extended wrestling match? Like Jacob with the stranger at the Jabbok, the preacher may cry out, "I will not let you go, unless you bless me!" (Gen 32:26). In situations where the text seems "wrong," lingering in the world before the text takes on greater importance. The question is not, "What does the text say?" but "How can we hear the text better as we listen to how it speaks to all in our community?"

The example of nineteenth-century Bible students dealing with the question of slavery provides helpful perspective. In that case, many careful biblical exegetes argued that slavery was acceptable. Others, however, who began by listening to the voices of slaves and then examining their own conscience, insisted that abolition of slavery was God's will. Seeing everyone in the community as a partner in bringing stories to and being formed by the biblical text may allow a life-giving meaning of the problematic passage to emerge as all struggle with the text, their world, and each other.[14]

THE WORLD OF THE TEXT: SHOCKING AND COMFORTING US

Preachers who honor the Anabaptist heritage will soon find their steps leading into the world of the biblical text itself. But here a preacher needs guidance to dance beyond simplistic readings. Much can be learned from early Christian students of the Bible, where the business of studying texts was taken very seriously. Four skills needed to be developed to elicit from texts their many gifts. First, students needed to learn textual criticism. All ancient students worked from hand-copied manuscripts, in which the possibilities of differences between manuscripts were enormous. Establishing for purposes of discussion that all were reading the same words and phrases could not be taken lightly.

Second, students learned to read the text out loud. Reading itself was a form of interpretation, for manuscripts had no capital letters, no periods or commas, and no quotation marks. Students needed to show that they could make sense of the text. What was being said? Who was speaking, and to whom?

Third, students took up the challenge of interpretation, or exegesis. They observed the definitions of words in the text and laid out the story line. They noted figures of speech, meter, and other elements of poetic style. When they had questions, they consulted other writings by the same author, because the author's "habits" were expected to be useful in coming to an understanding of a particular passage.

Only after these three skills had been exercised were the students ready for the fourth step, "judgment." It was then that they considered what in the text was useful for them.[15]

The seriousness of ancient textual study offers challenges to twenty-first century preachers working with biblical texts. Are they willing to work so hard, to take their Scriptures that seriously? As veteran preacher William Willimon puts it, a larger problem of biblical interpretation is not the gap between the world before and the world of the text, but that contemporary readers are used to thinking of reading as a simple, "user-friendly" activity. They are unpracticed in recognizing, let alone interpreting, the "thickness," or "surplus of meaning," in the text.[16]

A preacher might not be as systematic as the ancients in uncovering the many levels of richness in biblical texts, but it is helpful to have a plan as he begins to dance in the world of the text. Some steps can be suggested by the following questions:[17]

1. Is the passage poetry, narrative, letter, or law? What difference does its genre make?

2. How does the passage fit into the material surrounding it? Where does it fit within the overall outline of the book in which it is found?

3. How does the text sound when read aloud?

4. What do you notice when you outline the text or write it out showing the flow of the ideas as you heard them in reading aloud?

5. What words or phrases are emphasized or repeated? What is the range of meaning for words emphasized in the passage?

6. What technical, geographical, or historical terms are in need of definition?

7. Does the text call up visual images, color, or light? Does it suggest tastes, or smells?

8. What spaces does the text leave open? What does your imagination do with those spaces as you reflect on them? How might God's voice be found in those wordless spaces?

9. How does this text remind you of other biblical texts? How does God's Word throughout Scripture add to, clarify or question this text?

10. What invitation or challenge does the text offer? How might God be speaking through that invitation or challenge?

The pattern of the dance through the world of the text will move in two additional directions. First, preachers must consider the relationship between the English version(s) and the original languages of the text. Those who have the necessary training and time to translate from Hebrew or Greek will often discover additional exciting meaning possibilities from their efforts. Others may turn to a commentary that provides translation notes. Still others, who have skill in more than one modern language, may compare the way a passage "sounds" in English to Spanish, or Swahili, or Chinese. The translation question does not have one correct answer, but it is essential that the dance within the world of the text maintain a lively awareness that the Bible the preacher and the congregation use is indeed a translation. Activities that heighten this awareness are always appropriate.

A second question is what kinds of "helps" aid preaching preparation. Many preachers are tempted to turn immediately to a trusted commentary. However, if the preacher takes seriously her own participation in the interpretive dance, it is crucial to start with personal encounter with the text. Since all biblical commentaries, dictionaries, and handbooks are themselves interpretations, none can stand in for personal effort. Yet neither is ignorance useful, and all preachers need access to a good set of biblical commentaries plus Bible dictionary or handbook. Although study Bibles may provide helpful information, it is important to be aware of the editorial bias of the usually anonymous writers who provide the information in such Bibles. "Helps" provide the greatest assistance after the preacher has spent her own time with the text.

The preacher can engage the world of the text without being afraid of missing its "meaning." If he works carefully, taking time to let it soak into mind and body, with faith that God can speak, then the text will offer up something useful for the sermon in preparation. Often he will be surprised by what he finds; he will sometimes be shocked and at other times comforted. When he returns to the same text later, whether through another sermon, a Bible study, or personal devotions, he is likely to discover that even more meaning is present.[18] That is the gift of a lifelong commitment to dancing in the world of the text. Yet when preachers have engaged the Bible as fully as they can in one experience of sermon preparation, they have not yet finished the dance. They still need to circle into the world behind the text.

THE WORLD BEHIND THE TEXT: ROOTING US IN OUR STORY

It may be tempting to let this part of the dance to experts. For the Bible, which developed in the Mediterranean region, is now being read around the world, more than fifteen hundred years after it was collected in the form now in use. While early Christian students of the Bible had asked some historical questions about the text, seeing the Bible as a historical document is one legacy of the eighteenth-century European Enlightenment. Certainly sixteenth-century Anabaptists did not think primarily of the Bible as an ancient book. Indeed, some radical Anabaptists with an eschatological bent were convinced that the text's end-time visions literally described their own era.[19]

Today's congregations differ from both citizens of the biblical world and our sixteenth-century ancestors. Although the reality of biblical historicity is unavoidable, different responses to this reality have shaped the church. Some understand what the Bible says as mostly relative—and relatively distant from the present, since it comes from particular ancient times and places. Its historicity then means that its message cannot be timeless.

Others have adopted the modern worldview that only scientifically demonstrated facts are "true." Thinking this way means that everything in the Bible must prove historically accurate in the modern sense to be useful for the church.

Still others, especially those who struggled with readings that claimed to be the same for everyone in every century, have discovered fresh meaning in pictures emerging from the world behind the text. Seeing the archeological find of an inscription from the temple of Paul's day forbidding Gentiles to go beyond a certain point, for example, heightens the power of the apostle's call for Gentile inclusion within the Jesus community.[20]

All of these diverse responses have taken place in a setting where historical criticism has been the predominant scholarly approach to biblical study. It has often seemed that critical biblical study concerned itself primarily with "the author who composed (the text) or the world in which it was composed."[21] Modern assumptions led many biblical scholars to claim that they could uncover assured "scientific" results for the history behind the text. Yet in the twenty-first century there is still much disagreement, for example, about specific details of the life of the historical Jesus or how the Pentateuch developed.

In addition, since the 1970s many other approaches to biblical interpretation have challenged historical criticism. The idea that the world before the text matters is an important part of this challenge. Thus a migrant agricultural worker in the Southwest United States, a middleclass housewife in Pennsylvania, and a Sudanese refugee being resettled in a major urban area, will all find unique points of contact with the text.[22] The understandings of those who live on the "underside" of our world often challenge mainstream interpretations of the Bible.

Equally important for preachers is the challenge to historical criticism by scholars such as Schneiders and McKnight, who recognize that a heavy emphasis on historical criticism has often done little to strengthen the role of the Bible in the church. Yet neither would they say that historical understandings should be discarded. The question is how to profit from historical knowledge as well as allowing insights from other perspectives to enrich biblical study.[23]

Historical understandings underline that the Bible comes from a world very distant and different from the one in which today's preacher lives. She need not hesitate to take steps into the world behind the text, however. Many recent studies, some in the selected reading list below, offer to be her partners.[24] These works describe, for example, that people of the Bible thought of their universe as a tiered cosmos of three, seven, or many levels, with the earth as its center. In contrast, she knows we live on a tiny planet-speck in a small solar system at the edge of one galaxy within an infinitely expanding universe. People of the Bible lived in a world where many gods and other spiritual powers such as demons or angels were active. Unconsciously if not consciously, she shares the modern presupposition that spiritual and secular realms are separate. People of the Bible lived in a world where the honor or shame of the community overrode the significance of an individual. It was a world of patriarchy, of many slaves and few masters. She lives in a world where personal liberty, freedom of expression, and individual prerogative are central values, at least from within the middle and upper class.

One historical reality about the biblical world, however, connects more closely to the present. The twenty-first century has opened dominated by an imperial power, while most of the world's people suffer the oppression generated by the exercise of that power. It makes a difference, then, to recognize that the compilers of what Christians call the Old Testament worked in the face of the destruction of their homeland by the superpower Babylon. It is also important to think about what it means that Jesus lived and taught, and died as a political criminal, in a colonial territory of the Roman Empire. Paul, as well as other early Christian witnesses, traveled, preached, and suffered martyrdom within that same empire. Such understandings point toward interpretations that recognize the underlying biblical theme of liberation and the sociopolitical as well as personal spiritual dimensions of the salvation to which the Bible calls.[25]

The historical dimension of the biblical story not only links this world and the worlds of the Bible, however. History also calls to a further conversation with our Anabaptist ancestors, one of whose approaches to biblical interpretation is sometimes labeled "Christocentrism." This concept has been described in the saying, "When two texts disagree, Jesus is the referee."[26] Our faith forebears asserted that the Bible was not all the same—some passages carried more weight than others. At the center of sixteenth-century Anabaptist biblical interpretation was Jesus' teaching in the Sermon on the Mount. Rather than being dogmatic and legalistic in its understandings, Anabaptists who thought Christocentrically drew on this passage because they believed that it taught the fruit of correct interpretation as the way believers lived.[27]

History connects the circles in which stories of believers, from the times of the Bible through the centuries to the present, are found. The preacher who claims this heritage owes it to himself to reflect on why the Anabaptists grasped the centrality of Jesus' way for scriptural interpretation. Could it be that their marginal status and suffering shaped such an understanding? The challenge of the world behind the text is, more than anything else, to connect the story of the preacher and the congregation with the story of God's people—which the Anabaptists understood as their own story of following Jesus faithfully in life. This is the way of the small ones, powerless in worldly perspective, nonviolent, and committed to living into God's reign in the world. It is a vision to work for, and to pray for. Descendants of the Anabaptists who cannot identify with the Jesus of the margins are invited to enter into deeper fellowship with Christian brothers and sisters of diverse ethnic, gender, and economic identities in their societies, and with those around the world who extend the invitation to join them in being Jesus' people for the twenty-first century. With a joyful response, the preacher has danced full circle, back into the world before the text.

CONCLUSION

For preachers seeking to rightly interpret the Bible in preaching, then, the dance metaphor opens new possibilities that the image of a bridge does not. For a bridge implies a means of transit that offers passage in only two directions, from here to there and back again. Further, a bridge is built to transport freight from one end to the other, as if meaning is something separate from who we are and what we experience.

To dance, in contrast, means to move in many directions, to be part of the Bible's meaning, rather than only carrying its meaning with us. Encountering the world before the text, the world of the text, and the world behind the text helps us to take the Bible seriously, while not assuming that just one method provides the best or the only interpretation. As dancing requires partners, sometimes one, sometimes two, and sometimes many, so this approach to biblical interpretation always involves the Bible, Jesus Christ as God's Word, and all of us.

Finally, to dance requires some kind of rhythm—which may be the best way to understand the work of the Holy Spirit throughout the whole process. With the throbbing of the Spirit's wings in our ears, let us be ready for what God is saying to break through, eternal and ever fresh, into our lives.

SELECTED READING LIST

Anderson, Bernhard W. with Katheryn Pfisterer Darr. *Understanding the Old Testament*. Abridged Fourth Edition. Upper Saddle River, N.J.: Prentice Hall, 1998.

Charlesworth, James and Walter P. Weaver, eds. *Jesus Two Thousand Years Later*. Harrisburg, Pa.: Trinity Press International, 2000.

Coogan, Michael D., ed. *The Oxford History of the Biblical World*. New York: Oxford University Press, 1998.

Ehrman, Bart D. *The New Testament: A Historical Introduction to the Early Christian Writings*. New York: Oxford University Press, 1997.

Freedman, David Noel, Allen C. Myers and Astrid B. Beck, eds. *Eerdmans Dictionary of the Bible*. Grand Rapids, Mich.: Eerdmans, 2000.

Rousseau, John J. and Rami Arav, eds. *Jesus and His World: An Archeological and Cultural Dictionary*. Minneapolis: Fortress, 1995.

NOTES

1. See also chapter one, by Michael A. King.

2. Edgar V. McKnight, *Jesus in History and Scripture: A Poetic and Sectarian Perspective* (Macon, Ga.: Mercer University Press, 1999), 112-113.

3. McKnight, *Jesus in History and Scripture*, 117 (emphasis author's). See also McKnight's description of the diverse congregations in which he has led studies on biblical interpretation, viii, ix.

4. Sandra M. Schneiders, *The Revelatory Text: Interpreting the New Testament as Sacred Scripture*, 2nd. ed. (Collegeville, Minn.: The Liturgical Press, 1999), 29.

5. Colin J. D. Greene, "'In the Arms of the Angels': Biblical Interpretation, Christology and the Philosophy of History," in *Renewing Biblical Interpretation*, ed. Craig Bartholomew et al. (Grand Rapids: Zondervan, 2000), 206.

6. In this article, I am taking liberty with the way the idea of the "world before the text" is often used in hermeneutical discussions. My use refers largely to the world of the congregation's experience, rather than more strictly the world where the reader's experience and the text's subject matter intersect. See Robert M Grant with David Tracy, *A Short History of the Interpretation of the Bible*, 2nd. ed. (Philadelphia: Fortress, 1984), 159-160.

7. McKnight, *Jesus in History and Scripture*, 313; see also the outline of Schneiders' work in *The Revelatory Text*, which uses a chapter outline including these three perspectives for consideration of biblical texts. Throughout, both Schneiders and McKnight offer a great deal of additional historical background and theoretical insight related to the task of biblical interpretation, which will be useful to some readers. This article is deeply indebted to the work of both authors, but takes considerable freedom in its use of the models they offer.

8. Origen, Commentary on Psalms 3, in Joseph W. Trigg, ed., *Origen* (London and New York: Routledge, 1998),70-71.

9. McKnight, *Jesus in History and Scripture*, 283-284.

10. Stanley Hauerwas, "Practice Preaching," in Erskine Clarke, ed., *Exilic Preaching: Testimony for Christian Exiles in an Increasingly Hostile Culture* (Harrisburg, Pa.: Trinity Press International, 1998), 65. Hauerwas suggests that preaching is the only place in our society where many people will hear something that painful, hard to listen to, or prophetic.

11. Schneiders, *The Revelatory Text*, 172. Schneiders provides the analogy of the biblical scholar to the artist, but does not discuss the additional process of making what has been gleaned by biblical study and reflection accesible to others. Her work is helpful in providing a more theoretical description of the process by which those who study the Bible also have a live encounter with the text.

12. See also chapter three by June Alliman Yoder.

13. Stuart Murray, *Biblical Interpretation in the Anabaptist Tradition* (Kitchener, Ont.: Pandora Press, 2000), 157-185, describes in great detail the sixteenth-century Anabaptist practice of the hermeneutical community. See also Murray's call for participatory sermons as necessary in twenty-first century churches, at http://churchoutreach.com/archive.

14. Schneiders, *The Revelatory Text*, 177; Wayne Meeks, "The 'Haustafeln' and American Slavery: A Hermeneutical Challenge," in Eugene H. Lovering, Jr., and Jerry L. Sumney, eds., *Theology and Ethics in Paul and His Interpreters: Essays in Honor of Victor Paul Furnish* (Nashville: Abingdon, 1996), 232-253.

15. Trigg, *Origen*, 5-7.

16. William H. Willimon, "Postmodern Preaching: Learning to Love the Thickness of the Text," in Clarke, *Exilic Preaching*, 110-111.

17. This article does not discuss how sermon texts are selected for preaching. It assumes, however, that it is important for some thoughtful process of text selection to be in place. It is imperative that biblical interpretation in preaching not fall prey to the special interests or perspectives of the preacher.

18. Willimon, "Postmodern Preaching," 116.

19. See McKnight, *Jesus in History and Scripture*, ch. 10, "How to Read and How Not to Read the Bible," a discussion of the interpretational understandings of the Münster Anabaptists.

20. See McKnight's description of his own moves from one kind of biblical interpretational method to another, and the freeing impact of historical understandings, *Jesus in History and Scripture*, 309-310.

21. Fernando F. Segovia, "'And They Began to Speak in Other Tongues': Competing Modes of Discourse in Contemporary Biblical Criticism," in Fernando F. Segovia and Mary Ann Tolbert, eds., *Reading From This Place*, vol. 1, *Social Location and Biblical Interpretation in the United States* (Minneapolis, Minn.: Fortress, 1995), 1-32.

22. Segovia, "And They Began to Speak," 1-32.

23. Schneiders, *The Revelatory Text*, 99-100; McKnight, *Jesus in History and Scripture*, 276. See also Al Wolters, "Confessional Criticism and the Night Visions of Zechariah," in Bartholomew et al., *Renewing Biblical Interpretation*, 90-117.

24. See Jacob A. Loewen, *The Bible in Cross-Cultural Perspective* (Pasadena, Calif.: William Carey Library, 2000), for an in-depth discussion of the evolution of biblical cosmology throughout the period that the Bible was written and compiled.

25. See Ched Myers, *Binding the Strong Man: A Political Reading of Mark's Story of Jesus* (Maryknoll, N.Y.: Orbis, 1988); Richard A. Horsley, ed., *Paul and Empire: Religion and Power in Roman Imperial Society* (Harrisburg, Pa.: Trinity Press International, 1997); Richard A. Horsley, *Jesus and Empire: The Kingdom of God and the New World Disorder* (Minneapolis: Fortress, 2002).

26. This is a formula that I learned from students in my Bible classes at Eastern Mennonite University.

27. Murray, *Biblical Interpretation in the Anabaptist Tradition*, ch. 4.

Chapter 4

Preaching and the Bible: First We Have to Read It

Mary Schertz

When the millennium turned, my congregation did our fall Bible study on Revelation. It seemed timely. As part of that series, we asked a professor from the nearby Seventh Day Adventist school to preach for us one Sunday. At the end of the service, one of our members, a highly educated and sophisticated professional, confessed that although she did not agree with some of what the brother said, she really liked his biblical preaching. She wished we had more of that kind of preaching in our church. What she said is also what we hear at the seminary. What the people in congregations want is biblical preaching. Sometimes these desires are expressed in a critical vein—as in the charge that the seminary is not delivering preachers who preach biblical sermons. More often it is offered in a spirit of nostalgia, a musing about what seems lost in our tradition.

As a New Testament professor, allow me to be defensive for a moment. Some things are worth defending and in the normal course of my work, I do ponder the issue of "biblical preaching." I teach preachers to read a biblical text closely and empathetically. With Perry Yoder, my Old Testament colleague, I have written a book[1] in which we encourage pastors to think clearly and passionately about the "points of attachment" between a text and the congregation to whom they are preaching. The entire premise of that book is that the biblical texts have the capacity to nourish preachers, first of all, and to nourish their congregations as well.

Furthermore, although we did not quite have the guts to put it in the book explicitly, what we really mean is that unless the biblical text nurtures us we are not being nurtured. There is no substitute for the text. It is foundational. Dynamic delivery, riveting sermon illustrations, pertinent thematic material, solid theology and the warmth of a Holy Spirit filled faith are important aspects of preaching. But the heart of the preaching matter is the biblical text, the word of God. What we teach preaching students to do is to work with a text and to work with it well; to preach from a text and to preach from it well.

Now, having made my defense, I will also confess that I wonder sometimes whether what we do and teach is exactly what the people of the church mean when they call for "biblical preaching." Perhaps dedicated exegesis of a text and careful connection to the needs of the congregation, important as they are, are not all people are looking for when they think of biblical preaching. What I would like to do in this chapter is to look more carefully at the issue I think people are really raising when they call for biblical preaching and what we can do to help fulfill that yearning.

PREMODERN CONTEXT AND BIBLICAL PREACHING

I suspect that what people generally mean by biblical preaching is more or less what I grew up with on the drained-swamps-turned-fertile-fields in central Illinois. Many of these sermons were very long. We would settle into our pews after the Sunday school hour. We would begin the service by singing a stanza of "Jesus, Stand Among Us," followed by a spoken call to worship, two more hymns, the Scripture reading, and the pastoral prayer. The sermon itself began fairly precisely at 11:15 and went until at least noon—for a customary sermon. But often he—and it was always he—continued a few minutes past noon. The congregation's level of tolerance visibly and audibly faded at about 12:15 and all our regular preachers honored that edge. Occasionally a guest preacher would ignore the obvious and preach past 12:15.

The issue of length, I suggest, is a central and crucial issue to biblical preaching. Not in itself, of course, but in the scope of what the preacher was able to do with those extra minutes. Preachers in those days did not face expectations for pastoral care, pastoral counseling, meetings with groups of other ministers and conference work as heavy as those we impose on today's pastors. But they were also often doing something, such as farming or teaching, to put food into their children's mouths. In actuality they had no more time than today's preachers to prepare sermons even though they preached more than twice as long as most preachers do today. What they did, as nearly as I can recall, was to spend the first fifteen or twenty minutes on the text of the day. Then, having exhausted the results of their study for the week as well as their ideas about that text, they most normally started ranging through the biblical canon. It might be a recital—the biblical story from Genesis to Revelation. Or it might be more thematic—connecting all the places in the Bible where the main idea of the text for the day occurred. Or it might be something more creative—a story in the Old Testament that resonated with the story from the New Testament, or the other way around. At any rate, the second half was a "spin-off" of some sort from the text which had been read before the sermon began.

Was this good preaching? Is this what I want graduates to do when they move into their first pastorates? Well, probably not, even if today's congregations would stand for it. A lot about this kind of preaching was frankly awful. It was sometimes repetitive and boring. It was occasionally ill conceived and lacking in careful thought. It played its role in numbing minds and turning young people off church entirely.

But in all this preaching, some good, some awful, a lot of it mediocre, there were also powerful factors at work that were nurturing, that people rightfully appreciated as good sound biblical preaching, that people in congregations still want today. Perhaps the most important was the part I, as a youth in the church, liked the least. The section after the discussion about the text for the day, the part where the preacher ranged through the Bible, was, after all, a means of putting the text into its canonical context. It was a way of assessing the text, giving it weight or reducing its weight in light of the biblical canon. Even as our attention dipped in and out, something dynamic and useful was being achieved. At least three important goals were met in this canonical rambling.

Gift one: A range of biblical voices

First, the preachers were letting us in on a range of biblical voices. We certainly understood that the ultimate author was God speaking to us, the church. But despite these certainties, it was also abundantly apparent that God as ultimate author spoke in different ways over the years and across the cultures. God spoke in two testaments, for instance, and the second was different and probably "better" than the first, although these earlier preachers were not New Testament supercessionists in the contemporary sense of the term. In ways that are somewhat unusual today, the Old Testament functioned as Bible for us. That is to say, we were almost as apt to hear sermons on the Old Testament as the New. Moreover, it was not just Psalms, Isaiah, or the more palatable Proverbs that lent gist for the sermon mill. We also heard sermons on the various exploits of the patriarchs and the kings and the minor prophets. It was a fairly eclectic biblical menu.

In addition to the differences between the testaments, it was also evident that there were differences of point of view within the testaments. We would never have heard of source theory, the Yahwistic or Priestly documents, the Synoptic Problem, or redaction criticism. If we had, we would have dismissed them as attempts to make us doubt and stray from true faith. However, because we knew the scope of the biblical text well, we could not escape an awareness of the contradictions. We knew some of the Gospels left out important parts of the story of Jesus. We struggled to reconcile the Jesus of the Gospels and the Lamb of Revelation. We did not know quite what to do with the business of Paul telling the women of Corinth to wear coverings when they prophesied, then telling Timothy women were not to speak in church.

Gift two: Still the Bible coheres

If the diversity of the texts was one message that came through all those years of half-listening as the preachers at Cazenovia Mennonite droned on through the seasons, another message was that the Bible essentially cohered despite the diversity and contradictions. These preachers also gave us a sense that there was a "big picture," a pattern, a sense of flow and direction that could be derived from the biblical text. The voices in the text might be diverse, but there was an assumption that behind this diversity lay a basic unity. I am sure that these preachers, consciously or not so consciously, hurried over some of the critical problems in the text. Certainly, even when some difficulties were noted, individual explanations were not always or uniformly persuasive and compelling. The unity was expressed in simple ways—perhaps sometimes too simply. Still the basic themes emerged—God's love and providence, human sin and divine salvation, the work of God through history to bring about his will. Not only did these basic themes emerge with clarity, but we also gained a sense of reliance, of trust, of assurance that we could build our lives upon and around these texts.

We were not, as a congregation, aware of the higher biblical criticism making its mark in the scholarly world of the time. I do not know whether our preachers were aware of those trends or not. Certainly the seminary-trained men, of whom we had some, would have had some knowledge of such studies. In the end, we got what mattered—this sense of a larger coherence that transcends the smaller contradictions.

As it turns out, some decades later, the pastors and the congregations listening to them might have been better off not paying too much attention to what was happening in the disciplines of biblical studies and biblical theology at that time. To say this is not to suggest that these many years of dedicated study by biblical scholars have been in vain. As the apostle Paul would have said, by no means! Those years have been particularly fruitful and productive. We are, contemporary biblical scholars and congregations alike, indebted to the men and women who made textual studies their lives' work in more ways than we can say. To question some of the fruits is only to say that the service of biblical scholars is such that congregations should not and do not need to go through all the scholarly gyrations to arrive at a fruitful point. In the end, while the coherence of the biblical text has taken a battering in scholarly studies, more and more people of stature within the fields have begun once again asserting the basic unity of the texts.[2]

At any rate, living with the text necessitates some basic trust that the texts cohere. Biblical preaching has a duty to instill this trust. Outside our tiny church, the corn grew in the sultry July sun or the winter wind howled across the prairies and rattled the windows. Inside, our knowledge and appreciation of the biblical canon was being formed, a lifelong gift that would not be recognized by many of us for another half a lifetime.

Gift three: The preacher's role

The third gift of biblical preaching as I experienced it at Cazenovia had to do with the role of the preacher himself. It was evident that the preacher believed that not only was there, among the diversity of voices, a basic coherence but it was that it was our responsibility as Christians to see and to use this coherence. Our lives were to be in continuity with this pattern, even though it was sometimes difficult to see. However, especially when it was difficult to see the pattern, it was important, crucial even, to try. This effort constituted faith. We learned this basic faith stance in many ways, both in and outside of the Sunday morning service.

But one important way we learned this "bottom line" was through having the preacher up there in the pulpit every Sunday weaving a text into the canon and weaving the canon into his and our experience. We could and did criticize the various pastors that ministered to us. They were human and limited in their pastoral gifts and we were typical in our expectation that they would be more than human and unlimited in their pastoral gifts. But the one thing we neither questioned or criticized, to my knowledge, was these pastors' recognizable and consistent effort to live life in relation to the biblical text and to help us also live similarly. Although we might rake the minister over the coals for some real or imagined slight of his "Christian duty," we never questioned or criticized his basic use and appreciation of the Bible. We might and did question certain interpretations, such as what women could or could not do in church. That the minister cared about the biblical text and was living within its guidelines as he perceived those guidelines was never doubted.

Our preachers gave us these three gifts—at least—the gift of the diversity of the texts, the gift of their unity and, perhaps most important of all, the gift of their central role in human and ecclesial life.

This analysis of biblical preaching decades ago would not be complete, of course, without mentioning certain habits that supported what the preachers were doing from the pulpit. They did not bear the entire weight of the congregation's biblical knowledge by any means. We did not have the wonderfully creative curricula with which we are blessed today.

Nevertheless, most the adults in the congregation in which I grew up spent time each morning in devotions. Much of their private devotional time was devoted to Bible study, often through correspondence courses for which they received diplomas. Wednesday evening prayer meeting often included some Scripture study—and always for the children who were not usually expected to join in the rather lengthy intercessory prayers that took the bulk of the adults' time. Sunday evening worship was given to visiting missionaries, singing groups or other special programming. Still, there was almost always a Scripture read somewhere in the course of these evenings and a few comments made on the text.

Last, but hardly least, there was the two weeks of Bible school in June. Not only did Bible school play a significant role in the education of the children. Our church was quite small and the Bible school was quite large since many community parents were glad their children had something to do besides get into trouble around town. Consequently, almost every adult was pressed into teaching, even many of the farmers, there being a bit of a lull in the field work after planting. It is, of course, a cliché to say that one learns best by teaching, but it is my guess that this situation contributed significantly not only to the children's learning of Bible but to the adults' Christian education as well.

The preachers of those bygone days were not preaching into a biblical void. While many or even most people in their congregations would have had no more than a high school education, these were not people who were biblically illiterate by any means. If not terribly sophisticated in their hermeneutics, they were nevertheless people with a wide and deep, basic knowledge of Scripture.

POSTMODERN CONTEXT AND BIBLICAL PREACHING:

Life in our contemporary churches has changed drastically, not least in the matter of biblical literacy. Preachers no longer have the liberty of taking forty-five minutes or an hour Sunday morning to exposit Scripture. Nor are these Sunday morning sermons any longer primarily exegetical in many churches. When sermons are based on biblical passages, the association may sometimes be quite a loose one, the Scripture serving as an entrée into the topic but little else. Some sermons do not even pretend or claim to be biblical in nature. Of course there are needs and places for thematic, narrative, or topical sermons. As someone raised on a steady diet of "biblical preaching," I would certainly attest to the need for some variation on occasion.

Many preachers do, of course, preach diligently and well on biblical texts, following the lectionary, doing Bible book studies, using committees to select texts, and in other ways undergirding their preaching. However, sermons based on Scripture are often focused on a single text. Again I am not being critical here but simply trying to describe the differences. Certainly, many of our preachers do an exceptionally fine job of putting texts before congregations in ways that they can not only understand but also appropriate. But what seems to be lacking today, something we once received as a matter of course, is the canonical work.[3] Rarely do we hear anyone ranging through the canon, connecting texts on a theme or even just telling the biblical story from beginning to end. In fact, I have a distinct memory of a preaching class I took in which a colleague was rather thoroughly criticized by both peers and instructor for "throwing the whole Bible" at the congregation in "one fell swoop."

This canonical focus that we used to chafe under but also take for granted is, as far as I can determine, only present in the contemporary scene by the use of the lectionary in some congregations. When my present congregation started using the lectionary, for instance, the matter of biblical diet was mentioned. We turned to the lectionary because preachers admitted to their tendency to use favorite passages and because our hunting for passages to meet our needs was obviously wearing a little thin. While the use of the lectionary is solid practice, it does not quite serve the same purposes the preachers used to fulfill by "throwing the whole Bible" at us frequently.

The biggest difference is, of course, that we have to connect the dots for ourselves. In the long run, this may be the best way to do it, but how many of us take the time and energy to think about the texts that we've been hearing all year and wonder how they relate to each other? In addition, the lectionary itself is not the canon. It is a truncated, theological selection that often leaves much to be desired. Its limitations can be seen in individual readings when, for instance, the difficult, awkward, or violent verses of a Psalm are omitted. It is also limited in its selections from individual books—how many lament Psalms are included in the lectionary? Most glaring, however, is the absence of huge sections of the canon, particularly in the Old Testament, but also in the New. Where are the historical books represented? Where are the minor prophets represented? Rarely are the epistles of 1 John used or Philemon or Revelation. Even when preachers are diligent about using the biblical text for sermons, we simply use much less of the biblical text than preachers used to.

Not only do we hear less of the text on Sunday mornings, but there are far fewer opportunities for congregations to read and study Bible outside of the Sunday morning worship service. Sunday school, which used to be taken for granted for adults as well as children, is less well attended. The uniform lessons, which also used to be taken for granted as the main curriculum for Sunday school, have been supplanted with books on theology, psychology, or other topical studies. Wednesday night prayer meetings are history as are Sunday evening services in most congregations. Bible schools are a week long instead of two weeks and are often joint projects of several churches involving fewer students and fewer adults.

In short, what energy and money we do have for Christian education we spend on the children—adults have virtually no venues outside the public reading of Scripture and the sermon to relate to the Bible in other than a private way. Furthermore, our busy lives have, for most adults, precluded substantive devotional interaction with the text.

In addition to the shrinking dimensions of our relationship with the biblical text, the nature of our consensus about the text as well as our controversies about the text have changed dramatically. I do not mean to understate the kinds of controversies that plagued our conferences and denominations in time long past. Some of those were bitter and hard fought. Nevertheless, in at least what was once called the "Old Mennonite Church," in days gone by, the fights were mostly between groups who differed on specific interpretations of what Scripture said while essentially agreeing on the most basic hermeneutical assumptions of what role the Bible plays in life. Today many of our differences are between groups who have very different hermeneutical assumptions about Scripture and, consequently, what sort of place we ought to give it in our lives.

WHAT THEN SHALL WE DO?

In retrospect, the "good, old days" do have some things to commend them—and perhaps are worthy of a modicum of nostalgia, especially in this age when staying "in" and "with it" consumes more of our time and energy than most of us would actually confess. But I am not really making a value judgment here. Rather I am trying to be descriptive about the issues of biblical literacy and how it, or the lack of it, affects preaching today.

Certainly there are many things about the present era of biblical study that I would not trade for anything out of our past, even if I could. Our knowledge of the text has increased. We have a better understanding of what the Bible is and how it came to be the canon for the church. We have a greater database of historical research and information that simply was not available years ago. We also have ways of studying the Bible that illumine the text in fresh and exciting ways. Two major new methods of biblical study have flourished in these years, namely different kinds of linguistic, discourse and literary analysis as well as different kinds of social analysis. These new methods have both corrected some of the mistakes we have made in the past as well as added their own findings to our general understanding.[4] Technology has made available information and the tools of biblical study to a wide, although by no means universal, clientele.

Most important, women, people of color, people in developing nations all over the world have added their voices to the symphony of interpretation. Base communities in Latin America, gatherings of women theologians in Africa, Asian scholars of the Bible, and many other people and groups have all contributed in significant ways to our appreciation of the text. Again, these interpreters have in some cases challenged certain assumptions and conclusions and corrected mistakes, but also have contributed many fresh and elegant explanations of texts that would not have emerged from the more truncated and limited perspectives of the Western, white, male scholarship that dominated the scene for so many years.[5] All these opportunities and more are reasons to delight in the changes that the years have wrought for biblical preaching.

Nevertheless, despite all these wonderful advances, we are in serious trouble in many respects both with the issues of biblical preaching and indeed with the issues of living by the word of God at all. Unless we attend to the matter with vigor and a willingness to rediscover old ways as well as invent new ways to provide our congregations with a sense of the biblical whole, we will soon lose the very vitality that has been a part of the church down through the ages.

Thankfully, there are some things, old and new, that we can try. Whether in family Bible reading, reading groups, or simply individuals reading on their own, the most interesting observations and questions arise when people are actually reading. One of the finest services a preacher can offer a congregation is simply to encourage its participants to read the text. We have tended to dismiss "read through the Bible" programs as archaic, but I would like to see them revived. For some people, all that is needed is that small bit of structure. A group of ministers in our area got together and decided to publish a chapter of the New Testament a day in the local paper. That's a small and simple thing—but has the power to create a reading community. I would like to see more congregations making these kinds of efforts.

But the whole Bible is too daunting for many people and often, as in the case of our local paper's effort, what gets cut out is the Old Testament. What if, however, a congregation decided they would read an Old Testament book in conjunction with a New Testament book, such as Daniel and Revelation, Isaiah and Luke, Deuteronomy and Romans, or Genesis and Acts? These are more limited goals that would invite believers to read one part of the canon in light of another part. Moreover, this kind of reading would circumvent the common notion that the New Testament is always the more profound of the two.

Another simple reading strategy is to read through an entire Gospel as if it were a novel. That does not mean assuming that the Gospel is fiction but rather reading it "for the story." Read it in as few sessions as possible; read it fast. When I ask my students to read Luke-Acts this way, we have the most amazing conversations afterward. These are seminary students—rarely is my course their first Bible course and never do I have students who are new to these texts. Yet most of them have never read any part of the Bible in other than the piecemeal, fragmentary fashion we use for public or devotional reading. My first question in the discussion period following such a reading is invariably "What surprised you?" Sometimes that is the only question I have to ask.

Reading aloud for "entertainment" may also be almost a lost art, but it too can be revived. One night I was visiting in the home of some friends, and as the evening grew to a close they invited me to join their evening devotions. What they were doing with their three teenage children was reading through Judges. Amid good-natured groans and gentle teasing, the family settled down to wade through some of those strange stories and odd comments about events in them. Certainly some of the questions the teens raised were less than reverent. This was as it should be—what those stories and comments mean for people of faith should raise honest questions. What was important from my perspective, aside from all the benefits for family dynamics, was that they were reading, and reading in a sustained, disciplined manner. Furthermore, what they were reading was creating interest and stirring the imaginations of the three teens—building that all-important reading context for the next generation of believers.

In addition to ways pastors and preachers can encourage individuals and families to read the biblical text, there is also much that can be done to nurture Bible reading in church groups. Sunday evening worship, Wednesday evening prayer meetings, and even adult Sunday school may be lost causes. But believers are continuing to meet in groups. Small groups meet, men's and women's groups meet, youth groups meet. As long as the church exists, there are likely to be smaller groups within the larger body that draw together. As long as smaller groups within the larger body draw together, there is hope for Christian education and for biblical literacy. Furthermore, these groups are often looking for ways to focus and bring energy to their group experience. While personal support and individual growth are sometimes the main concerns of these groups, and are often the reason the groups form in the first place, these concerns often cannot sustain the liveliness of the group over time. Bible reading and study can provide nurture for all sorts of groups if handled rightly.

In these situations, especially with adults, but even with teens, simply reading through a portion of text and allowing questions to arise may be adequate. These sessions may well crystalize a cluster of questions in which the group may wish to invest further—either by commissioning some additional study or by asking a more skilled and specialized teacher to join them for a session or two. But there are some simple exercises that can be quite powerful in a small group experience.[6] To these I now turn.

EXERCISE: AN EXAMPLE

One exercise we at the seminary have found useful is a process outlined in *Seeing the Text.*[7] This exercise is particularly helpful in bringing human experience to bear on the text and bringing the text to bear on human experience, a goal not only in keeping with small group life but one of the most important reasons to meet as a small group at all. In addition, the exercise plays a vital role in creating and assessing the canonical context of biblical texts—one of the dynamics so lacking in contemporary congregations.

This exercise involves asking participants to name the ten biblical texts "without which you cannot live." It can be set up in various ways—but usually works best if group members have some time to work at it on their own, thinking through the question, reading and rereading portions of the Bible, making and revising their lists.

The question is indeed a simple one, but answering it is often not such a simple matter. It gets to the heart of who we are as individuals as well as what we think is the heart of biblical faith. It is well worth taking time and putting effort into this part of the exercise. These lists are unlikely to remain exactly the same as one goes through life. They are unlikely to be exactly the same from person to person. But that is not the point. The point is the practice of deciding which of all the biblical texts are the most life-giving for a particular individual. There could be more or fewer, of course. There is no particular magic in the number ten. On the other hand, we have found ten to be a good number with which to work—it both provides generous scope yet limits the work.

The real magic is in the interaction that takes place between the members of the group and the biblical text as people begin to talk about the texts they chose and why they chose them. Or, in some cases, about the texts they did not choose and why they did not choose them. Both individuals and groups learn much by doing this exercise. It is self-revelatory, in that the reasons for the choices can sometimes be found in the person's experience. A text that was meaningful at a particular point of crisis in life often shows up on these personal lists. Older persons, in fact, sometimes use this exercise as a way to reflect on their journey through life. But these sorts of reflections can be a rich source of ideas for living life in both younger and older people.

But the range of texts over the canon, the proportion of Old and New Testament texts, even the order in which the lists are arranged, can reveal insights about different ways we approach Scripture and different attitudes we have toward the Bible. The exercise also, in ways surprising to many people, reveals what basic commonalities are shared by people with widely divergent views of Scripture and of the issues we often try to settle with appeals to Scripture. People with a wide divergence of views on such issues as war and peace, sexuality and homosexuality, or such value of life issues as abortion and capital punishment can still find that their ten most relevant texts overlap.

WHY TRY?

As cultures and as peoples, we have a strong tendency to remake our religious figures in our own image. If one studies the ways Jesus has been characterized, for instance, one can plot the values of the culture portraying him. We have a premodern Jesus, a modern Jesus and a postmodern Jesus—or rather, many postmodern Jesuses. We have a vast capacity to domesticate, own, and tame our most profound experiences of the divine. We fall prey, time and time again, to the golden calf phenomenon.

But the biblical text is "other." If we continue to read it, not just the parts we like but the canon in its entirety, it will confound our efforts to make it entirely and unhelpfully our own. It defies our attempts to master it. It continues to stand apart from us, with its strangeness, its foreignness, its obscurities and absurdities. While we sometimes wish it wasn't so hard to understand, that is part of its power. For the Bible, coming to us in strange squiggles across the miles and the centuries is what it claims to be—the work and word of God, a book that can nurture us and call us to account, assure us of God's compassion, and make us aware anew of God's holiness. But first, we have to read it.

NOTES

1. Mary H. Schertz and Perry B. Yoder, *Seeing the Text: Exegesis for Students of Greek and Hebrew* (Nashville: Abingdon, 2001).

2. See, for example, Brevard Childs, *Old Testament Theology in a Canonical Context* (Philadelphia: Fortress Press, 1983); James Sanders, *From Sacred Story to Sacred Text* (Philadelphia: Fortress, 1987); James Dunn, *Unity and Diversity in the New Testament: An Inquiry into the Character of Earliest Christianity*, 2nd. ed. (Philadelphia: Trinity Press, 1990).

3. There are many fine books on preaching from biblical texts. See Paul Scott Wilson, *The Four Pages of the Sermon: A Guide to Biblical Preaching* (Nashville: Abingdon, 1999); Ronald J. Allen, *The Teaching Sermon* (Nashville: Abingdon Press, 1995). Also very useful are Leander E. Keck, *The Bible in the Pulpit: The Renewal of Biblical Preaching* (Nashville: Abingdon Press, 1978) and Eugene L. Lowry, *The Homiletical Plot: The Sermon as Narrative Art Form* (Atlanta: John Knox Press, 1980). For a more complete explanation of weighing a text in light of its canonical context see pp. 133-148 of Schertz and Yoder, *Seeing the Text*.

4. The literature in these newer disciplines is too expansive to list here. But for examples of good, literary criticism see Robert Tannehill's two volumes on Luke and Acts, *The Narrative Unity of Luke-Acts: A Literary Interpretation,* 2 vols. (Philadelphia: Fortress Press, 1986, 1990) or Ulrich Luz, *Matthew 1-7: A Commentary* (Minneapolis: Augsburg Press, 1989). An example of sociological criticism is David A. deSilva, *The Hope of Glory: Honor Discourse and New Testament Interpretation* (Collegeville, Minnesota: The Liturgical Press, 1999).

5. Two collections of essays on the general topic of social location and biblical interpretation are Fernando Segovia and Mary Ann Tolbert, eds., *Reading from This Place,* vol. 1, *Social Location and Biblical Interpretation in the United States* and *Reading from This Place,* vol. 2, *Social Location and Biblical Interpretation in Global Perspective* (Minneapolis: Fortress Press, 1995). Contributions by persons of color include Virginia Fabella and Sun Ai Lee Park, eds., *We Dare to Dream: Doing Theology as Asian Women* (Hong Kong: Asian Women's Resource Center for Culture and Theology, 1989); Susan Brooks Thistlethwaite and Mary Potter Engel, eds., *Lift Every Voice: Constructing Christian Theologies from the Underside* (San Francisco: Harper & Row, 1990); R. S. Sugirtharajah, ed., *Voices from the Margin: Interpreting the Bible in the Third World* (Maryknoll, N.Y. Orbis, 1991).

6. A classic resource for congregational Bible study is Walter Wink, *Transforming Bible Study: A Leader's Guide* (Nashville: Abingdon Press, 1980). Others include Charles F. Melchart, *Wise Teaching: Biblical Wisdom and Educational Ministry* (Harrisburg, Pa.: Trinity Press, 1998) and James Wilhoit and Leland Ryken, *Effective Bible Teaching* (Grand Rapids: Baker Books, 1988). The various volumes in the *Believers Church Bible Commentary* series (Scottdale, Pa.: Herald Press, founded 1979, first volume appeared 1986) are also helpful, particularly in the sections identified as "The Text in the Life of the Church."

7. Schertz and Yoder, pp. 136-138.

Chapter 5

God's Word in The World: Prophetic Preaching and the Gospel of Jesus Christ

Dawn Ottoni Wilhelm

I have given them your word, and the world has hated them because they do not belong to the world. . . . Sanctify them in the truth; your word is truth. —John 17:14-17

In the gospel of John, it is not only evident that God loves the world (3:16) but also that God's people often find themselves at odds with the world. Filled with grace and truth, the gospel of Jesus Christ is not only a source of divine comfort but also holy confrontation; those who would preach the fullness of the gospel are challenged to speak not only of God's mercy but also of God's justice. Amid the tensions and realities of this blessed but broken world, the prophetic impulse in preaching arises out of our loving engagement with others and our passion to give voice to God's loving intention for all of creation.

To be sure, some pastors would rather limit their preaching role to that of public nurturer or counselor. Many others, however, recognize the importance of both nurturing and challenging the church in its journey of Christian discipleship and know that to be pastoral is also to be willing to be prophetic.

For Anabaptists, the prophetic voice in preaching has been enlivened through its particular social and religious contexts as well as its distinctive modes of testifying to God's Word in worship. In contrast to topical approaches to social justice preaching prevalent among many North American homileticians today,[1] an Anabaptist understanding of prophetic preaching offers a distinct, biblically integrated, and theologically sustained approach to preaching that may help inform and enliven the prophetic witness of the church. The purpose of this chapter is to (1) offer a definition of prophetic preaching based on biblical and theological commitments guiding an Anabaptist understanding of prophetic preaching; (2) explore the social conditions and worship practices conducive to prophetic preaching for Anabaptist communities of faith; and (3) name three essential elements of prophetic preaching that provide guidance and direction for preachers who would give voice to God's Word in the world.

DEFINITION OF PROPHETIC PREACHING

Because prophetic preaching is referred to through such diverse categories as social justice preaching, charismatic or Spirit preaching, crisis preaching, and public issues preaching, it seems helpful to begin with a definition of prophetic preaching that is based upon biblical and theological commitments guiding an Anabaptist approach to prophetic preaching:

In accordance with the prophetic tradition of Israel and the ministry of Jesus Christ as recorded in Scripture, prophetic preaching may be understood as divinely inspired speech enlivened by the Holy Spirit in the gathered community of faith. Prophetic preaching proclaims God's Word from within the Christian tradition against all that threatens God's reconciling intention for humanity and for all that creates and sustains a vital and necessary ministry of compassion to neighbors near and far. Because it is not exclusively either moral exhortation or predictions regarding future events, prophetic preaching envisions past, present and future concerns within the context of the reign of God realized in Jesus Christ and empowered by the Holy Spirit.

At least two components of the foregoing definition are crucial for a consideration of prophetic preaching among Anabaptists. First, this definition identifies an understanding and practice of prophetic discourse that is biblically informed and establishes an indispensable connection between the biblical witness of the prophets (and that of Jesus Christ in particular) and the practice of prophetic preaching today. Although a topical approach to prophetic preaching may address issues of social concern that arise in a given time or setting, the understanding of prophetic preaching proposed here honors the full range of prophetic expression and narrative contexts of the prophetic voice throughout Scripture. Such an approach gives priority to the prophetic urgency of God's Word as it addresses the needs and struggles of the world. Thus prophetic ministry is viewed as arising out of God's Word (proactive) and is not only in response to the very real crises and questions of any given time (reactive). Set within the larger context of God's ongoing redemptive relationship with humanity, this approach values the breadth of the biblical writers' concerns as well as the depth of humanity's ongoing struggle to live toward God's promises and the hope of God's reign.

Second, this definition assumes that prophetic preaching requires the preacher's theological reflection. Because the preacher speaks not only from "within the Christian tradition" but also through particular theological commitments that greatly influence her or his interpretive process and preaching practices, this definition and the discussion that follows value several theological commitments that have helped shape an Anabaptist approach to prophetic preaching. Among these are the following:

(1) The *Spirit of Jesus Christ* has long been the source of interpretive insight, inspiration, and empowerment of the prophetic witness for individuals and communities of Anabaptist believers who have sought divine guidance in private and corporate expressions of worship. A lively pneumatology has long existed among Anabaptists who, although sharing many theological views in common with other Protestant and Catholic faith communities, have also asserted that "divine authority was based on *Scripture and Spirit together*, rather than the *Scripture alone* of Protestantism."[2] In other words, Anabaptist worship has anticipated the lively presence of the Holy Spirit amid the gathered community to bring new understanding and empowerment to the people of God as they engage in biblical reflection and faithful response to God's Word.

(2) The Holy Spirit not only moves within the lives of individual believers to interpret Scripture but Anabaptists have also emphasized the

Spirit's authoritative presence *amid the gathered community*, calling God's people to corporate and visible participation in the prophetic urgency of the gospel. As the worshiping community is challenged by new interpretation and exhortation from its members, both community discernment and individual responsibility for voicing the Spirit's leading are integral to the church's ministry. The tensions that may arise between individual prophetic utterance and a community's resistance to alternative views may generate divisiveness as well as create new possibilities for ministry within the community of faith. Because an Anabaptist understanding of prophetic preaching assumes the ongoing work of the Spirit in the life of the community, it is vital that the prophetic preacher identify and give voice to the Spirit's creative and redemptive work amid God's people. In discerning God's will for the church's ministry and service to the world, individual insight must attend to community interpretation just as the gathered community is also challenged to receive new leadings of the Spirit through the voices of its individual members.

(3) Yet another theological commitment of many Anabaptists reflected in this definition is the assertion of *God's reconciling intention for humanity*. God's way of reconciliation known to us in the life, death, and resurrection of Jesus Christ forms the basis for our relationship with others as we not only speak *against* all that threatens God's peaceful intentions for the world but also *for* those activities that encourage and engage a ministry of compassion to neighbors near and far. Not only offering a critique of all that threatens God's redemptive activity in the world, as we realize and anticipate God's reign among us we may also seek to engage and energize others to extend the witness of peacemaking and compassion beyond boundaries of our own choosing. More than moral exhortation or future predictions, this definition of prophetic preaching seeks to develop ways of drawing on the Spirit's active presence amid the worshiping community to offer critique and energy for the prophetic witness of the church.[3]

Therefore, in contrast to a topical approach to preaching about issues of social concern, this definition seeks to identify a biblical and theological orientation to prophetic preaching informed by the witness of Scripture. Such an approach responds not only to the needs of the world but also to the creative urging of the Spirit of Christ, who is present in the gathered community to inspire and empower the church for prophetic ministries of peace and compassion. Because Anabaptists identify the locus of theological reflection and response to God's Word within the gathered community of faith, it is important to recognize those elements of community life and worship that may help or hinder, encourage or discourage the prophetic impulse in preaching.

COMMUNITY LIFE AND WORSHIP PRACTICES CONDUCIVE TO PROPHETIC PREACHING

In his examination of prophetic activity in both ancient and modern societies, Robert Wilson insists that "any study of prophetic behavior in Israel must take into account the role of social groups in creating prophets and in shaping their behavior."[4] Whether these groups function on the periphery of society or within the central social structure, prophetic intermediaries arise out of and are subject to group expectations about how they are to speak and act. Wilson's work and that of other biblical scholars strongly supports the assertion that "there can be no socially isolated intermediaries."[5]

Building on Wilson's notion of peripheral prophets and the social requirements of prophecy, Walter Brueggemann names several conditions within subcommunities of faith that may generate prophecy, all of which may be found within past or present expressions of Anabaptist worship.[6] He describes a subcommunity that is conducive to prophetic activity as one in which—

> there is a *long and available memory* that sinks the present generation deep into an identifiable past that is available in song and story;
> there is an available, expressed *sense of pain* that is owned and recited as a real social fact, that is visibly acknowledged in a public way, and that is understood as unbearable for the long term;
> there is an *active practice of hope*, a community that knows about promises yet to be kept, promises that stand in judgment on the present, and;
> there is an *effective mode of discourse* that is cherished across the generations, that is taken as distinctive, and that is richly coded in ways that only insiders can know.

Brueggemann also asserts that such a community "knows itself to be positioned for the long-term in tension with the dominant community" and then suggests that the church as a subcommunity in the U.S. may conceive of itself as such an alternative community of prophetic discourse.

As members of the free church tradition, many Anabaptists already perceive of themselves as holding religious views and practices that stand in contrast to the dominant social and political order.[7] Both the historical circumstances surrounding the emergence of Anabaptism in the sixteenth century as well as the theological commitments and practices that have informed diverse expressions of Anabaptist faith throughout the centuries have contributed to a distinct understanding of prophetic discourse and faith.

Historically, the act of rebaptizing previously baptized adults was not only an offense to the religious sensibilities of sixteenth-century Europe but was also an affront to the political power holders of the church and state. The practice of believers' baptism posed a significant threat to civil authorities, since infant baptism not only conferred membership into the church but also granted automatic citizenship, allowing civil authorities to tax and conscript persons into military service.[8] Thus the religious freedom required by believers' baptism was deemed seditious and dangerous to political stability by virtually all political authorities and Anabaptists were punished and/or persecuted for their faith and practices. From their earliest beginnings, the diverse group of believers known as Anabaptists insisted upon an alternative vision of church membership and Christian practices that often put them in conflict with civil authorities.[9] In terms of Brueggemann's outline of the conditions encouraging prophetic activity in subcommunities of faith, Anabaptists have a long and available memory as well as an expressed sense of pain that has arisen out of a history of religious persecution that continues to influence their identity as Christians.

In addition to these historical circumstances and political realities, the prophetic impulse among Anabaptists has also been influenced by particular theological commitments and an orientation to faith that has emphasized the reconciling intention of God in Jesus Christ. Empowered by the Holy Spirit's ongoing involvement in the life of the faith community (noted above), Anabaptists have not only underscored the participation of all baptized members in the ministry of the church and the worship of God but have done so while maintaining and developing a commitment to reconciliation and nonviolence in the witness of the gospel. With regard to Anabaptist worship practices that encourage the prophetic impulse in the gathered community, at least two features of traditional Anabaptist worship are worth exploring.

First, some of the most moving testimonies of faith and alternative visions for living may be found in the numerous hymns and songs composed by Anabaptists throughout the centuries. Several of these reflect the history of suffering and hope that has persisted among Anabaptists for generations. This sense of shared pain and hope is communicated in worship through hymn texts related to the cross of Christ, the need to follow Christ in our love for enemies, the lives of the martyrs and hymns that include pleas and protests toward persecuting governments. Of the 750 or so hymns written by Anabaptists between 1527 and 1570, nearly half are martyr or historical songs. The *Ausbund* (the sixteenth century hymnal of the Anabaptists) as well as numerous subsequent collections not only celebrate the lives of the martyrs but offer hope in a vision of God's sovereignty and power.[10] Through corporate acts of singing, Anabaptists have long sustained and encouraged the hope of Christ in services of public worship.

A second area of worship life of great relevance to a consideration of the prophetic impulse among Anabaptists is the tradition of *Zeugnis*, or "bearing witness," immediately following the sermon. Although early worship practices may be glimpsed from only a few court records, it is evident that following the Scripture reading and sermon, persons gave spontaneous and immediate response to the preacher's message and were expected to further expand upon the text's meaning as well as bear testimony of their experience of God's Word in their lives.[11]

According to historian Alvin J. Beachy, for the early Anabaptists the sermon was not considered a definitive offering of the Word of God (as it was for other church reformers who held a more sacramental view of preaching) but was the basis of shared admonition and witness regarding what God had done and was doing in their daily lives.[12] From their earliest experience of worship it appears that the Anabaptists had a strong sense of communal responsibility for interpreting God's living Word and viewed the sermon as one way of engaging the community in its ongoing interpretation of Scripture and discernment of the Spirit in their midst.

To be sure, most Anabaptist worship services today do not allow for such open periods of community response and the collective spiritual discernment of God's Word in corporate worship. However, some Old Order groups share the preaching responsibility among several ordained speakers who expand upon the text's meaning in relation to the previous preacher[13] and many other Anabaptist faith communities give regular opportunities for non-ordained members of the fellowship to preach and speak at various services of corporate worship and encourage individuals to offer prayers (prepared or spontaneous) and testimonies of various kinds to bear witness to a sense of God's presence and power in their lives.[14]

Far more problematic are occasions when the preacher as prophet is challenged to speak a word not received by the community of faith but instead resisted within the fellowship of the church itself. In terms of being disposed toward the prophetic interests of Scripture, many communities of faith either do not recognize the prophetic urgency of God's Word or do not see themselves as prophetic agents of God's compassionate, reconciling reign on earth. To be sure, there are communities of faith that have so isolated themselves from the concerns of larger society or that, conversely, have so identified with the struggles of society they are not able to hear a new and challenging word. On such occasions, the prophetic preacher is challenged not only to patiently love God's people but also to know when and how to question the resistance of the local faith community. In such settings, it is vital that the preacher cultivate at least two orientations to prophetic preaching that may enhance and encourage the community's engagement with prophetic ministry.

First, the prophetic preacher in the local congregation is wise to remember that the prophetic role is intimately related to the pastoral. It is within the multiple functions of community leadership in the local congregation that the preacher gains authority and is trusted to speak forth prophetically on matters of faith and ministry.[15] The prophetic preacher needs to intentionally cultivate ways of encouraging a caring community of faith as the context within which challenging words of prophetic passion and purpose may take root and grow.[16] If prophetic ministry is related to the caregiving ministries of the church, and if the preacher as prophet is also perceived to be the preacher as pastor, even difficult words of challenge may be received as expressions of God's greater concern for others.

Second, as the prophetic preacher meets with resistance within and beyond the local community of faith, he or she must also be aware of resources beyond the congregation when seeking to check and/or validate his or her perception of God's Word for others. In addition to the counsel of Scripture (whose interpretation is itself in need of community discernment for most Anabaptists), it is wise for the prophetic leader to consult other trustworthy sources of authority—including spiritual leaders of other congregations and traditions whose kindred sense of prophetic urgency may offer the companionship and critique needed to discern a true and gracious word from God. Whether in the form of ecumenical pastors' groups, larger denominational gatherings or leadership events, the preacher as prophet needs to be in conversation with those who will offer honest critique and genuine support for his or her prophetic vision.

Amid these challenges, the prophetic preacher hopes to cultivate communities of prophetic witness willing to bear testimony in word and deed to God's compassionate, reconciling intention for the world. Since "the bearer of the prophetic task is the whole people of God,"[17] Anabaptist worship and preaching seeks to develop discourse that opens the way for the Spirit to inspire and speak through the gathered community of faith. In terms of having a *long and available memory, an expressed sense of pain, an active practice of hope, and an effective mode of discourse* (the four conditions cited by Brueggemann), the socio-historic conditions and theological commitments of Anabaptism contribute to its experience as a religious subcommunity of the larger society, able to give human voice to divine concern and offer prophetic insights subject to group consideration and validation. As the church attends to the prophetic urgency of the gospel, the voice of the Spirit may move in our midst to inspire and empower the prophetic voice in preaching.

THREE ESSENTIAL ELEMENTS OF PROPHETIC PREACHING

Because the living Word of God revealed in Jesus Christ is central to Anabaptist faith and preaching, the gospel accounts of Jesus' life, death and resurrection provide a wealth of material for Anabaptists and others who would explore the prophetic voice in preaching. Although it is not possible within the scope of this essay to review all four Gospel accounts as they relate to the prophetic and theological interests of each gospel writer, it is nevertheless possible to identify a few key elements running throughout the Gospels that permeate Jesus' prophetic ministry and are worthy of consideration for preachers today. At least three essential concerns emerge when considering Jesus' own prophetic preaching and activity as recorded in the Gospels.

Prophetic preaching voices God's passion for others

As the incarnate Word of God, Jesus embodies and gives voice to God's passionate engagement with humanity. From his scandalous beginning in a manger, through his inaugural address at Nazareth (Luke 4:16ff) and subsequent ministry marked by parabolic preaching and teaching, healing the dis-eased, communing with outcasts, and suffering an ignoble death on a cross, Jesus embodies God's love for all humanity. And through his resurrection, he makes known to us the transforming power of God's passion.

For the prophetic preacher, two observations may be made regarding Jesus' passionate engagement with and ministry for others. First, the prophetic ministry of Jesus Christ suggests that God's passion is intimately related to the suffering of this world and is the basis for our compassion toward others. Remembering that the English word *passion* is derived from the Latin term *passio*, meaning "suffering," the prophetic ministry of Jesus not only testifies to God's loving zeal for humanity but also speaks of Christ's willingness to suffer on behalf of others. As one who offered himself in service to others ("emptying himself" to the point of death, Phil. 2:5-11), God in Christ looks toward the interests of others with humility and compassion. The passion of Christ is not only at the heart of the gospel, it is also essential to the prophetic impulse to witness to God's love and reconciling intention for all the world.

For those who would proclaim the fullness of the gospel, it is vital for preachers to speak on behalf of our passionate God, who is present in the world and whose suffering is intimately related to the suffering of others. This is not an invitation to the glorification of suffering or guilt ridden attempts to identify with those who are impoverished or destitute. Rather, it is an awareness of the ways in which passion leads to compassion, a willingness to suffer with others just as God in Christ suffers with all of broken humanity. Just as Christ witnesses to us of God's compassion for those who are despised (Mark14:1-9), diseased (Luke 6:18-19), or in need (Jn. 6:1-14), the prophetic preacher gives voice to God's passion for those who suffer injustice, abuse, or neglect. A passionate articulation of the gospel commands our heart, soul, mind, and strength in such a way as to let love have its way with us; moving us beyond boundaries of our own making and toward those whom the world teaches us to despise.

A second observation that may be made regarding Jesus' passionate engagement with others is that his words and deeds reveal a greater degree of anguish than anger. Although Jesus sometimes expressed outrage and communicated his anger toward those for whom a misplaced passion for material possessions or pride led them away from compassionate outreach to others (Luke 12:13-32), he also expressed compassion toward enemies (Luke 6:27-33) and showed considerable forbearance toward those who challenged his teaching and authority. He may have overturned the tables in the temple (Luke 19:45-46), but it was only after weeping over the city of Jerusalem (Luke 13:33-35) and lamenting that God's city of peace would not recognize the things that make for peace (Luke 19:41-42). More than acts of righteous indignation or words of moral condemnation, the prophetic urgency of Jesus' ministry was realized through words and deeds that reflect God's compassion for others. The prophetic preacher who embraces the passion of Christ and seeks the transforming power of Christ's Spirit is therefore wise not to mistake anger for passion.

The passion of Christ's prophetic ministry suggests that the language of lament is crucial to the prophetic voice in preaching. Whereas many preachers are comfortable with the language of praise and petition and even, to a certain extent, confession, the language of lament is largely ignored in many North American congregations. However, lament permeates the biblical account, including some forty percent of the psalms, as God's people give voice to their grief, remorse, fear, and anguish. The capacity to grieve what is not right in our own lives and in the lives of others opens the way for us to engage the just and compassionate intentions of God amid a broken and beloved world. Before we resort to despair or vengeance, lamentation turns us in the direction of a powerful, loving God whom we trust with our sorrows and by whose wisdom we begin the process of discerning that for which we also hold responsibility in our present calamity. Indeed, how can we begin to face the truth of human suffering and our own complicity in the injustices of this world without the God-given language of lament?[18]

For the prophetic preacher who hungers and thirsts for God's righteousness, the language of lament gives voice to anguish and confesses faith in God who is able to bear our grief and transform our despair as we pray for creative and life giving ways to respond to the crises we face. Lest anger lead to vengeance, we bring our rage to God who suffers on behalf of all people and gives understanding of our enemies and all that opposes God's justice and reconciling intention for the world. In the words of Miroslav Volf, "By placing unattended rage before God we place both our unjust enemy and our own vengeful self face to face with a God who loves and does justice."[19] The language of lament addresses God whose passion for others opens the way for our compassionate engagement with the world, recalling us to the One who is the source of all justice and mercy.

Prophetic preaching proclaims the promises of God

Just as God in Christ embodies divine passion for the world, the prophetic ministry of Jesus speaks powerfully of God's promises and impending reign. Beyond lamentation and amid the trials and tragedies of the church and world, the gospel speaks forth an alternative vision of hope, redemption, and divine blessing. For those who preach and hear the gospel, the promises of God resound throughout the Old and New Testaments, calling forth God's redemptive purposes on earth. It was God's loving promise that called Jesus from the grave,[20] and it is the living promise of a risen Lord that continues to surprise us today with intimations of divine compassion in the church and world.

There are two ways in which the proclamation of God's promises may be deemed essential to the prophetic voice in preaching. First, proclamation of divine promises not only voices the commitments of God but, even more important for the church in its witness to the world, recalls the One who makes promises and is entrusted with their fulfillment. Just as lamentation is directed to God, the proclamation of God's promises directs our attention to God the source of our hope and empowerment. However much we may rely on human agency and well-intended efforts to participate in God's gracious, just, and reconciling mission on earth, the efficacy of divine love is not conditioned upon human accomplishments. As we give voice to God's promises we recollect ourselves as God's people and point toward the One whose redemptive and creative power are effected through the Spirit of Jesus Christ active in the church and world. The church must never forget that although our response to God's grace and our participation in God's will are vital to the well-being of our lives and to those around us, ultimately and always the source of our empowerment and hope is God.

Second, the promises of God are not simply past announcements worth repeating. Rather, God's promises are enlivened in the present as we evoke God's intended future. Promises of divine companionship (Matt. 28:20b), the Holy Spirit as guide (John 16:13) and God's just reign (Mark10:28-31) permeate the gospel through an assertion of future fulfillment as well as insistence on present realization. Living between what is and what is yet to be, the prophetic preacher attends to both the corruption among us and the reality of divine hope that insists its way into the most desperate of situations. Thus, the prophetic preacher who is passionate about God's Word in the world is not simply concerned with renunciation of evil but listens for God's promises echoing in every generation and relates instances of faith, hope, and love as they are found in the church and world. As surely as sin is at work among us, so are the promises of God and the prophetic preacher is responsible for identifying and naming the ways in which God's intended future is realized in the present. In the words of Richard Lischer,

> The future has broken into our time in the death and resurrection of Jesus. . . . The future is not *more* history but the transformation of history in the One who will be all in all. Preaching too, because its subject and object is the risen Christ, not only announces this end but participates in it. It is a sign of the end. Preaching-as-promise strains forward to align itself to that finality which has been loosed among us.[21]

For Jesus, the present and future realization of God's promises are most fervently articulated in preaching the parables. The Greek word *parabole* itself refers to something "thrown alongside" something else and in Jesus' parables, God's kingdom is often seen as thrown alongside, indeed in collision with, this world's kingdoms. According to the parables, God's promised reign comes not only through the surprising reversal and upset expectations of religious and worldly leaders alike (Luke 10:25-37), but also through the dramatic confrontation of God's world with ours (Luke 12:13-21). Just as the language of lament gives voice to human and divine passion, the language of the parables asserts God's subtle and dramatic intrusions into our expectations and dares to voice God's promises amid corrupt and selfish interests of church and world.

The parabolic nature of Jesus' prophetic preaching suggests that God's promises not only fulfill our deepest longings, they also confront our every injustice; they not only anticipate future fulfillment, they also assert the reign of God among us even now (Luke 17:21). Thus the promises of God are essential to prophetic preaching not only because they recall the One who makes promises but also because they anticipate and evoke God's intended future for our present time and situation.

Prophetic preaching points the way to new possibilities

If prophetic preaching encourages the language of lament to give voice to our passion and the language of the parables to articulate God's promises active among us, it also urges us toward a language of imaginative possibility that engages the church with the world in its many hopes, struggles and terrors.

As surely as Jesus embodies the compassion of God for the world and his ministry evokes the future reign of God in the present, Christ also witnesses to new possibilities and alternative responses to all that threatens God's Word in the world. When confronted by religious leaders who hoped to bring him into conflict with political authorities, Jesus recalled them to their allegiance to God (Matt. 22:15-22; Mark 12:13-17; Luke 20:20-26). When confronted by those who would condemn a sinner, Jesus urged them to consider their own sinfulness (John 8:3-11). And when pressed to define what deed might ensure one's heavenly reward, Jesus pointed his questioner away from selfish considerations, toward the needs of others and the treasure found in giving up everything in service to God and neighbor (Matt. 19:16-30; Mark 10:17-31; Luke 18:18-25). His ministry was marked by insight, imagination, and prophetic creativity as Jesus sought ways of engaging others in relationships of love, justice and compassion.

Thus for those who would give voice to God's Word in the world today, prophetic preaching is not only concerned with witnessing to God's passion and promises but also to the possibilities of God's love and power among us. Just as Jesus sought alternate ways of engaging others and eliciting their loving response to God and neighbors, so may the prophetic preacher view church and world through God's eyes, calling forth creative responses amid the most challenging circumstances.

The prophetic preacher who would point the way to new possibilities for God's people in the world must therefore be concerned with two things. First, the prophet is concerned with evoking alternative ways of imagining God's loving and just purposes at work in the church and world. More than offering simple three-point solutions to the most difficult issues of our time, and beyond rational attempts to explain the overwhelming reality of evil and suffering, the prophetic imagination engages others in alternative views of reality. Passionate about the promises of God, the prophet speaks of God's just and reconciling intentions amid humanity's terrors and tragedies. The urge for creative and constructive engagement with others is offered not on our own terms but in terms of God's loving purposes revealed in Jesus Christ as the prophet seeks to engage the imagination of others in ministry to the world.

Evoking an imaginative response from God's people, the Old Testament prophets often used poetry rather than prose to communicate their wrestling with others and their mysterious encounters with the divine. In his book, *Finally Comes the Poet: Daring Speech for Proclamation*, Walter Brueggemann reminds us that

> Those whom the ancient Israelites called prophets, the equally ancient Greeks called poets. The poet/prophet is a voice that shatters reality and evokes new possibility in the listening assembly. Preaching continues that dangerous, indispensable habit of speech.[22]

For those who would speak of possibilities beyond that which the church and world now envision, the prophetic preacher uses language that blinds as well as illumines, laments as well as exults, breaks open our settled accounting of good works and grace, and stirs hope for new possibilities among us.

However, to evoke images is not enough. A second responsibility of the prophetic preacher is to provoke creative responses on the part of the hearers. In pointing the way to new possibilities the prophetic preacher is interested in encouraging a convictional response that arises out of the hearers' encounter with God's living Word. If the foremost concern of the gospel is to love God with heart, soul, mind, and strength and our neighbors as ourselves, the prophetic voice in preaching is concerned with cultivating an emotional, spiritual, intellectual and/or physical response to God's Word in the world.

More than rail against others, the prophet rallies others for God's loving purposes and actions, opening the way for the Spirit of Christ to move and energize God's people for ministry and mission. Whether opportunities for personal and/or corporate response are made explicit, implied, or suggested through careful questions to the congregation, the prophetic preacher hopes to elicit the imaginative engagement of others in response to God's Word.

The passion of Christ, the promises of God and the possibilities of the Holy Spirit are not only essential to prophetic preaching; they are essential to developing alternative ways of engaging the church in the world. For Anabaptists and other preachers who seek to proclaim the fullness of the gospel, the prophetic voice in preaching witnesses to God's compassionate concern and reconciling intention for all the world. Filled with grace and truth, God's Word is alive in the world, eager to engage our prophetic witness.

NOTES

1. For example: Walter J. Burghardt, S. J., *Preaching the Just Word* (New Haven: Yale University Press, 1996), William Sloane Coffin, *A Passion for the Possible: A Message to U.S. Churches* (Louisville: Westminster/John Knox Press, 1993) and J. Philip Wogaman, *Speaking the Truth in Love: Prophetic Preaching to a Broken World* (Louisville: Westminster John Knox Press, 1998).

2. C. Arnold Snyder, "Beyond Polygenesis: Recovering the Unity and Diversity of Anabaptist Theology," in *Essays in Anabaptist Theology*, ed. by H. Wayne Pipkin, Text Reader Series, vol. 5 (Elkhart, Ind.: Institute of Mennonite Studies, 1994), 13.

3. The critical and energizing functions of prophetic discourse are identified by Walter Brueggemann in his work, *The Prophetic Imagination*, 2nd. ed. (Minneapolis: Fortress Press, 2001), chs. 3-4.

4. Robert R. Wilson, *Prophecy and Society in Ancient Israel* (Philadelphia: Fortress Press, 1980), 87. In addition to examining the support groups necessary for prophetic activity, Wilson also notes three other requirements for prophetic activity that must be present in the larger societal context, including a belief in the reality of a supernatural power or powers, a further belief that these powers can influence earthly affairs and can in turn be influenced by earthly agents, and social conditions of crisis that require the services of a divine intermediary (i.e., war, natural disasters, rapid social change).

5. Wilson, 30. See also Joseph Blenkinsopp, *Sage, Priest, Prophet: Religious and Intellectual Leadership in Ancient Israel*, Library of Ancient Israel, Douglas A. Knight, ed. (Louisville: Westminster John Knox Press, 1995). In ch. 6 of Thomas W. Overholt's *Channels of Prophecy: The Social Dynamics of Prophetic Activity* (Minneapolis: Fortress Press, 1989), the author discusses Wilson's social prerequisites in his treatment of the "end of prophecy" beyond the time of the exile and asserts that the prophetic witness is threatened with extinction when the members of society fail to recognize the prophetic voice among them: "To say that in a given social context

prophecy came to an end is not to deny the theoretical possibility of valid prophetic activity but rather to note the failure of members of that society, at least for the moment, to credit (authorize) specific instances of prophetic behavior," 159.

6. Brueggemann, xvi.

7. In his outline of Anabaptist alternatives to the state churches emerging during the Protestant Reformation, Hans-Juergen Goertz insists that it is one of the distinguishing features of various Anabaptist groups that they not only critiqued the practice of infant baptism but "represented a common church-political front" that challenged political order and urged a measure of social unrest: "Given the dominance of the notion of the *corpus Christianum*, any attempt to form a breakaway community could not fail to be seen as an attack on the foundations of society. The free church, even if in the circumstances it could only comprise a tiny minority therefore became a revolutionary community." *The Anabaptists*, trans. Trevor Johnson (New York: Routledge, 1996), 86.

8. According to historian C. Arnold Snyder, "Given this political reality [of severe persecution] espousing Anabaptism in the sixteenth century was no 'purely religious' option, but rather was a faith decision that directly confronted and challenged the social, religious, and political status quo. Anabaptists were sought out, persecuted, jailed, dispossessed, exiled and put to death by Lutheran, Reformed and Catholic cities and rulers well into the seventeenth century . . . " *Anabaptist History and Theology: An Introduction* (Kitchener, Ont.: Pandora Press, 1995), 2.

9. From the sixteenth century *Martyrs Mirror* to twenty-first century collections of stories recounting Anabaptists acts of civil disobedience and alternative service in recent history (see Rachel Waltner Goossen, *Women Against the Good War: Conscientious Objection and Gender on the American Home Front, 1941-1947*, Chapel Hill: University of North Carolina Press, 1997), Anabaptists may be said to have a long and vibrant memory related to the ways in which religious commitments may lead Christians to live in opposition to state and civil authorities. See also Urie A. Bender, *Soldiers of Compassion* (Scottdale, Pa.: Herald Press, 1969).

10. See Paul M. Miller, "Worship Among the Early Anabaptists," *Mennonite Quarterly Review (MQR)* 30, no. 4 (October 1956): 235-246.

11. See John S. Oyer, "Early Forms of Anabaptist *Zeugnis* After Sermons," *MQR* 72, no. 3 (July 1998): 449-454.

12. "The Theology and Practice of Anabaptist Worship," *MQR* 60, no. 3 (July 1966): 163-178.

13. See Donald B. Kraybill and Carl F. Bowman, *On the Backroad to Heaven: Old Order Hutterites, Mennonites, Amish, and Brethren* (Baltimore: Johns Hopkins University Press, 2001), 156-160, 263.

14. Sometimes these opportunities have been referred to as moments of "praying and prophesying" among groups related to the Brethren. In the nineteenth century, in accordance with I Cor. 11:4-5, there is evidence of women whose speaking ministries were so moving that they were also invited to share in the regular preaching activities of the congregation. See Nancy Kettering Frye, *An Uncommon Woman: The Life and Times of Sarah Righter Major* (Elgin, Ill.: Brethren Press, 1997).

15. See William H. Willimon, *Preaching About Conflict in the Local Church* (Philadelphia: Westminster Press, 1987).

16. For a thoughtful analysis of how preaching may cultivate a caring community, see G. Lee Ramsey, Jr., *Care-full Preaching: From Sermon to Caring Community* (St. Louis, Mo.: Chalice Press, 2000). Although Ramsey does not provide an in-depth discussion of the relationship between pastoral and prophetic modes of discourse as these further the larger ministries of the church, his work reveals a strong degree of concern for the social dimension of the gospel as this, too, may express the community's care for itself and others (88-118).

17. John Howard Yoder, *For the Nations: Essays Public and Evangelical* (Grand Rapids: William B. Eerdmans Publishing Company, 1997), 217.

18. See Don Saliers discussion of the sense of truth in worship in *Worship Come to Its Senses* (Nashville: Abingdon Press, 1996), 56-60.

19. *Exclusion and Embrace: A Theological Exploration of Identity, Otherness and Reconciliation* (Nashville: Abingdon, 1996), 124.

20. See Robert W. Jenson, *Story and Promise: A Brief Theology of the Gospel About Jesus* (Ramsey, N.J.: Sigler Press, 1989), chs. 3-4.

21. "Preaching and the Rhetoric of Promise" in *Word and World* 13(1), 78.

22. Walter Brueggemann, *Finally Comes the Poet: Daring Speech for Proclamation* (Minneapolis: Fortress Press, 1989), 4.

Chapter 6

The First Covenant in the Twenty-first Century: Mining the Old Testament for the Postmodern Anabaptist Pulpit

David A. Stevens

*H*alf the sermons I preach are from the Old Testament. I have practical reasons. The Old Testament remains an under-mined resource in the Christian pulpit. As such, sermons from this less-used part of the Bible can bring a freshness and adventurousness, both to me and my listeners. The new-sounding Old can be energizing for younger and established congregations alike.

There is another reason I am attracted to the first covenant Scriptures for preaching: I simply love them. I owe this love to Tom McDaniel, my Old Testament professor from Eastern Baptist Seminary, who guided me from strawless bricks to eagles' wings and everywhere else in between. Through Tom's close reading of texts I never failed to discover surprises and power that I hadn't seen before—even in "familiar" stories. I was hooked and thirsty for more.

But has my love been blind? That's a legitimate question. The truth is, until now, I've never intentionally reflected on what I do and why I do it when I prepare a message from an Old Testament text.[1] I simply preach. Have I been walking in the shaky footsteps of Aaron, week after week just melting earrings and serving up calves?

This much is certain: Proponents of preaching from the first three-quarters of the canon face many challenges. Nevertheless, I am convinced that postmodern Anabaptists will find rich ore in the pages of the Old Testament for crafting relevant and transforming sermons.

THE CHALLENGES OF PREACHING FROM THE OLD TESTAMENT

The case against the use of the Old Testament in the church is at least as old as Marcion.[2] More importantly, Marcion's challenge lives on among many in a continuing hesitancy or even aversion toward Old Testament preaching today.

In part this reluctance is understandable. Whereas preaching from the New Testament is more or less self-evident and self-authenticating, preaching from the Old Testament raises serious questions. Some of these questions engage all Christians equally while others address Anabaptists with particular vigor.[3] While space does not permit a detailed investigation, it is important to at least briefly mention where some of the trouble spots lie.

First, is it possible for Christians to hear and proclaim the Old Testament in its "own voice"?[4] The answer will depend on one's understanding of the nature and relationship between the testaments.[5]

Second, even if possible, is it legitimate for Christians as Christians to hear and preach the Old Testament in its own voice? Or, said another way, does "in its own voice" mean "as if it were the Hebrew Bible" or "as if the New Testament did not exist"? Christians proclaim Jesus Christ. But the Old Testament does not witness to Jesus Christ in any obvious or direct way. So, for example, Matthew discerned in Isaiah 7:14 a prediction of Jesus' birth, and Christians can legitimately claim God "fulfilled" that verse in Jesus[6]. But Isaiah's words were recognized as prophecy and Scripture centuries before Matthew. The very existence of the book of Isaiah means a legitimate and relevant word of God was heard through this prophet without reference to Jesus. Few postmodern preachers in the Anabaptist tradition practice the same hermeneutics as the early church, which often inappropriately allegorized, christologized or spiritualized the Old Testament. But the practical question remains: Precisely how may the church of today use the first covenant writings in its proclamation of the gospel? For instance, must all Old Testament texts used in preaching be paired with a New Testament text or pass through a doctrinal "filter" to be truly Christian proclamation?[7]

Third, the distance from the Old Testament world to ours is even longer than that between the New Testament and our world.[8] Are there interpretive guidelines and procedures that will keep Christian under-standings and applications of Old Testament texts within limits that re-spect the Old Testament context?[9]

This representative list of challenges to preaching from the Old Tes-tament could be greatly expanded.[10] The above examples are sufficient to demonstrate the reality and complexity of the problems. Neverthe-less, despite the difficulties, significant rewards await Christian preach-ers who journey into the "mines" of the Old Testament.

THE VALUE OF THE OLD TESTAMENT
FOR THE POSTMODERN ANABAPTIST PULPIT

There are what we may call "external arguments" (that is, external to the content of the Old Testament) in support of Old Testament preach-ing. These external arguments include the following: Some form of the Old Testament was the Bible of Jesus and the early church; its message and text were clearly essential to the missionary preaching attested in Acts; the New Testament explicitly affirms the Old Testament's value (e.g., Matt. 5:17, Luke 24:44-45, Acts 8:32-35, Rom. 15:4, I Cor. 10:6, 2 Tim. 3:16-17);[11] the very preservation of the Old Testament as part of the Christian canon, in the face of significant opposition, attests its en-during worth.[12]

Perhaps most significant for preachers, however, are the "internal reasons" for valuing the Old Testament as a resource for Christian proclamation. To be precise, its message is relevant for us today. Get your pick ax!

For example, the sheer breadth of life circumstances recorded in the first covenant Scriptures makes it exceedingly "minable" for the preacher: The Old Testament explores good things happening to good people (Ruth 2-4), bad things happening to bad people (much of

Judges), bad things happening to good people (the person Job), good things happening to bad people (Ps. 37, Jer. 12:1-2, Job 21) and death happening to all people (the book of Ecclesiastes., Ps. 49).

The Old Testament often displays a dizzying tolerance for theological pluralism. For instance, its pages include not only a very practical and conventional piety (the book of Proverbs) but also its intellectual dismantling (the book of Job) and, in turn, a record of the resignation when both the conventions and the protest have exhausted themselves and crumbled to the rug like an over-tired preschooler (the book of Ecclesiastes.).

The Deuteronomistic History (Jos.-2 Kings) understands foreign invasion and exile as Yahweh's just punishment for Israel's violation of covenant (Deut. 28:47-68, 1 Kings 8:46-51, 2 Kings 17:7-18). Lamentations, however, considers such punishment to grossly exceed the crime. But most surprising of all, Psalm 44:17-22 proposes there has been no crime at all; rather Yahweh has been unjust and "asleep"!

Leviticus expends much of its energy tediously expounding the details of the sacrificial system. But prophetic texts (e.g. Isa. 1:12-17, Amos 5:21-24, Mic. 6:6-8, Jer. 7:21-23) and psalmic texts alike (e.g. Ps. 40:6, 50:7-14) seem not only to discredit abuses in the system but question the very system itself!

Obedience to God's commandments is the essence of Israel's very life (Deut. 30:15-20). But in Ezekiel, God says, "I [purposely!] gave them statutes that were not good and ordinances by which they could not live" (20:25). Is King Manasseh the epitome of all evil (2 Kgs. 21:1-18) or a paradigm of repentance from evil (2 Chron. 33:10-13, 18-20)? Is our hope in a God who changes his mind (Jon. 3:10) or precisely in a God who refuses to change his mind (1 Sam. 15:29)?

Examples of this theological pluralism could be almost endlessly multiplied. That the Old Testament has allowed this stunning variety to survive the "smoothing" effects of textual transmission is nothing short of astonishing.[13] As twenty-first-century Anabaptist congregations struggle with their own contexts of pluralism, the Old Testament exemplifies a willingness to invite many positions to the table and pass them a microphone.[14]

The Old Testament has much to say to the postmodern hunger for a life that is whole instead of fragmented. For example, while we postmoderns are vulnerable to compartmentalizing religious life and civic

life, the Old Testament integrates them. So Psalm 14:1, 4 defines athe-
ism as unethical behavior; Amos 5:18-24 defines true religion as the
practice of social justice;[15] Leviticus chapter 19 defines "holiness" (19:2)
in terms of upright human interactions (19:3ff).[16]

The quest for an integrated life is addressed in other ways by the Old
Testament. In our day, many Christians have come to understand care
for the environment as part of devotion to God. The Old Testament has
already anticipated this connection.[17] For the first covenant people, life
was a seamless garment; "vertical" and "horizontal" relationships are in-
separable.[18]

Yet another valuable contribution that the Old Testament makes is
its refreshing honesty about human beings. It makes absolutely no attempt to hide the unsightliest warts of even its most prominent protag-
onists. So, right alongside the teflon-coated David of Chronicles, stand
the "unedited" intrigues of the Succession Narrative.[19] Jacob/Israel, the
very man for whom God's people are named, is repeatedly "caught on
camera" as a fit-for-the-tabloids liar, schemer, supplanter, and fugitive.
The Old Testament's stark humanizing of Israel's heroes is a way of indi-
rectly showing us a long-suffering and gracious God who works out the
divine plan not because of these "clay jars" but despite them.

Even more refreshing is the fascinating breadth of emotions which
the Old Testament deems acceptable in "spiritual life." The Psalms are
full of self-pity, self-promotion, conceit, rage, vengeance, and a whole
host of other feelings many Anabaptists find unseemly enough expressed in person-to-person conversation, much less toward God.[20] But
the Old Testament is a promotional photo shoot of the cast from "Spirituality Beyond Nice"; it challenges us to redefine piety and to expand
our understanding and practice of prayer. Old Testament faith invites
the whole self not just the "presentable" self before God.[21]

Equally astounding—the Old Testament mine contains seams that
constitute the voice of Israel's self-criticism. This amounts to a considerable body of material, attested in, but not limited to, the writing
prophets, the deuteronomic traditions (the Book of Deuteronomy, the
Deuteronomistic History, deuteronomistic redactions to Hosea and Jeremiah, and so forth), and "alternative" wisdom materials (Job, Eccl.).
So, for instance, the limitations placed on kings by Deuteronomy
17:14-20 sound specifically aimed at Solomon; Leviticus 18:18 is an
implicit critique of the patriarch Jacob. But far in excess of these brief

passages is the Old Testament's nearly continual refrain of corporate Israel's unfaithfulness.

This self-critical voice is especially valuable for the postmodern church in an age when Mennonites, in much of North America at least, are experiencing enormous pressures to practice the values of the dominant culture—values like individualism, litigation (along with the need for excessive insurance that goes with it), consumerism, narcissism, and militarism. Relevant to this situation, Daniel and his companions (see Dan. chapters 1-6) can be seen as the original self-made Gen-X'ers who show us how to be "in the world but not of the world." The Old Testament's witness to Israel's self-examination encourages postmodern Christians to examine their life styles, to dismantle acculturation and to re-center life on God and Christ.

Above all, what confronts us in the Old Testament is a passionate God, a God of lavish grace and uncompromising demand.[22] This same God who sent Jesus Christ is portrayed as wrathful enough to slay innocent and guilty indiscriminately (Ezek. 21:1-7). But God is also portrayed as nostalgically misty-eyed enough to recoil at the mere thought of punishing the "toddler" Israel whom God taught to walk (Hos. 11:1-9). Yahweh is an exalted, all-powerful God before whom the nations are like drips from a bucket (Isa. 40:12-26). Yet Yahweh is also a tender and intimate God who midwifes us into existence (Ps. 22:9-10, 71:6; Isa. 46:3); who knows our skeletal system and inner thoughts (Ps 139); who is moved by overhearing the groans of the brutalized (Exod. 2:23-25); who forgives us like a compassionate father (Ps. 103:8-14) and bounces us on the knees like a playful mother (Isa. 66:12-13).

However complicated this incomparable legacy may sound, all of it is true to Israel's experience—and, perhaps, to ours.

MINING OLD TESTAMENT TREASURES FOR PREACHING

How then do we harvest first-covenant ore to refine it into metal for Christian proclamation? Preaching is much more than a discrete task; it is a lifestyle. In light of this, it is helpful to consider two aspects of our question: (1) Preparing ourselves to approach the Old Testament homiletically and (2) acts of homiletical engagement with the text.

In terms of preparation, all the steps prerequisite to preaching in general apply to Old Testament preaching. These include commitments to prayer, to regular reading and reflection on the Bible, to observation and reflection on contemporary life, to acquiring and using exegetical skills.

In addition to these general prerequisites for preaching, several preparatory steps are especially useful for homiletical interaction with the Old Testament. First, we can make it a goal to become familiar with all of the Hebrew Scriptures, not just Genesis, Isaiah and the Psalms; we can make them a part of our regular devotions. What we find may surprise us. We will find that genealogies and lists often contain fascinating anecdotes.[23] Terse proverbs can espouse dense theologies (e.g. Prov. 16:9) or deeply reflective philosophies of life (e.g. Prov. 30:8b-9) or suggest personal experiences that lie behind the poetry (e.g. Prov. 31:10-31). Narratives frequently introduce unsung, even nameless characters whose stories ache to be told.[24] When reading legal materials, we can concentrate on larger concepts and values[25] without getting mired in the technical minutia of the sacrificial or judicial systems. We discover that Old Testament law is more dynamic than static as well as more representative than comprehensive.[26] The dynamic nature of Old Testament law is an implicit encouragement to communities of faith to engage in ongoing spiritual discernment.

Second, we can be honest about any presuppositions or prejudices we have toward the Old Testament and be willing to examine them. We can ask ourselves these questions: Do I find the Old Testament unappealing in terms of morality, theology, politics? Does it seem remote in terms of relevance? Am I put off by certain texts that contain military or other kinds of violence?[27] Does the Old Testament seem to describe a God different from the God revealed in Jesus Christ? We can test traditional ways of distinguishing the testaments—law versus (New Testament) grace, promise versus fulfillment, God of war versus Prince of Peace—to see whether those paradigms accurately describe specific texts. When we clear the slate for a fresh encounter with the Old Testament we may be astonished!

Third, we can read secondary works on the Old Testament that provide solid background for preaching. Able theological treatments of the Old Testament often spark the homiletical imagination.[28] A number of Old Testament scholar-preachers have published collections of sermons. These provide models of how first covenant texts may be used in the pulpit.[29] While commentaries should never be substituted for one's own ground work and creativity, two recent series are especially theologically and homiletically sensitive, namely, the *Interpretation Commentary* and *The New Interpreter's Bible*.[30] These may be profitably read even outside of sermon preparation. Journals like *Interpretation*, directed to a pastoral audience, devote at least one of four issues a year to a specific biblical book, while other issues address biblical themes. Moreover, each issue contains a section entitled "Between Text and Sermon," wherein the theological and practical implications of several texts are presented in essay form.

These elements of a homiletically oriented life provide indispensable background for preaching. Of course backgrounding is not enough. Eventually the preacher confronts a specific collection of verses with the goal of producing a sermon. Therefore it is essential to have a strategy for textual engagement that will best use exegetical results for homiletical purposes.

I have found Stephen Farris' understanding of preaching as creative analogy to be particularly helpful. According to Farris, a sermon enables a conversation between a portion of the Bible and the world of the listeners—a truly crosscultural experience! Analogies help bridge the two worlds by acknowledging both the similarities and differences between them. "To 'draw an analogy' is to make a comparison between the similar features or attributes of two otherwise dissimilar things, so that the unknown, or less well known, is clarified by the known."[31]

An analogy between an Old Testament text and our world might have any one of several focal points. For example, drawing analogies between Old Testament and present-day characters can bring the biblical stories to vivid expression. Consider these attempts:

(1) Hagar is a homeless, jobless single parent whose husband turns her out for another woman (Gen. 21).

(2) David is a successful executive who at midlife succumbs to sexual misconduct (2 Sam. 11)

(3) The Babylonians are a military and economic superpower, hated by the developing nations they take advantage of (Ps. 137).

Even in one-sentence summaries, we can grasp the power of such analogies. However, while the comparisons to postmodern times are broadly true, we should also recognize the important differences between the "conversation partners": Hagar does not live on the streets of a U.S. city, David does not head a Fortune 500 corporation, and there are no more Babylonians![32] In using analogies, we must be aware that vividness and distortion occur together.

In addition to character correspondences, another focal point for a preaching analogy is the dynamics in the text. Here are some possibilities:

(1) The large amount of space in the call narrative of Moses (Exod. 3:1-4:17) devoted to Moses' objections to God provides abundant opportunity to examine our own resistance to God's calling or to change generally.[33]

(2) Jeremiah buying real estate in a country overrun by invaders (Jer. 32) suggests that to have hope, we all must make some concrete investment in the future, no matter how uncertain the road ahead.

(3) The human tendency to make quick judgments based on incomplete information, sometimes with unfortunate consequences, is vividly portrayed in Joshua 22

(4) God's people experienced the erasure of the familiar during the exodus and the (Babylonian) exile. Their need to reconstruct a viable identity is comparable to that of historical Anabaptists, who also experienced settlement, persecution, dispersal, and re-formation of faith community. The exodus and exile also speak to present-day refugees around the world, even to the "voluntary exile" of present-day North American Anabaptists who adopt life-styles alternative to the surrounding culture.

(5) Psalm 55:4-8, 12-14, which describes the pain of violation from someone close and trusted, is relevant to victims of abuse.

(6) God led Israel through the desert "by stages" (Exod. 40:34-38; Num. 9:15-23; cp. Eccl. 3:1-8), that is, not all at once. Those recovering from surgery or in the consuming time of caring for an infant also need to understand life as having stages.

(7) The reconciliation stories of Jacob and Esau (Gen. 33) and Joseph and his brothers (Gen. 45-50) remind us that restoring relationships takes time and is often an incomplete process.[34]

These examples are sufficient to illustrate the rich resources available to those who mine the caverns of creative analogy.[35]

It is precisely our affirmation of one God, of Old and New Testaments, and postmodern times, that encourages comparison between what God has done and what God is doing. If within the pages of the Bible itself God's blessings on his people were perceived to have far-reaching ripple effects (Gen. 12:1-4a; Isa. 19:23-25; Acts 3:25), then they still do. If God was present at the birth of mountain goats, got a bang out of the wild ox because no human could domesticate it (Job 39:1-4, 9-12), made giant bath toys to play in the ocean (Ps. 104:26), talked to the snow, hail, frost, wind, and water (Ps. 147) and longed to set free creation from its bondage (Rom. 8:19-21), then God still does. If God humbled himself and "came down" to deliver his people (Exod. 3:8; John 1:14; Phil. 2:5-11), then God still does.

CONCLUSION

To many, a plea for Old Testament preaching may well sound like a voice crying out in the wilderness, if not a prophet from the bottom of a cistern. The challenges are both formidable and in a very real sense insoluble. Yet the rewards are equally considerable and the "ore" more accessible than often imagined. Techniques like the use of creative analogy help bring the treasures to light.

Postmodernity is the age of the church's reinvention. At such a time as this, exodus and exile have much to say to Anabaptist congregations. But how will they hear without a preacher (Rom. 10:14)?

Will we preach from the Old Testament? As we each ponder our own personal answer, it may help us to remember that Jesus passed through the wilderness. And Jesus passed through the Jordan. And when he came out, he came out preaching (Mk. 1:9-15). We can too!

NOTES

1. I believe that legitimate Christian preaching is preaching *from a biblical text*.

2. Marcion was a second century Christian-become-heretic. Marcion's canon excised the entire OT (and a good bit of the NT as well) as unfit for Christian proclamation.

3. Among those questions vigorously accosting Anabaptists, the most obvious are Old Testament war texts.

4. The very terminology *Old Testament* is Christian; it implies another testament, the New, to which the Old stands in relation. But beyond mere terminology or the bare fact of having a "sequel," the Old Testament is arranged differently, and is therefore physically different, from the Jewish or Hebrew Bible. The Christian Old Testament is something of a hybrid, containing the same books as the Hebrew Scriptures but generally in the order of its Greek translation, the Septuagint.

These two distinct arrangements have different theological implications. For example, the Christian Old Testament ends with the so-called writing prophets, specifically, with what corresponds in the Jewish Scriptures to the Scroll of the Twelve (or in Christian tradition, the Minor Prophets). The end of that scroll, commonly called the Book of Malachi, concludes with the expectation of the coming of Elijah as precursor to the "great and terrible day of the Lord." In the New Testament, the ministry of Jesus opens with the appearance of a new Elijah, namely, John the Baptist. The Jewish Bible, in contrast, ends with Chronicles. What then do we mean by the Old Testament's own voice? Do we mean its hybrid Greek-Septuagint voice or its Jewish-Hebrew voice?

5. There is a long-attested tradition in the history of Christian biblical interpretation, Anabaptism included, which understands the testaments to stand in a relationship of promise and fulfillment. John Howard Yoder among others has noted that ultimately this interpretive template ill-fits not only the Old Testament but the New Testament as well, since it too is a promise awaiting fulfillment. Rather, Old (in either Septuagint or Hebrew order!) and New Testaments are alike in being eschatologically oriented. See Mal 4:5-6, 2 Chron. 36:22-23, Rev. 22:17, 20. John H. Yoder, "The Authority of the Canon" in Willard M. Swartley, ed. *Essays on Biblical Interpretation: Anabaptist-Mennonite Perspectives*. Text-Reader Series, vol. 1 (Elkhart, Ind.: Institute of Mennonite Studies, 1984), 265-90.

6. Jesus "fulfilling" the Old Testament, in part or whole, can be understood as involving both continuity and discontinuity with the meanings of first covenant texts.

7. "While denying a christological center to the Old Testament, we still affirm a christological center to our preaching," says Paul Scott Wilson, *The Practice of Preaching* (Nashville: Abingdon Press, 1995), 75. Amen! But we must still answer the question, Precisely when is a sermon "Christ-centered"? In my opinion, the fulcrum of the debate about christocentrism in preaching is its identification in practice. Christocentrism can be viewed narrowly or broadly. Is it the citation of a New Testament or Gospel text that makes a sermon christocentric? Is it the explicit mention of Jesus, with or without direct quotation of a text? Is it reference to accepted Christian doctrine? Is it pointing to Christ-likeness without any explicit mention of text or Jesus?

While the debate is unlikely ever to be settled, my own preference is for keeping the definition of christocentrism relatively broad. There are occasions when the Christ-likeness of Jeremiah or Ruth or God in the Old Testament (!) is a sufficient witness to the "gospel" to stand on its own without needing to be "baptized" by Matthew or Paul.

8. While space does not permit an extended analysis, it should be stated that these two bridges are qualitatively different, not merely quantitatively so!

9. "The sermon's task is to extend a portion of the text's impact into a new communicational situation, that of contemporary hearers listening to the sermon," says Thomas G. Long, *Preaching and the Literary Forms of the Bible*, 33. If that is a reasonable definition of the task of preaching, the challenges are two: (1) By what criteria is the text's "impact" determined; (2) What are the parameters for legitimate "extending" into the new situation? To the second question we can respond that no universally accepted set of norms exists. Nevertheless, since there are things that a given text does not and cannot mean, there are limits within which homiletical appropria-

tions of the text must fall. Those boundaries may never be perceived any more clearly than through a glass darkly; if we have to "grope" after God (Acts 17:27), can we expect any less with textual meanings? But however elusive, the boundaries are there. There is a range into which legitimate interpretation and application must fall—a set of possibilities that is finite.

10. For additional challenges, see for example, Donald E. Gowan, *Reclaiming the Old Testament for the Christian Pulpit* (Edinburgh: T&T Clark, 1980), 3-6.

11. Consider also the pervasive use of Old Testament language, allusions and imagery in the Book of Revelation. This is a different kind of affirmation of the Old Testament's value but a positive valuation nonetheless.

12. There is even an implicit value present in the age of the Hebrew Scriptures. The writings of the Old Testament come from a period of perhaps 1000 years while the New Testament materials span under 100 years. The New Testament reflects more or less a single period of the church's ascendency, albeit amidst resistance and persecution. However, in the Old Testament's ten-foldgreater expanse, we witness the life of the community of faith encountering numerous successes, failures and complete reinventions of itself in response to overwhelming catastrophes. The Old Testament's witness to Israel's theological adaptations during over a millenium of formation and reformation of its identity is a significant resource to a postmodern church which is also reinventing itself.

13. The overwhelming witness of this theological pluralism has caused Walter Brueggemann in his *Theology of the Old Testament* (1997) to completely abandon the idea of a theological "center" to the Old Testament, at least a center understood as a unified theology. A previous generation of scholars, represented for example by Walther Eichrodt and his own Old Testament theology *magnum opus*, were more confident about the existence of a textually verifiable, unified theological center to the Old Testament (in Eichrodt's case, covenant). The trend to accept a chorus of theological voices as a foundational assumption for Old Testament study continues, as evident in a work like Ehrhard Gerstenberger's *Theologies [!] of the Old Testament*.

14. The Old Testament's "theological pluralism" should not be understood as complete disunity. The message of the Old Testament comes to us from a choir rather than from a soloist. But just as a choir anthem has many parts and a unity, so the Old Testament is unified by its witness to God and Israel bound together in relationship. The variety of theologies in the Old Testament are not the result of theological arbitrariness or laxity. Rather they come from different voices of the one people wrestling with the meaning of bondedness to God over centuries of changing life circumstances. The Old Testament invites us into that continuing journey of theological reflection. Especially in postmodernity, it is this wrestling that attests the Old Testament's authenticity, authority and relevance.

15. Josiah defended the cause of the poor and needy. Yahweh asks, "Is not this to *know* me?" (Jer 22:16). Spiritual vitality, knowing God, is viewed as inextricable from ethical behavior.

16. As further examples of the Old Testament's integration of the religious and secular, we may consider Proverbs 20:13, 23 which uses the religious word "abomination" to describe unjust commercial practices; in a chapter devoted to the festal

calendar, Lev 23:22 inserts gleaning laws to benefit the disadvantaged.

17. See for example Ps 85:10-12; Jer 14:1-15:9; Lev 26:3-6. Moreover, Job chapters 38-41, where God answers Job out of the whirlwind, aims an incisive rhetoric at the idea that human beings are the sum total of all God's concerns—a view which has greatly contributed to the present ecological crisis.

18. Therefore Jesus' delineation of the two great commandments (to love God and neighbor, Mark 12:28-34 and parallels) is his theological synthesis of a pervasive Old Testament theme already established.

19. The (Throne) Succession Narrative can be delimited as 2 Samuel 9-20, 1 Kings 1-2.

20. Spiritual "ecstasy" and imprecation can even come together (see *all of* Psalm 139)!

21. That Old Testament "spirituality" should include the broadest range of human affect is hardly surprising from writings which begin with a description of the person as part divine (Gen. 1:26-27) and part dirt (Gen. 2:7).

22. Israel's Scriptures understand God as *holy*. God enacts this holiness as what we might call an involved separatist. That is, God is intimately and vitally involved in the life of Israel. But as holy, God is also "other." Moreover, God is other not only in essence and location but also in perspective and action (see e.g. Isa. 55:8-11). To western civilization, which regards the rights of human individuals as the highest good, the Old Testament gives a necessary reality check: a holy God who can act "for his own sake," i.e. without any reference to human need (see e.g. Ezek. 36:22-32). As Leander Keck says, God's holiness relativizes us. See Leander Keck, *Who is Jesus? History in Perfect Tense* (Columbia, S.C.: University of South Carolina Press, 2000), 135.

23. Consider for example, "Enoch walked with God; *then* he was no more." (Gen. 5:24, italics mine. The meaning is that Enoch's "walking with God" describes his earthly life. This brief anecdote in the midst of a genealogy piques my curiousity: what was Enoch's walking with God like?); 1 Chron. 7:24, within a male genealogy, describes Sheerah, a woman architect, general contractor, building financier, or, perhaps, all three!

24. Consider for example, the women pioneers of Transjordan (Num. 32; see especially 32:26-27); the tragic figures of David's wife Michal and her second husband, Paltiel (2 Sam. 3:14-16); the adaptive and peacemaking Israelite slave girl of Aramean general Naaman (2 Kings 5); the boy Joash, heir to the throne, who hid with his nurse for six years in a temple bedroom to escape the purge of Athaliah (2 Kings 11:4-20; 2 Chron. 22:10-23:21); the peacemaking prophet Oded (2 Chron. 28:8-15).

25. We can ask, What does this commandment imply about God, God's relationship to the people, and the people's relationships with one another?

26. Consider for example, Lev. 6:5-6 (Eng: 6:12-13) and the law derived from it, but attributed to the Pentateuch (!) in Neh. 10:34; Lev. 24:10-23; Num. 3:11-13, 40-51, 9:1-14, 15:32-36, 27:1-11, 36:1-12, 2 Chron. 30:17-20; the deuteronomic "updates" to the Covenant Code (Exod. 23:19).

27. It is important to observe that "war texts" in the Old Testament are more var-

ied than sometimes acknowledged. The Old Testament contains at least three kinds of war passages: (1) victory texts (e.g. Jos 6); (2) defeat texts, which often portray the horrors of war (e.g. Lamentations, Psalm 74); (3) alternative texts (e.g. Isa 2:2-4//Mic 4:1-4, Isa 19:23-25).

28. One example in the genre of "Old Testament Introductions" is Bruce Birch, et.al. *A Theological Introduction to the Old Testament* (Nashville: Abingdon Press, 1999).

29. Representative are Walter Brueggemann, *The Threat of Life* (Minneapolis: Augsburg Fortress, 1996); James L. Crenshaw, *Trembling at the Threshold of a biblical Text* (Grand Rapids: Eerdmans, 1994); Hans Walter Wolff, *Old Testament and Christian Preaching.* Trans. Margaret Kohl. Philadelphia: Fortress, 1986; Donald E. Gowan, *Reclaiming the Old Testament for the Christian Pulpit* (Edinburgh: T&T Clark, 1980).

30. In particular, *The New Interpreter's Bible* ends each exegetical treatment with a provocative section called "(Theological) Reflections."

31. Stephen Farris. *Preaching That Matters: The Bible and Our Lives* (Louisville, Ky.: Westminster/John Knox, 1998), 8. Farris, while certainly not the first homiletical theorist to exploit the concept of analogy, provides a thorough and accessible exposition of its possibilities.

32. To be honest and helpful in using analogies, preachers can signal to listeners that their analogies are impressionistic rather than exact with qualifying language like, "If _____ were alive today, I wonder if she would be something like _____ ."

33. It is ponderable that Luke 5:1-11 might be thought of as a kind of call narrative of Peter, complete with the element of objection!

34. A real danger inherent in using human character and behavioral analogies is creating sermons that detract from the vertical dimension. To Farris' credit, he fully recognizes this risk. See Farris, 114.

35. Figurative language in the Old Testament is another type of expression of analogy already present in the text. Metaphors, similes, allegories, and so forth invite the exploration of comparisons and the making of new ones. Such imagery can itself be the basis for a sermon (consider for example Isa. 55:10-11).

Chapter 7

Collaborative Preaching in the Community of Interpreters

June Alliman Yoder

*T*he preaching event as we know it today barely resembles what some of the early Anabaptists might have experienced. The gatherings of persecuted believers huddled in forests and caves of Europe, worshipping in secret places and in fear for their lives were so different from how we in North America worship today. Our sixteenth-century forebears were deeply committed and gathered despite the threats of persecution that hovered about them. Unfortunately, when you are worshiping while your life is being threatened, you are not likely to be keeping a journal or diary of worship. We know little about what actually happened in those worship services. Though some evidence exists, it is scarce; and though the search continues, it has not been very fruitful.

In regard to my topic of collaborative preaching, it is interesting that even though there is little evidence to support it, "for several decades Mennonites have laid claim to a clear, incontrovertible hermeneutical method. The most difficult of Scriptures must yield their meaning to the body of believers who function within what is called the hermeneutical community."[1] In other words, the task of interpreting the Scripture was the work of the community of believers.

Though there were leaders among the early Anabaptists, and records show that only a few people were given the authority to baptize, many were given the opportunity to speak in public worship. They would listen to and respond to one another. One person preached and another (or others) would respond in agreement, with questions, or with concerns. There are records of this "preach and response" pattern happening in a number of ways, but these records are very rare—so rare in fact that one can hardly declare with any certainty that this was a hermeneutical pattern. However, that pattern points to a theological ideology which modern Mennonites have embraced in theory if very little in practice. Indeed, in theory it came close to being the "priesthood of all believers" which they claimed for themselves. Baptism was their ordination. One of the great sins for church leaders was to be accused of "running alone."[2] Anyone who preached and taught what was considered contrary to the Scriptures was disciplined by the hermeneutical community in hopes of bringing the wandering preacher back into the fold. After all, the whole Reformation focused on the issue of biblical interpretation. So among the radical reformers, biblical interpretation was a central issue for their preaching.

It seems safe to say that for some sixteenth-century Anabaptists, preaching was *an interpretation of the Scripture followed by a response from one or more of the other gathered believers.* Sometimes the response was in the form of standing up and walking out, sometimes in the form of a discussion.

This paradigm may sound vaguely familiar to preachers who hear their sermon discussed in church hallways and at Sunday dinner. For the most part, however, today's preacher works at sermon preparation in isolation and gets relatively little feedback. The isolation in which most preachers work today stands in bold contrast to the hermeneutical community Oyer referred to. Many factors lead to this isolation, and I think it important to examine some of them and be aware of what brings us to our current condition.

ISOLATION OF PREACHERS

Before we look at the many factors that contribute to the preacher's isolation, it is important to notice that first and foremost the paradigm is what has changed. The shift from a witness and discussion pattern to a monologue in the public address mode is a huge shift. It is one that was not made quickly, but it is a change that reflects the changes in ecclesiology. *As the church changed, preaching changed* and the monological nature of public address came into common usage. This is important because often we blame preaching for something that is symptomatic of the state of the church.

The first factor leading to isolation of preachers was the change in the roles of leaders. Ministers were called out, and the preacher's voice was no longer just another voice. Now there was a voice more influential than the others. When that voice was educated, it carried even more influence in the preaching role. The minister became the expert on all things biblical and theological. As the minister began to receive financial remuneration, the expectation was that the minister was the most capable preacher and that this was part of the task for which the minister was hired. It became the duty of the minister to preach, even as others in the congregation were relieved of the assignment. What once had been a whole choir of voices was now a solo performance.

But other factors also have served to isolate the preacher. One of the things children educated in North American schools run into is the admonition to "Do your own work." The notion of consulting with others is educated out of us at a fairly young age by describing it as a form of cheating. If you are talking to other people about your work, you are borrowing at best and being dishonest at worst. Collaboration has overtones of plagiarism, thus young people quickly learn to go to isolated places to do their writing and studying. This negative connotation lingers long and deep. Team sports are something of an antidote for this mindset, but that is play, not work.

Another isolating notion is the corporate model of efficiency prevalent in many churches. Sometimes congregational leaders other than the minister come from management in business or other professions, and they want the church to be run with the same efficiency. The pastor's job description says "prepare and preach sermons"—so it is the preacher's job to get a sermon together and no one else's. The idea of less efficient ways of working, or of "wasting" more than one person's time, seems genuinely counterproductive.

A further isolating factor is that many people think coming up with a sermon every week is something that only ministers can or should do. It is the calling of the minister to preach. Lay people are called to be mechanics, or teachers, or work at the donut shop; it is the minister's job to put a sermon in place. Lay participants can fulfill many tasks of the congregation, but it is the minister's job to baptize, serve communion, marry, bury, AND preach.

Meanwhile, pastors may think that if they do not protect this turf, they may have no job left. If everybody can do everything, then there is nothing left that is solely the ministers? Therefore, some preachers guard preaching as their sacred prerogative.

Another isolating factor is that much of a minister's work—counseling, studying, visitation—is private and confidential. It is work that most of the congregation knows little or nothing about. But preaching is public. Here everyone sees what a preacher is doing. So some ministers come to protect preaching as something "I did."

It is interesting to reflect on these isolating factors. On the page they may not look that substantial, yet they drive how many preachers work. Preachers know the desperation that comes when they sit alone feeling the solitary pressure to compose a sermon. Not only is such isolation difficult and lonely—it is unnecessary. Collaboration is important to make preaching rich and robust. While finding meaningful partners is not the most efficient way to do sermon preparation, it does bring us to satisfying and nurturing encounters with the Word of God.

COLLABORATION

Collaboration is most simply defined as working together, to echo the meaning of the word *partnership*. One difference, however, is that collaboration can include partners not immediately thought of as allies. The two parties in a new collaborative relationship have become partners even if not originally allies. I am reminded of a story told to me a number of years ago; it provides a vivid picture of collaboration.

Some women were in graduate school together in a rigorous social work master's program. They began to enjoy each other's company and to study together. Once, as a part of their research, they participated in a sacred ceremony among a tribe of Native Americans. The ceremony involved a ritual of passing a pipe around the room and punctuating the silence occasionally with the word "ho," which was a rough equivalent of the Baptists' penchant for saying "amen." It was a word for praise and peace.

Now it came to pass that these young women were about to finish their academic work and be tested. The philosophy of the school was that quality depends upon a certain number of people being selected out at every stage—at admission first of all and then at the point of candidacy for the degree. The process at this particular exam was to have all the candidates—all five young women—stand in front of the room to answer a barrage of questions fired at them from the panel of professors. This system would dramatize for everyone, especially the students, which were worthy and which not.

The first woman to answer a question did so brilliantly. The woman beside her quite unselfconsciously blurted out, "Ho!" When she herself answered the next question well, the first woman responded with a "ho." The spirit began to infect everyone. Soon every question was followed by exclamations of "ho." There was so much "ho"-ing going on that all the weeds of doubt and fear were torn out and every woman came to know her own power. Instead of battling each other, they allowed their connectedness to emerge. Everyone passed the exam.

In education circles collaborative learning remains an elusive step. The notion of turning adversaries into allies runs contrary to the custom of doing work in isolation so you can do better work than the other and thus achieve a better grade, a promotion, or the approval of those who have power over you. This non-collaborative and non-cooperative mode keeps preachers operating in ways that are least helpful for preparing effective sermons and ministering to the needs of congregations.

As a teacher of preaching, one struggle I have every year is to try to convince my students that not only do they not need to do their work all by themselves, but they will do better work if they work collaboratively. Though I encourage them to talk to each other about their work, some are not able to overcome this deeply rooted isolation. Anabaptist theology and ecclesiology both yearn for a communal discernment in collaborative relationships.

COLLABORATIVE RELATIONSHIPS

In the next few pages I want to highlight some of the important collaborative relationships that preachers can have, and explore how these relationships can enrich the sermons that we preach and bring us back to a more egalitarian relationship with others in the church. If we think of preaching as more conversational and dialogical, we will be reaching toward a more thorough understanding of what it can mean to be a priesthood of all believers as well as what it can mean to do public address well.

Holy Spirit

Perhaps it seems odd to begin the conversation about collaborative relationships with the Holy Spirit, but there are many who view the human spirit and the Holy Spirit as being in competition somehow. Contemporary preachers relate to the Spirit of God in different ways. Nearly everyone agrees that the Spirit is somehow a part of the picture or a piece of the puzzle, but not everyone understands how it fits together in the same way. Carol Lakey Hess in "Educating in the Spirit" writes of two ways ministers often relate to the Holy Spirit.[3] One way of understanding how the Holy Spirit and the human spirit work together is the concept of "the Spirit of the gaps." The preacher does whatever s/he can do and the Holy Spirit is expected to fill in the gaps. The Holy Spirit becomes an explanation for the x-factor which is not covered by human efforts. In this relationship, whatever the preacher can do the Holy Spirit does not have to do, and the better the preacher is the less frequently the Holy Spirit will have to be called upon and the less the Spirit will be asked to do.

When the Holy Spirit is unintentionally marginalized like this, the preacher disposes of his/her prayerful reliance on the Spirit. Lakey Hess uses the analogy of the relief pitcher who comes in to clinch the win only if the regular players are in trouble. Otherwise, the Spirit just sits on the bench and waits for the next crisis. Preachers must give care not to presume independence from the Spirit and turn to basking in personal skills and accomplishments. The preacher who uses the Spirit as a relief pitcher calls on God mostly on Saturday night when God is very busy with other pastors in crisis.

A second way of understanding how the Spirit works in preaching is the opposite extreme. In this view, the Spirit is in charge of the whole preaching event and the preacher is neither blamed nor credited for what happens during the preaching event. The preacher is the one marginalized in this scenario. This understanding of the Holy Spirit's work in preaching is most familiar to the Mennonite Church of the Swiss-

German heritage. Years ago the group of ministers, referred to as the bench, would meet just before the service to decide who was going to preach that morning and what the text would be. It is clear that with such a practice the preacher of the day would turn the event over to the Spirit for inspiration and a message, and that such a preacher would carry little responsibility for how preaching went that morning.

I propose that preaching is the work of both the human being and the Holy Spirit. It is a true partnership. A partner is someone you work with on a big project neither of you can do alone. If you have a partner, it means you can never give up, because your partner is depending on you. I dare say that first and foremost the preacher is a collaborative partner with God. Thus the task that is most important, for the preacher, is to be in a healthy, listening relationship with God. Regular prayer, Bible reading, and quiet reflection are required for the Spirit of God to be an integral part of the preacher's life and work. This is not a Saturday night crisis relationship, but rather one ongoing throughout the week.

Scripture text

Another significant collaborative relationship the preacher participates in is with the biblical text. Anabaptists hold the Scripture in high regard as a source of communication from God. Biblical authority is highly valued, and sermons in this tradition almost always are launched from or centered in a biblical text. We come to the Scripture because we believe. We believe it is in the Scripture that we will meet God, and if we linger there we will hear a message regarding new and right living in Jesus. It is not primarily that we believe in the Scripture, rather we believe in the One we come to encounter and know through Scripture. The events of long ago and far away begin to have a claim on the here and now. So it is that the preacher goes regularly to Scripture not only to be nurtured and re-created but also to find the message that will shape the Christian formation of the congregation.

Thomas Long in *The Witness of Preaching* speaks of going to the meeting ground of Scripture. He says that "throughout its history, the church has discovered that when it goes to the Scripture in openness and trust, it finds itself uniquely addressed there by God and its identity as the people of God shaped by that encounter."[4] It is perfectly understandable that Mennonites around the world name their seminaries biblical seminaries instead of theological seminaries. It is the Bible that stands at the center of our understanding of God, the work of Jesus, our relationships with one another. The preacher must be rooted in the Bible and in the Jesus whom the Scriptures proclaim.

Expert knowledge and opinions

I want to include scholars as part of the tapestry of collaboration for the preacher because scholars are one of the most easily accepted partners. Both preacher and congregation recognize the invaluable assistance of lexicons, commentaries, and other research produced by scholars over the centuries. We read and study the experts in biblical studies and theology. Books and libraries appear like an oasis to the preacher facing next Sunday's sermon. It is not odd to me that preachers reach for materials scholars provide. What intrigues me is that for so long such materials have been the only acceptable partner outside of the Holy Spirit and the Bible.

Today the experts present themselves in many electronic forms as well. Video documentaries on archeological digs, website commentary on lectionary texts, and articles online all call to the preacher. The number of web sites for preachers and computer programs for sermon preparation is growing with no end in sight. The preacher crumbles under the mass of material with which she or he might collaborate.

Periodicals dedicated to preaching and sermon preparation, whether online or in print, offer to make preaching easier and quicker. The weekly task overwhelms many, and the writers know it and seek to bring relief. The temptation to some is not collaboration and partnership with these experts, but to let them do the job. At a ministers' conference a few years ago a pastor whispered to me, "I use Thursday to look for a sermon." He didn't use Thursday to focus on preparing a sermon; rather he used Thursday to find one ready-made.

The accessibility the electronic era provides to scholarly materials regardless of proximity to a library is wonderful. The challenge is to see these many materials as partners with which we collaborate in the sermon preparation process. In the same way that we don't expect the Spirit of God to do the sermon preparation without the preacher's participation, so we should not be willing to give over preparation to another person who does not know us, our congregation. or our circumstances. There are so many experts willing to tell us what we should say, yet none know us nor are we able to dialogue with them. They offer one-way communication. At best they can be part of the collaboration, but they are not the last word; sermon preparation should not be given over to them.

Sometimes these resources offer to make sermon preparation easier. I suppose that is acceptable, but sermon preparation is not easy. To look for things that make it easier may be acceptable, but it is a mistake for the preacher to think sermon preparation will be easy. There is a difference between looking for fresh ingredients to make the sermon good and looking for the thaw-n-serve dinner that makes sermon preparation easy.

Up to this point we have suggested collaborating with the Holy Spirit, Scripture, and scholars and experts who produce commentaries, books, articles, and periodicals either on paper or on web sites. All are profoundly helpful, but they are not all there is to the collaborative conversation. They overlook other partners available to the preacher. Lets look at some.

Congregational analysis

I use congregational analysis here in the broadest sense of the word. The sociology and demographics of the congregation are important influences on the sermon. A preacher who knows the needs and concerns of the congregation better understands the gospel message most participants need to hear on any given Sunday.

This same congregation will help the preacher decide what kind of language and images will communicate best. Congregation analysis will help the preacher understand how the congregation thinks and what motivates participants' lives. The preacher who does not take exegeting the congregation seriously misses a major collaborative partner.

In *Preaching as Local Theology and Folk Art,*[5] Lenora Tubbs Tisdale moves the focus of the preaching event from the preacher and the text to the congregation. This shift is a helpful corrective for most Mennonite preachers. With our elevated view of Scripture, we tend to overlook the important role that the listener plays in communication. One does not have effective communication if the receivers of the message are disregarded. Though Tisdale's homiletic may overplay the role of context, it is a useful corrective and should certainly be added to the collaborative mix. In her way, Tisdale is inviting the whole congregation into the pulpit. Her awareness that the preacher speaks out of a context as well as to a context points to the interactive nature of preaching as she understands it. The recognition that the preacher and the congregation live in a congregation, in a community, in a nation, in the world—each with a history and a future—is a significant partnership for the preacher. The preaching is still done with the solo voice of public address, but the other voices of the congregation are present in the sermon.

People within the congregation

It is interesting to note that within the last decade, two books have been written to address one of the most central Anabaptist principles of preaching—that of valuing equally the thoughts and concerns of each one in the community of faith. Each author writes a homiletic of inclusion and shared voice.

Lucy Atkinson Rose, in *Sharing the Word: Preaching in the Roundtable Church,*[6] invites preachers to conversational preaching that grows out of connectedness and mutuality with the worshipers. She particularly desires to speak on behalf of those marginalized by the homiletic process. Her non-hierarchical roundtable includes everyone equally and meaning is found through the conversation. Though the preacher continues to preach with a solo voice in public address form, what is preached is gathered from the roundtable church conversation and is designed to stimulate and nourish the conversations the congregation is having at various places in the congregation and in the world.

John McClure's The *Roundtable Pulpit*[7] describes a similar desired outcome with more structure. Again, the issue is how to move from a leader-centered style of preaching to a style that is inclusive and dialogical. Like Rose, McClure is not suggesting that the sermon be an actual pulpit dialogue. Rather, he is advocating a dialogue with members of the congregation around the sermon texts, the needs of the congregation, and the experiences and insights of the group. Out of that conversation comes the raw material from which the sermon will emerge. At the following week's meeting, the group discusses last week's sermon and begins again to look at the text for the next week.

The "roundtable" group of about ten congregation members is committed to the process for an agreed upon period of time. Then participants leave the group and new people move into the roundtable. This plan provides a systematic way of including all the voices of the congregation. All must be empowered to contribute in their way and all must be taken seriously. There are other benefits to this process too. It is a significant way for pastors to get to know the congregation members better and an important step in helping congregation members understand the preaching task.

But most significant of all is the collaboration between the preacher and the congregation. In this model they become partners in the activity of finding God's voice in the text and interpreting that text for this particular congregation. On Sunday the preacher gives witness to what God has revealed to them and through them as a committed and representative group. To me this sounds a lot like the description of preaching among the early Anabaptists given at the beginning of this essay. *Preaching was giving witness to what God had revealed to the gathered group through Scripture followed by a response from one or more of the other gathered believers.* People who have used McClure's method remark about how carefully people listen to the sermon because they know it is a message discerned by the group.

The worship setting

The longer I teach preaching, the more I am impressed by how much of the preaching event is shaped by the congregation and the worship setting in which it occurs. The context of the hearing creates the message. I often think about that when I read my Bible. Reading at home in private I hear some things; reading with my Bible study group I often hear something more; then hearing the same text in the context of Sunday worship it sounds still different. In the first setting I hear only with my ears, but in the second two settings I hear also with the ears of those around me.

Public worship is not so much about the nurturing of individuals as the remolding of the community of believers. It is a group event, and as we sit in worship the group is changed by what we hear, and the group changes what we hear. All of us who preach have been amazed to hear people leaving the worship service comment on something that was said during the sermon, something we know we did not say. Again I am reminded of the communication theory principle: It is not what you said, but what the listener heard you say that was communicated.

The physical space is an important factor in the preaching partnership of public worship. Is the preacher high and lifted up? Does the preacher sit in a circle with the congregation? What is the relationship of the pulpit to the communion table? These and other questions highlight factors that speak to the congregation and the preacher about what the congregation believes about preaching, whether conscious of it or not.

After public worship, the sermon moves from its public phase and enters a personal phase. After the congregation has heard the sermon in the company of one another, each person now goes her or his separate way, and together we become the scattered church. We walk away from public worship as solo bodies, but we are always a part of the community of believers and the work of the sermon continues in each of us as a part of the group.

CONCLUSION

Collaborative preaching, as I present it in this chapter, is not so much a *style* of preaching as it is a way of *viewing* preaching. Books have been written on each of these collaborative factors: the Holy Spirit, the role of the Scripture texts, the knowledge and opinions of experts, congregational analysis, conversations with people of the congregation, and the influence of the worship setting. All these factors can be influential in the preparation of the sermon and should be considered with care. Each factor can be inappropriately overemphasized, overlooked, or minimized. The care and the mix, the proportions and the particular topic, are what shape a given sermon.

But I dare say that never does an effective sermon rise fullblown from the head of the preacher alone. Always it emerges as the result of many factors in collaboration. Part of the preacher's job is to cultivate the relationships with God, with the Scripture, with the experts, and with the congregation that will help the congregational participants strengthen their relationship with God and one another. Indeed we come full circle. For the task of the preacher is to listen to and care for the hermeneutical community from which our sermons come.

NOTES

1. John S. Oyer, "Early Forms of Anabaptist Zeugnis After Sermons," *Mennonite Quarterly Review*, 62, no. 3 (July 1998): 449.

2. Cornelius J. Dyck, "The Role of Preaching in Anabaptist Tradition," *Mennonite Life* 17, no.1 (January 1962): 23.

3. Carol Lakey Hess, "Educating in the Spirit" in Jeff Astley, Leslie J. Francis, and Colin Crowder, eds. *Theological Perspectives on Christian Formation. A Reader on Theology and Christian Education.* (Grand Rapids: Eerdmans, 1996), 119-131. The section "The Spirit of the Gaps" appears 119-121.

4. Thomas G. Long, *The Witness of Preaching* (Louisville: Westminster/John Knox Press, 1989), 50.

5. Lenora Tubbs Tisdale, *Preaching as Local Theology and Folk Art* (Minneapolis: Fortress Press, 1997). Tisdale's chapter three on "Exegeting the Congregation" is particularly useful in the collaboration discussion.

6. Lucy Atkinson Rose, *Sharing the Word: Preaching in the Roundtable Church* (Louisville: Westminster/John Knox Press, 1997). I especially point readers to the introduction and chapter one of this book which outline the general focus of her homiletic. Chapter four focuses on the marginal voices that need to be heard in preaching.

7. John S. McClure, *The Roundtable Pulpit: Where Leadership and Preaching Meet* (Nashville: Abingdon, 1995); chs. 2 and 3 are most helpful in outlining his "Collaborative Homiletic."

Chapter 8

Theological Preaching in an Age of Doctrine Lite

Mark R. Wenger

My in-laws recently cleaned out a few keepsakes from Grandmother. Among the assorted yellow newspaper clippings and photos were a few books. My wife asked if I had interest in any of them. A volume caught my eye—*1000 Questions and Answers on Points of Christian Doctrine.* Written by Daniel Kauffman and published by Mennonite Publishing House in 1908, this little book contains forty-four doctrinal topics— salvation, self-denial, ordinances, pride, heaven, and so on—probed by 1000 questions and answered with simple declarative sentences buttressed by lots of Bible references. It is one of a host of materials published during what has been called the "doctrinal era" of the Mennonite church, dated 1898 to 1944, whose influence has lingered into the 1980s and beyond in some circles.[1]

This torn and worn booklet is emblematic to me of the place of doctrine in many North American Anabaptist circles at the beginning of the twenty-first century: it feels out-of-date and old-fashioned. Anabaptists are by no means unique in this respect. Where teaching Christian doctrine and theology as truth was once a priority for right living in this world—and secure preparation for the world to come—the very notion of truth for many today has become more diffuse. Preachers cannot assume that most of their listeners know the basic beliefs of the Christian faith. In addition, a myriad of competing theologies abound, each with its own angle for interpreting the Scriptures.

In a recent book, Robert Hughes and Robert Kysar call this state of affairs a "doctrinal defoliation."[2] They enumerate several ecclesial and cultural reasons for this loss of theological acumen. Catechetical teaching and preaching in the church has been slighted; preaching now tends to focus on social and personal issues. Theology is perceived by many as boring, unconcerned with the practical issues of living. Doctrinal questions can be dangerously divisive; it's safer to steer around them. "Teaching sound theology in preaching," Hughes and Kysar declare, "seems to have gone the way of the Edsel."

They also identify several cultural factors adding to theological erosion in the pulpit and congregation. Consumerism with its individualistic assumptions makes it more difficult to form a cohesive theological community. Television offers up pat answers with lots of emotional punch. Radical secularism makes God seem distant and irrelevant. New spiritualities offer experiences of God that are not dependent on biblical understanding or theological formulation. Postmodernism deconstructs and dissolves assertions of universal truth. The new always seems to trump the old.[3]

While this state of theological knowledge in the church is not entirely new, some leaders have a sense of growing urgency. One Anabaptist-related missions leader recently confided to me that he has lost confidence in the ability of Protestant Christianity in the West to hold onto historic Christian tradition and theology. A pastoral friend recounted how he had been attracted to the Mennonite church because of its clear doctrine and theology; lately, however, he is wondering whether the church has lost touch with its roots. Another pastor of a large and growing Anabaptist congregation in the Midwest tells me that newcomers to the fellowship soon want to know "what it is that this church believes."

These anecdotal comments, together with the assessment of Hughes and Kysar, point to a situation sensed by many in congregations today—the need for effective and intentional theological preaching—in other words, creative and faithful preaching which aims toward the theological grounding and formation of the congregation and its members. Such preaching requires attention both to the abiding doctrines of Scripture and church tradition as well as to contemporary human experience in all its myriad colors. Doctrinal preaching is not easy preaching; sermons with theological depth require knowledge and wisdom. The need for and the difficulty of theological preaching are two suppositions that underlie this chapter.

Clarifying some terms would be helpful at this point. *Doctrine* and *theology* have and will be used somewhat interchangeably in this chapter. The distinction between them is one of scale and scope rather than kind. *Theology* is the more general, sweeping term and refers to reflection and articulation on the nature, character, and activity of God in relationship with humanity. Christian theology is centered on a powerful story, the good news of what God has accomplished in Jesus the Christ. Other modifiers are frequently attached to theology for purposes of category or type: systematic theology, liberation theology, Anabaptist theology, and so forth

Doctrine is a more specific word. It refers to a discrete theme or subject lifted from the whole of theology. Doctrine carries a more positional and teaching connotation. A synonym for doctrine is *dogma*, which may sound harsher still to contemporary ears, though its Greek root means, "what seems good, fitting, becoming." Dogmas or doctrines are a "restatement of the Christian mysteries" in the words of poet-writer Kathleen Norris. They "undergird the faith" and are part and parcel of Christian worship and preaching.[4]

How then can we preach theologically in an age of doctrine lite? We can first recognize that *all* preaching, in a sense, is theological. Something theological is apparent even if God barely makes an appearance in the sermon. Whether the concerns of the sermon are social, psychological, ethical, or scriptural, the preacher addressing a faith community in worship is doing theology by broad definition. Preaching is also always teaching; *kerygma* is *didache*. Regardless of the sermon form or purpose, one can fairly ask—What is being taught here?

The question in focus for this chapter, however, deals with preaching on theological themes and doctrines in more direct rather than indirect ways. How can preachers intentionally strengthen the theological character of their sermons rather than leave it to happenstance? The old Puritan Plain-style approach to preaching made a deliberate move to doctrine in every sermon—*exposition, doctrine, and application.*

Many preachers, myself included, are tempted to steer away from doctrinal sermons. We do so because we know that such sermons have the tendency to gather weight and dull the senses. The language of faith is impenetrable for some; for others it is tired jargon. Concentrated theological propositions are rarely God-revealing and life-giving. "The letter kills, but the Spirit gives life" (2 Cor. 3:6, NIV).

When we preach, we don't aim to indoctrinate our listeners; we long to bring them into the mysterious place where God revealed in Christ Jesus encounters them in truth and grace. Teaching a congregation to recite the Apostles' Creed or the Confession of Faith is not the same thing as preaching theologically among them. Knowing a creed or confession of faith is not at all the same thing as knowing God, just as looking at a map is not the same thing as traveling there yourself. There is no substitute for making the journey.

Doctrine and theology, however, can function like a map, a diagram of faith voiced by those who really did know God. The map outlines pathways of faith that have stood the test of time and experience for others and thus commend themselves to us. We explore and follow these pathways together, describing their features in colloquial and accessible language. This is the image I like to hold in front of me when preaching deliberately on Christian doctrine or theology: I am a map-reader on the road of experience with listeners, studying the pathways from Scripture and tradition, listening to the wind of the Spirit, pointing out the ancient and always new way to God in Christ Jesus.[5]

METHOD AND POETRY

Many of us preachers, though, need something more specific than a metaphor to help us preach theologically. Two authors approaching preaching from very different angles provide useful advice and insight.

Paul Scott Wilson, professor of homiletics at Emmanuel College in the Toronto School of Theology, has written a textbook for preaching entitled *The Practice of Preaching*. He includes a chapter addressing "Theology in the Sermon."[6] Wilson insists "something needs to happen theologically in the sermon if preaching is to reach its potential as God's event." The goal of the preacher is to create with words and ethos "hospitable conditions for the relationship with God" of which the preacher is speaking.[7] He suggests several ways that preachers can work theologically. He draws these "lessons" from two basic theological approaches: systematic theology and homiletical theology.

Methodological helps from systematic theology

Among methodological helps grounded in systematic theology are these:

(1) Keep God in the center of the sermon rather than at the periphery. We are preaching God, not just about some doctrine, truth, story, or text. The sermon is God's event; God chooses to be encountered through preaching. "When the sermon goes well, information concerning God is not the purpose of the event so much as God's formation of us in Christ's image. The sermon we listen to is less an intellectual exercise than it is our being reclaimed by Christ as God's own."[8]

(2) Imitate the theology of those, including great preachers, who stand as models for the church. These should be persons who have shown a keen sensitivity to the realities of congregational life. This might include persons from general church history, from other cultures, or within one's own faith tradition. Who are the giants whose life and preaching commend themselves to the contemporary congregation?

(3) Test the logical consequences of any doctrinal position taken. Ask what is at stake for the church if this position is held. For example, how does a peace and justice theological stance affect the church's self-understanding, or its relationship to society, government and the global church? In what ways does God's grace color these interactions? Obviously one sermon cannot explore all the implications of a doctrinal position, but some basic lessons can be drawn.

(4) Identify as clearly as possible your own theological method or approach which should be at least broadly compatible with the congregation. Is it orthodox, liberationist, Anabaptist, evangelical, liberal, feminist, charismatic? This kind of internal clarity will help communication between preacher and congregation.

Methodological helps from homiletical theology

(1) Concentrate your preaching on only a few core or great doctrines of the church. In other words, avoid the trivial and idiosyncratic. What are these central doctrines? They are identified for us by our faith tradition. For Anabaptist groups these would usually be found in a preferred confession of faith or in the practical wisdom of the faith community itself.[9]

(2) Find movement within theology to develop some direction for the sermon. This may be some logical movement within a doctrine—

need identified . . . solution provided—or theological transitions within a biblical text. For instance, if we are preaching about the reality of human suffering, we could move to typical human responses (God's apparent absence) and then to God's response (entering into suffering in a redemptive way). The apostle Paul's writings provide a good example of theological movement and direction. His analytical diagnosis of the human condition at the outset of Romans leads directly to the prescribed remedy—salvation through faith in Christ Jesus.

(3) Employ theological intervention with your text if it has no apparent theological theme, no explicit focus on God or on Christ Jesus. This entails bringing to bear the broader canon, tradition, or faith to help with interpretation and teaching. For example, many of the Proverbs sound like standard self-help clichés. Yet these Proverbs can be developed in theological or doctrinal directions—use of money, care for the widow, sexual ethics—by incorporating broader biblical teaching. Perhaps a text has no explicit focus on God (Esther) or Jesus Christ (a text from the Old Testament). With care one may legitimately inject a theological theme, e.g. Christology, which may not be present in the primary text.

Kathleen Norris in *Amazing Grace: A Vocabulary of Faith* offers a poetic perspective for preaching theologically which is very different from that of Wilson.[10] Norris, a writer-poet, returned to church as an adult after twenty years away and felt "bombarded by the vocabulary of the Christian church. Words such as 'Christ,' 'heresy,' 'repentance,' and 'salvation' seemed dauntingly abstract . . . even vaguely threatening."[11] Worship itself, not lectures, became the way in which she began to inhabit this strange landscape of theological language. *Amazing Grace* is a record of her intriguing and thoughtful interaction with some of the words and doctrines of the Christian lexicon that most attracted or troubled her. She attempts to "remove the patina of abstraction or glassy-eyed piety from religious words, by telling stories about them, grounding them in the world we live in as mortal and often comically fallible human beings."[12] Under the heading "God-talk" she writes,

> I've come to believe that even in preaching, one is wise to avoid much theological terminology. I don't mean that pastors shouldn't speak of God, or Christ, or salvation—they'd be foolish not to. But when a sermon is little but biblical or theological language that the preacher has not troubled to digest, to incarnate . . . so

that it might readily translate into the lives of parishioners, it is often worse than no sermon at all. . . . Half an hour after a sermon like that, I'm hungry again. The preacher has not done what I consider the real work of writing, and if the sermon is so full of God-talk as to lack a recognizably human voice, the presence of a person behind it all, why should other people trouble to listen to it? (212)

Norris' point is sharp and penetrates throughout the book: theology and doctrine is a strange and abstract language unless internalized and expressed in recognized congregational idioms. It is not enough to know the code words and repeat them with insider flourish. Norris' lexicon of theological terms is a prime example of the inventive and creative ways preachers can interact with the language and doctrines of faith and "taste them again for the first time." There is no substitute for the hard work of re-languaging, reimaging and, in a sense, reliving the tradition of Christian church. We as preachers face the joyful toil of finding new words for describing and new ways of looking at old pathways to God. It has been suggested that the "preacher is a 'reverse theologian,' seeking to discover new images for doctrines that already exist."[13]

NORMS AND GUIDES

Wilson and Norris offer contrasting and beneficial pointers for preaching Christian doctrine in the current environment. One focuses on theological method in sermon preparation; the other explores meaning of religious terms in a poetic manner. Both assume and address elsewhere in their books an aspect of theological preaching that is basic, especially for those who claim an Anabaptist heritage: the key role of the Bible.[14] Historically, Anabaptist theological work has been predominantly biblical theology, focusing on guidance for right practice. North American Mennonites named their seminaries *biblical* rather than *theological*. Mennonites have produced few systematic theologies.

One exception to the pattern, however, is a major systematic theology by Thomas N. Finger, *Christian Theology: An Eschatological Approach*. Finger declares near the beginning of this two-volume work, "Scripture is the norm of theology. . . . Theological reflection must be grounded in and be evaluated by fidelity to the distinctive way in which the biblical writers speak."[15]

"All Scripture is inspired by God and is useful for teaching, for re-proof, for correction, and for training in righteousness" (2 Tim. 3:16 NIV). A doctrinal sermon without the Bible is like a tree without roots. It is cut off from the soil that keeps it green and growing, the story of God's gracious outreach strategy to reconcile the world to himself.

The Bible is not a static book; it is dynamic. The content of the Scriptures does not change, but to express the substance of the Christian faith in vital and authentic ways, the form and manner in which this takes place will change. In the words of Thomas Finger, "If Scripture or past theological formulation is simply quoted, the kerygma [gospel story and teaching of Christ] will often sound archaic and irrelevant, unlike the living dynamism that it really is."[16]

Having affirmed the normative place of Scripture for Anabaptist theological preaching, preachers do well to remember that context and experience are crucial factors for effective communication. In a real sense, doctrinal preaching means doing *local theology*. The sermon is delivered before a given congregation of listeners in one place and one time. Truth claims of universal scope may be spoken, but the sermon is intended for a specific setting, people and time. Theological preaching is not a commodity like pork bellies that can be frozen one place, then thawed and cooked up on order at another. A sermon needs to be prepared fresh and local to fit the moment and address the needs of the people with God's Word.

Another important piece of context is the faith tradition of the congregation. Earlier we highlighted Paul Scott Wilson's recommendation that preachers concentrate their theological work on a few core doctrines of the church identified for us by our particular faith tradition. These central doctrines are also clarified by knowing something about the history of the congregation, its neighborhood location, its socioeconomic status, its theological conflicts, and sense of God's missional call for the future. Informal religious affiliations and the nature of the relationship to the denomination can also be important indicative factors. Creeds, confessions of faith, and worship traditions and styles are useful markers of the basic beliefs and values shared in common by a congregation. From this constellation of points, we preachers chart what doctrines to emphasize and in which theological direction God is calling.

For many Mennonites the 1995 *Confession of Faith in a Mennonite Perspective* is a relatively recent primer for preachers on the theological and doctrinal matters currently shared broadly across the church. Its twenty-four articles are arranged in four groupings.[17] This *Confession of Faith* along with its commentary can be pretty dry reading, but it does provide guidance for Mennonite preachers as they work theologically with biblical texts, cultural issues and doctrinal topics. Two of the stated purposes of the *Confession of Faith* are to "anchor Christian belief and practice in changing times" and to "aid in sharing Mennonite belief and practice with other Christians, members of other faiths, as well as with people of no faith" (back cover).

The role of experience in theological preaching is one other angle that cannot be overlooked. Historical and authoritative argument from Scripture will not suffice for many contemporary listeners. There is a "fundamental pragmatism inherent in most of our listeners."[18] People want to know how to make life work successfully. God often seems hopelessly beyond comprehension and experience. And Christian doctrines can appear to have little to do with the struggles of ordinary daily life. The preacher's challenge is thus to bring all that tangled experience to God, to frame the experience in theological language that helps to make sense of life's confusions and aspirations.

I know this mandate for the preacher can feel daunting, maybe even impossible. And indeed our reach almost always exceeds our grasp. But the task becomes more manageable when we realize that theology and doctrine are not antithetical to human experience. In fact the common experience among believers over time—similar pathways that have been traversed again and again—lies beneath every Christian doctrine. Every doctrine has its feet planted on the ground of human experience. "Behind every doctrine there is a common experience of believers that has surfaced again and again and has finally been named 'sin' or 'sanctification' or 'regeneration.' Doctrines do not drop out of the sky nor do they represent the emotional euphoria of one person or one congregation or even one age. . . . Doctrines have stood the test of time."[19]

The goal for us preachers then is to uncover and understand the durable human experience of God behind doctrines and help contemporary believers come to the place where they are encountered by this same divine presence. Our responsibility, dependent on the Holy Spirit, is to breathe life and blood into dry bones of doctrinal statements with words and images that create hospitable conditions for a God-meeting, language that touches the heart, teaches the mind and moves the will.

One simple way is to develop a case study from contemporary experience and explore how a particular Christian doctrine can shine the light and truth of Jesus Christ into the experience. For example, a drive by any shopping mall on a typical Sunday afternoon will find it packed with shoppers. Many people today feel over-busy and stressed to the max with demands on their time. A sermon could explore, in light of this shared experience, what the biblical doctrine of Sabbath might offer as a sanctuary in time—space for rest and relationships and uncluttered worship of God.

Other examples abound. Destructive habits and addictions provide room to speak of confession, repentance and forgiveness. Marriage, infidelity and divorce offer analogies for addressing God's covenant relationship with his people. A hospice nurse in our congregation has observed publicly that "Believers die well." We all are shadowed by death. In this context the preacher could choose to speak of God's judgment and salvation or of the hope of the believer in Christ. Theological truth has always grown from the lived experience of people in encounters with God. That is still the case.

SUGGESTIONS FROM MY OWN EXPERIENCE

I have been preaching regularly in a congregational setting for more than fifteen years. In the interest of being yet more practical and concrete, I briefly describe a number of ways I have sought to enhance the theological formation of the congregation through sermons.

(1) *Complement the worship actions of baptism, the Lord's Supper, foot washing and anointing the sick with oil.* Variously referred to as sacraments, ordinances, signs or symbols, these ancient ritual actions of the Christian church are not dependent on sermonic accompaniment for meaning and efficacy. Nonetheless, celebrating them within the faith community creates a distinctive worshipful space for preaching on the core doctrines and values of the church. The goal should not be to capture or restrictively define the meaning of the ritual action, but to give verbal and poetic input to enlarge the conditions for a faith-filled God-encounter in their communal enactment.

(2) *Follow the seasonal rhythms of the Christian year.* Advent, Christmas, Epiphany, Lent, Easter, Pentecost, and Ordinary Time all offer unique opportunities for preaching doctrine. Advent lends itself to

preaching of the reign of God, the second coming of Christ at the end of time, and God's saving initiative in Christ for humanity and creation. Christmas celebrates the incarnation, God taking on flesh and blood in a great rescue mission. Epiphany refers to God showing himself and might be an occasion to preach on revelation, witness, and mission. During Lent, marking the weeks before remembering Christ's crucifixion, one could preach of sin and repentance, prayer, the cross, and the work of Jesus Christ the Savior. Easter is the most joyous Sunday of the Christian year. Themes of God's triumph over death and evil, resurrection, and hope are especially fitting in this season. The day of Pentecost and following weeks provide wonderful opportunities for teaching concerning the Holy Spirit and the church.

(3) *Preach through one of Paul's letters to the churches.* These epistles preserve some of the earliest theological reflection and formulation of Christian doctrine. Paul's theological reasoning about the Christ-event, Jewish history, and life in the Spirit of Christ is a fine model for preachers. I know preaching from Paul can be difficult. I'd much rather take narrative material and develop a sermon. But I have discovered that when I do the hard, consistent work required to appreciate Pauline material, I am forced to think more creatively about theology and doctrine. The rewards are more valuable as a result. Most recently I preached through Colossians with its incomparable Christology.

(4) *Preach a series on denominational faith distinctives.* Shortly after my wife and I began to co-pastor the congregation we serve presently, the worship commission came to me and requested sermons on Mennonite faith distinctives. Some topics I selected were: discipleship, covenant, community, peace and nonresistance, evangelism-service, baptism, and faith and practice.

(5) *Preach a series on "What do we believe about . . . "*This series was especially well received; people seemed to want to know what the Bible teaches and the church believes about experiences and ideas they encounter in many arenas of life. This series was also riskier for me personally. One sermon in particular—"Heaven & Hell: The Great Separation"—produced unusual consternation. Here is a sampling of the other sermon titles and doctrinal foci: "The Immanuel Principle" (outreach & missions); "The Virus of Violence" (peace of Christ); "Sex, Lies, and Truth" (sexual norms); "Are There Many Ways to God?" (Christology); "Am I a Monkey's Uncle?" (creation).

In conclusion, one additional point begs to be made. From reading this chapter one might get the impression that preaching theologically is mostly a matter of technique. Honing methods, skills, and practice is crucial—but can never replace the more basic spiritual commitments and devotion of the preacher. To preach theologically, the preacher must *live theologically*, beginning with a sense of divine call to the task. This divine call is disciplined, sustained, and refreshed through attentiveness to God in the ugly and sublime of life. We preachers have no business pointing persons toward God through faith in Christ Jesus unless we are joyfully and committedly on that same journey ourselves.

Let's face it; we preachers can easily fake it. Eugene Peterson makes this point in *Working the Angles: The Shape of Pastoral Integrity*. The public activities of pastoring, the ones we get paid to do, he says are like the visible sides of a triangle—preaching, teaching, and administration.

> People hear us pray in worship, they listen to us preach and teach from the Scriptures, they notice when we are listening to them in a conversation, but they can never know if we are attending to *God* [emphasis original] in any of this. It doesn't take many years in this business to realize that we can conduct a fairly respectable pastoral ministry without giving much more than ceremonial attention to God.[20]

The ultimate shape of our ministry, however, is determined by the angles that connect the lines together, making a whole. The angles that form the lines of ministry into a triangle are Scripture reading, prayer, and giving spiritual direction. These are the basic, quiet, and frequently neglected disciplines of attentiveness to God for the preacher.

I believe there can be no more fitting way to close this chapter than to remind each other that we preach in the service of Another. Nurturing our relationship with God in all of life, amid a community of faith reaching for the same answers, is the real beginning of preaching theologically about things that matter.

READINGS IN DOCTRINE

Blackwood, Andrew W. *Doctrinal Preaching for Today*. New York: Abingdon Press, 1956.

Browning, Don S. *A Fundamental Practical Theology*. Minneapolis: Fortress Press, 1991.

Carl, William J. *Preaching Christian Doctrine*. Philadelphia: Fortress Press, 1984.

Confession of Faith in a Mennonite Perspective. Scottdale: Herald Press, 1995.

Carroll, Colleen. *The New Faithful: Why Young Adults are Embracing Christian Orthodoxy*. Chicago: Loyola Press, 2002.

Ellingsen, Mark. *Doctrine and Word: Theology in the Pulpit*. Atlanta: John Knox Press, 1983.

Erickson, Millard J. & James L. Heflin. *Old Wine in New Wineskins: Doctrinal Preaching in a Changing World*. Grand Rapids: Baker Book House, 1997.

Finger, Thomas N. *Christian Theology: An Eschatological Approach, Vol. I*. Scottdale: Herald Press, 1985.

Gross, Leonard. "The Doctrinal Era of the Mennonite Church." *Mennonite Quarterly Review* 60 (January 1986): 83-103.

Holmer, Paul L. *The Grammar of Faith*. San Francisco: Harper & Row, 1978.

Hughes, Robert and Robert Kysar. *Preaching Doctrine*. Minneapolis: Fortress Press, 1997.

Martin, Gerald. *Great Southern Baptist Doctrinal Preaching*. Grand Rapids: Zondervan, 1969.

Norris, Kathleen. *Amazing Grace: A Vocabulary of Faith*. New York: Riverhead Books, 1998.

Peterson, Eugene. *Working the Angles: The Shape of Pastoral Integrity*. Grand Rapids: Eerdmans Publishing, 1987.

Sangster, W. E. *Doctrinal Preaching: Its Neglect and Recovery*. Birmingham: Berean Press, 1953.

White, James F. *Protestant Worship: Traditions in Transition*. Louisville: Westminster/John Knox Press, 1989.

Wilson, Paul Scott. *The Practice of Preaching*. Nashville: Abingdon Press, 1995.

NOTES

1. Leonard Gross, "The Doctrinal Era of the Mennonite Church," *Mennonite Quarterly Review* 60 (January 1986): 83-103.

2. Robert Hughes and Robert Kysar, *Preaching Doctrine* (Minneapolis: Fortress Press, 1997), 1.

3. Ibid., 3-9. The foregoing two paragraphs summarize Hughes and Kysar's analysis of the responsibility the church and culture each bear in the disintegration of theological skill among average church members.

4. Kathleen Norris, *Amazing Grace: A Vocabulary of Faith* (New York: Riverhead Books, 1998), 324.

5. In a new book Colleen Carroll, editorial writer for the *St. Louis Post-Dispatch*, examines the phenomenon of young adults, steeped in relativism, embracing Christian truth claims in surprising numbers and confidence. *The New Faithful: Why Young Adults are Embracing Christian Orthodoxy* (Chicago: Loyola Press, 2002). In defining orthodoxy, Carroll cites G. K. Chesterton's phrase that "orthodoxy . . .

means the Apostles' Creed, as understood by everybody calling himself Christian until a very short time ago and the general historic conduct of those who heed such a creed," 13.

6. Paul Scott Wilson, *The Practice of Preaching* (Nashville: Abingdon Press, 1995), 82-97.

7. Ibid., 82.

8. Ibid., 23.

9. Don S. Browning, *A Fundamental Practical Theology* (Fortress Press: Minneapolis, 1991). Browning argues that faith communities are an "antidote to the corrosive acids of Western individualism and liberalism," 2. Using Aristotle's concept of *phronesis*—"practical wisdom"—Browning claims that faith communities do not "exercise practical wisdom in spite of their religious symbols and convictions; they exercise practical wisdom *because* (emphasis original) of their religious symbols and convictions," 10. This kind of perspective, in my opinion, may be especially useful for understanding theology in the Anabaptist tradition because of its historic emphasis on orthopraxis.

10. Kathleen Norris, *Amazing Grace: A Vocabulary of Faith* (New York: Riverhead Books, 1998).

11. Ibid., 2.

12. Ibid., 8.

13. William J. Carl, *Preaching Christian Doctrine* (Philadelphia: Fortress Press, 1984), 29.

14. Church historian James F. White maintains that at the time of the Reformation when all the Reformers claimed to hold a *sola scriptura* foundation, the Anabaptists were the most radical and "the most insistent on the sole authority of Scripture" in shaping their worship and fellowships. "Anabaptist Worship," in *Protestant Worship: Traditions in Transition* (Louisville: Westminster/John Knox Press, 1989), 81.

15. Thomas N. Finger, *Christian Theology: An Eschatological Approach, Volume I* (Scottdale, Pa.: Herald Press, 1985), 54.

16. Ibid., 54.

17. *Confession of Faith in a Mennonite Perspective* (Scottdale, Pa.: Herald Press, 1995). Articles 1-8 explore themes shared broadly within all Christian churches—God, Jesus Christ, Holy Spirit, Creation, Sin, and Salvation. Articles 9-16 look at the church and its practice—Church, the Signs of Baptism, Lord's Supper, Foot Washing, Discipline and Leadership. Articles 17-23 describe the life of Christian discipleship—Family Relationships, Stewardship, Peacemaking, and the Church's Relationship to Government. Article 24 describes the coming Reign of God.

18. Hughes and Kysar, 10.

19. Carl, 25.

20. Eugene Peterson, *Working the Angles: The Shape of Pastoral Integrity* (Grand Rapids: Eerdmans Publishing, 1987), 3.

Chapter 9

Thunderstruck to Hear Their Own Mother Tongues: Preaching in Multicultural Contexts

Nathan D. Showalter

"*T*hen when they heard, one after another, their own mother tongues being spoken, they were thunderstruck. They couldn't for the life of them figure out what was going on, and kept saying, 'Aren't these all Galileans? How come we're hearing them talk in our various mother tongues?'" (Acts 2:6-8, *The Message*)

The first sermon in a multicultural context was Peter's address on Pentecost to folks from Parthia and Pontus, Asia and Egypt, even (the text says) from Crete and Arabia. This polyglot group of worshipers couldn't figure out why they were hearing good news about God in their own mother tongues. They were thunderstruck to hear God's message in their heart languages.

That is what preaching in a multicultural context is about: sharing God's message in the heart language of our hearers. If we are not able to provide actual translation into that language, then we do what is next best—we share the message with the images and stories, the ideas and illustrations that help our listeners understand that God does indeed speak their mother tongue.

For three years in the early 1970s I worked with a multicultural congregation in Nairobi, Kenya, and for eight years (1990-98) served as pastor of Taipei International Church in Taiwan. Much of what I share here grows out of my learnings in those two congregations, where people came from more than a dozen different cultural and language backgrounds, with English as the common language for worship. Currently I am working in Lancaster (Pa.) Mennonite Conference, a regional association of Mennonite congregations where pastors increasingly find themselves preaching to multicultural audiences and where one in ten congregations worships in a language other than English. The great North American melting pot is more like a stewpot, with our various cultural backgrounds not absorbed but, like the ingredients of a stew, fully present to enrich the texture, aroma and flavor of the Christian community.

FROM BABEL TO PENTECOST

When people gathered in the land that today is Iraq to build a city with a tower whose top would reach to the heavens, God confused their language. Soon people scattered to the four winds, speaking a growing variety of languages and dialects that since Babel have made it hard for people from these various tribes and nations to live, talk, work, and play together (Gen. 11).

At Pentecost God began to heal the curse of Babel. People began to hear God's message in their own languages: the good news that God loves all peoples and welcomes them, through the Messiah, into an international, multicultural family of faith. Since that time there has been an inexorable gathering of peoples into the community of Jesus. Wherever this Good News has taken root, cultural and racial barriers have gradually given way in a remarkable civilization of the Spirit in which "there is neither Jew nor Greek, slave nor free, male nor female, for [we] are all one in Christ Jesus" (Gal. 3:28 NIV).

Today this civilization of the Spirit (kingdom of God) is Greek and Palestinian, African, Western, aboriginal, and Oriental. The Bible or parts of it is available in more than two thousand languages. A video presentation of Luke's gospel has its soundtrack translated and lip synched into nearly every language of the world with more than a million speakers. Christianity was not originally a Western phenomenon, and the "next Christendom" will be uniquely an expression of the southern hemisphere. African, Asian, and Latin American Christians will far outnumber those from Europe and North America, bringing their music, imagination, and cultures of worship to the twenty-first century church.[1]

It was Donald McGavran who reminded us that people like to become Christians without leaving home.[2] People may be initially bewildered when they hear in their own mother tongue about what God is doing. Many, however, are warmed and drawn to the good news that God is not far away but in the most familiar places of their community. God is intimately involved in each culture, bringing renewal, reconciliation, healing, and joy. "He set it all out before us in Christ, a long-range plan in which everything would be brought together and summed up in him, everything in deepest heaven, everything on planet earth" (Eph. 1:10, *The Message*).

> Sing to the Lord a new song;
> Sing to the Lord, all the earth.
> Declare his glory among the nations
> His marvelous deeds among all peoples.
> (Ps. 96:1, 3 NIV)

In creation God brooded over chaos to bring light, beauty, and love. Since Pentecost, God is orchestrating a new symphony in which all peoples everywhere are joining in the rehearsal for a great concert of every nation, tribe, people, and language, singing to the God who has died to bring healing peace (salvation) to the nations (Rev. 7).

IN TUNE WITH A NEW SONG

Preaching to a multicultural audience is done in the context of the new song the Spirit gives to people of various tribes and nations. We sing with all the melodies of our congregation, especially the new songs that are growing out of the life of God's people, expressing the deepest longings, the richest poetry of each culture where the Spirit is speaking the mother tongue. Ancient hymn texts are set to the new harmonies the Spirit gives in the life of the worshiping community. When there are no new songs, the preacher's voice becomes dull and the people hard of hearing. The sermon is always set in the context of the new song, the sign that God's Spirit is translating the message into the heart languages of the people. And the sermon is never an event by itself, but always a part of the worship of the faith community.

God's people of the Older Covenant were unmistakably a people of song. When Jesus came an angel choir sang to the shepherds, a despised underclass and an improbable audience. Although Messiah's coming in itself was eventually understood as a gigantic cross-cultural statement, Jesus mostly spoke Aramaic to a mostly monocultural audience. Soon after his death and resurrection Jesus' followers began to realize that the good news about God's nation was intended for all peoples everywhere (Matt. 28:18-20), not just for the descendants of Sarah and Abraham. And so the teachings of Jesus were recorded in Greek rather than in the language of the Hebrew Scriptures or the dialect Jesus spoke.[3]

It is no accident that the church was born amid an international, multicultural assembly. God's Spirit overwhelmed the group of Jesus followers, and there to witness was a group of worshipers from all over the Mediterranean world. Peter stood up to preach, reassuring his bewildered audience that the speakers were not drunk, proclaiming, if not yet fully understanding and accepting, God's intention to pour out his Spirit on every culture of people (Acts 2:17; Joel 2:28).

Preachers cannot accept the logic of Babel. Rather they speak in the power of the Spirit who brings astonishing renewal and reconciliation in every mother tongue. Their sermon is set to new music. It becomes a new song. They stand ready to receive the gift of tongues that is a sign of God's cross-cultural intention. Today as at Pentecost, people are thunderstruck when they hear the believers speak God's language in their own mother tongue. When they hear the good news, they sing a new song. And the sermon grows out of and amplifies that new song.

Perhaps nowhere is the new song illustrated more vividly than in African-American preaching. A suffering people heard the word and began singing a new song and preaching in a new voice in ways that continue to transform American culture and worship. The line between sermon and song is wonderfully hard to see:

> Up from the bed of the river
> God scooped the clay;
> And by the bank of the river

He kneeled him down;
And there the great God Almighty
Who lit the sun and fixed it in the sky,
Who flung the stars to the most far corner of the night,
Who rounded the earth in the middle of his hand;
This Great God,
Like a mammy bending over her baby,
Kneeled down in the dust
Toiling over a lump of clay
Till he shaped it in his own image;
Then into it he blew the breath of life,
And man became a living soul.[4]

Preachers who want to preach more effectively in a multicultural context will do well to listen to God's trombones—the voices of African-American preachers whose ancestors heard the gospel in the crucible of slavery and learned how to sing a new song when the dominant culture around them was preaching a flawed gospel. White preachers have much to learn about applied theology from the black homiletical tradition, and about the still unrealized dream of a nation where children "will not be judged by the color of their skin but by the content of their character" (Martin Luther King Jr.).[5] Even as our worship is being transformed by the rhythms and instruments of Africa, so our preaching will be enriched by the music, metaphors, rhythm, and poetry of black preaching.[6]

A MULTICULTURAL BOOK

In preaching to a multicultural audience. we soon discover that the sacred book from which we preach is itself multicultural, bilingual, and interfaith (Jewish-Christian). The Bible is written in two vastly different languages, Hebrew and Greek (with a few sections in Aramaic). Even the orthographies of these languages are different. The preacher helps people to understand this linguistic richness, not just by helping them reflect on original text meanings, but also by having the Bible read from time to time in the mother tongues of the congregation. (If there is no non-English speaker in the congregation, then a guest can on occasion help the congregation encounter the multi-lingual context of the larger Christian church.) It can be effective to have the same familiar text read in several languages, so people experience linguistic variety even while being reminded of a text they may know by heart. Helping people to learn a biblical word or phrase in Hebrew, Greek or modern (non-English) language is another way of helping Christians experience the multicultural context of the Bible.

Even though the growing variety of English Bible translations is sometimes frustrating in a congregation's teaching and worship, this diversity of biblical voices is a gift in a world in which English has become a global language. It constantly reminds us that God's Word is always interpreted in a particular cultural context. And it offers us a variety of readings that enrich our understanding of original texts written in languages no longer spoken and for which precise translation may never be found. A paraphrase like *The Message* is especially helpful in rendering ancient texts into fresh idiomatic cadences that jar us out of complacent readings that prevent God's Word from connecting with changing cultures and contexts. "Every part of Scripture is God-breathed and useful one way or another—showing us truth, exposing our rebellion, correcting our mistakes, training us to live God's way. Through the Word we are put together and shaped up for the tasks God has for us" (2 Tim. 3:16-17, *The Message*).[7]

The preacher needs to be sensitive to the presence of persons in the congregation who speak English as a second language. For those persons the use of a simpler English translation like the Contemporary English Version (American Bible Society) will be a great asset to understanding. And most native English speakers will discover new meanings by listening to a translation different from the one they normally use. The congregation will want to offer a Bible in the person's mother tongue, if available, and may be able to provide a bi-lingual translation for members or seekers—one that has both English and a second translation in the person's mother tongue. (The American Bible Society can provide information about non-English and bi-lingual Bibles: see 1-800-32-BIBLE or www.AmericanBible.org. A local Christian bookstore may also be helpful.)

Over the several thousand years of history that it covers, the Bible describes a constant interplay of cultures, ethnic groups, nations, and civilizations. In the Bible we meet nomadic shepherds, farmers, city folk, sages, soldiers, scholars, fishermen, queens, and poets. We read of blood and even human sacrifice. We learn about customs that involve sandals and the transfer of inheritance rights (Ruth 4:1-12). We hear about everyday rituals of foot washing (John 13) and head covering (1 Cor. 11) that have no ready reference in most of our cultures today.

To preach the Bible is to communicate about a variety of cultures and peoples. To preach effectively to a multicultural audience is to exploit this rich cultural tapestry in helping people from a variety of cultures encounter God in their own cultural context. This means not avoiding but rather illuminating the cultural complexity of the Bible. It means connecting the message of the Bible to our own mother tongue and to the mother tongues of our listeners.

To a multicultural audience in Taiwan it could mean helping people understand the relationship of First Covenant sacrifices and the contemporary Taiwanese practice of placing food on tables along the sidewalk as a way of showing honor to a Chinese god or goddess. In North America, the preacher helps a multicultural audience understand the way our various cultures illuminate the biblical story of Christmas with a rich variety of cultural accretions such as Christmas trees, gift-giving, and the more recent African-American celebration of Kwanzaa (a seven-day celebration from Christmas to New Year).

The preacher helps her audience understand the different kinds of textual materials and how they are expressed in the various cultures of that audience. Hebrew poetry is different from English poetry, and these differences may help people gain appreciation both for the Psalms and ancient Hebrew worship as well as for the different ways congregation members use poetry and music in home, school, and community.

IDENTIFICATION

Jesus identified with his listeners. Through his having paused at noon for a conversation with a Samaritan woman at Jacob's well in central Palestine, we are rewarded with a conversation, a parable, and a rich lesson in cross-cultural communication. Clearly Jesus was reading nonverbal cues when he began the conversation with a woman coming alone to the well at the hottest hour of the day. Jesus used a simple question to begin a conversation that quickly led to profound personal and faith issues.

"Will you give me a drink?" Just by making this request, Jesus affirmed both the woman and her culture. When the woman expressed surprise that a Jew would be asking her for an unkosher drink, Jesus pointed out that he could give her living water. Who wouldn't be interested? From there the conversation went deeper to the woman's own personal life and her need for healing. But not without the woman trying to shift the discussion to safer ground, to matters of religious controversy. Before long the entire village turned out to hear Jesus teach.

Jesus refused to allow cultural conventions or religious taboos to prevent him from offering life and healing to the Samaritan woman and her community. Without being dishonest to his own culture and theology, Jesus identified with another culture. He reached out with an invitation and a blessing to people Jews considered unorthodox.

When preaching in a multicultural context, we will affirm the cultures of our audience, while still offering an encounter with the God who creates and renews culture. The cross-cultural minister will look for all that is good in the culture and religion of his listeners, while still sharing a Christian invitation "with gentleness and respect" (1 Pet. 3:15).

"I have become all things to all people, that I might by all means save some," wrote Paul, an accomplished preacher in the multicultural context (1 Cor. 9:22b). Paul celebrated his own Jewishness, but was willing to "count it as garbage" to communicate Christ cross-culturally (Phil 3:8). In this Paul was following Jesus, who entered our culture (identification, incarnation), experiencing human life in every dimension. This radical identification with others is our model for preaching. We plunge deeply into the worlds of the people we pastor so that our sermons reflect their dreams and disappointments, engaging them in their sin and success. We develop an "empathetic imagination" that allows us to experience both the biblical text and the life situations of our listeners and through preaching connect the one to the other.[8]

TELLING THE STORY

The preacher in a multicultural context is always a storyteller.[9] Although Jesus' audience seems to have been mostly Jewish, he was still aware of the multicultural context of Jewish society. And he told stories that helped his listeners think cross-culturally. In the story of the Good Samaritan, Jesus shocked his audience by giving them a hero from a despised and theologically unorthodox minority group. To have the same impact, today's preacher might choose a story in which the hero is a

Muslim Arab American. And those who pass by are a pastor, a seminary professor, and a conference staffperson (my current role).

Most New Testament stories require translation beyond the text itself. We need to give our audience a *dynamic equivalent* of the parable Jesus told—a retelling of the story that helps our audience have the same emotional experience that the first century audience had when they heard the story. The parable of the Lost Son (Luke 15) can be re-told so that the audience imagines it happening to their family, to their son or daughter. The core truth of God's astonishing acceptance, love, and forgiveness then becomes vivid and real in each new cultural context, challenging the natural logic of exclusion (chauvinism) that seems present at the core of every culture. Some members of an American congregation could make use of the pop song about "tying a yellow ribbon to the old oak tree." For another congregation the story might include drugs and prostitution, or a life of parties and indolence at a church college.

POSTMODERN CULTURE

Many believe we stand on the threshold of a new era. We are watching, they say, the twilight of the modern era, of the Enlightenment, and are the first to see the dawn of a new age that is being called (for lack of a better name) postmodern. If this is indeed the case, then we are living through a time of change not unlike the Reformation or the birth of the industrial age. With a culture change of such vast proportions, we must learn to understand this emerging postmodern culture, and to sing the new songs of the rising generation. We must "demodernize" our preaching and learn to speak with a new voice.

Leonard Sweet, a student of postmodernity, challenges preachers to learn how to communicate with the "natives" (people younger than forty) in this new culture. Our preaching must become EPIC: we must move from rational to Experiential, from representative to Participatory, from word-driven to Image-driven, and from individualistic to Connected (communal).[10] Even as we learn to preach to a postmodern culture, we must at the same time anchor ourselves more firmly than ever in our ancient-future faith. "The postmodern world that surrounds us yearns for stability, morality, security, fidelity, faith, hope, and love," writes Marva Dawn.[11] Authentic Christian worship offers these gifts to people who doubt that Truth can be found but who hunger for it nonetheless.[12] Christian preaching in the context of rich, God-centered worship offers a spiritual feast for the postmodern soul.

In summary, preaching in a multicultural context means—

- Interpreting God's message into the heart languages of our listeners, being especially sensitive to those who speak English as a second language and helping people experience the linguistic textures of both Bible and congregation.
- Paying careful attention to the Bible as God's revelation to his multicultural people, using the cultural textures of the biblical stories to engage our hearers in their own culture-rich stories.
- Identifying with our listeners so that our vocabulary, images, metaphors, and stories connect deeply with the cultures of our congregation.
- Learning from African-American preachers how to "sing" the sermon in a way that bridges cultures, uniting the spiritual and the social.
- Telling stories like Jesus to open people's minds and hearts to God's Spirit who continues to remove the curse of Babel so that we can live and work together in peace.
- Understanding postmodern culture so that our preaching becomes more experiential, participatory, image-rich, and connective (EPIC).
- Realizing that a sermon never stands alone and ensuring that our preaching is always enveloped by rich, God-centered worship.

NOTES

1. "As Southern [hemisphere] churches grow and mature, they will increasingly define their own interests in ways that have little to do with the preferences and parties of Americans and Europeans. We can even imagine Southern Christians taking the initiative to the extent of evangelizing the North, in the process changing many familiar aspects of belief and practice, and exporting cultural traits presently found only in Africa or Latin America. We can only speculate what this future synthesis might look like. But underlying all these possibilities is one solid reality. However partisan the interpretations of the new Christianity, however paternalistic, there can be no doubt that the emerging Christian world will be anchored in the Southern continents," Philip Jenkins, *The Next Christendom* (New York: Oxford University Press, 2002), 14.

2. "[People] like to become Christians without crossing racial, linguistic or class barriers," Donald McGavran, *Understanding Church Growth* (Grand Rapids: Eerdmans, 1970), 198.

3. Lamin Sanneh has shown that Christian proclamation over the centuries is always about translation, relativizing, and at the same time renewing every culture through God's radical identification with each particular culture as Jesus begins to speak that mother tongue. "Christianity is remarkable for the relative ease with which it enters living cultures. In becoming translatable it renders itself compatible with all cultures. It may be welcomed or resisted in its Western garb, but it is not itself uncongenial in other garb." Lamin Sanneh, *Translating the Message* (Maryknoll, N.Y.: Orbis Books, 1989), 50. This results in a "radical pluralism" that brings cultural affirmation and renewal as a sign of God's missionary presence. Preaching is always translating—interpreting God's word into the vernacular, the language of the people, the language of the heart, 200-09; 232-34.

4. James Weldon Johnson, *God's Trombones* (New York: Viking Press, 1927, 1955), 20.

5. "Christian preachers of all races who are willing to progress toward racial reconciliation in America may discover new sources of inspiration both by experiencing black folk preaching and by engaging its hermeneutical, ethical, and political transcripts," Cheryl J. Sanders, "God's Trombones: Voices in African American Folk Preaching," in *Sharing Heaven's Music: Essays in Honor of James Earl Massey*, Barry L. Callen, ed. (Nashville: Abingdon, 1995), 164.

6. Paul Scott Wilson says that "Black preaching is strong because God matters: God is active, intervenes in history, acts on behalf of those in need, and connects with the lived experience of the listeners. God is the focus. Too much preaching and too much of biblical criticism leave God out," in *The Heart of Black Preaching*, by Cleophus J. LaRue (Louisville: Westminster John Knox, 2000), on the back cover.

7. Eugene Peterson, *The Message: The Bible in Contemporary Language* (Colorado Springs: NavPress, 2002).

8. The phrase "empathetic imagination" is from Fred Craddock, quoted in *Preaching Sermons that Connect* by Craig A. Loscalzo (Downers Grove, Ill.: InterVarsity Press, 1992), p. 28.

9. In a multicultural context the preacher "is best understood as a storyteller or narrator who creates bonds of *identification* between the sacred text of scripture and the particular text of the community addressed," David Augsburger and Mitties McDonald DeChamplain in William H. Willimon and Richard Lischer, eds, *Concise Encyclopedia of Preaching* (Louisville: Westminster John Knox, 1995), 96.

10. Leonard Sweet, *Postmodern Pilgrims* (Nashville: Broadman & Holman, 2000). Sweet develops each of these themes at length.

11. Marva Dawn, *A Royal "Waste" of Time* (Grand Rapids: Eerdmans, 1999), 69. "Premodernism asserted that there was an objective truth that could be known by those who had the skill to see it. Modernism objected that truth was relative, that different people saw truth differently according to their own situations. Postmodernism insists that there is no truth at all, that whatever truth there might be must be created by each person, for any larger claims to truth are in reality disguised bids for power. The meta-narrative of the Christian community compassionately demonstrates that Jesus is the Truth, an objective Truth who can be known," Dawn, 56. "Christians should not embrace a postmodern worldview," writes Sweet; "we must

not adapt to postmodernity. Jesus is 'the same yesterday, today, and forever' (Heb. 13:8 NKJV) (*Postmodern Pilgrims*, p. xvii).

12. The late missionary churchman Lesslie Newbigin can help the preacher maintain a clear distinction between multiculturalism and pluralism. "As we confess Jesus as Lord in a plural society, and as the Church grows through the coming of people from many different cultural and religious traditions to faith in Christ, we are enabled to learn more of the length and breadth and height and depth of the love of God (Eph. 3:14-19) than we can in a monochrome society. But we must reject the ideology of pluralism." Lesslie Newbigin, *The Gospel in a Pluralist Society* (Grand Rapids: Eerdmans, 1989), 244.

Preaching for a Hearing—The Sermon in Human Consciousness: Buttrick and Anabaptists

Lynn Jost

*H*ow do people hear sermons? This chapter probes that question using insights from David J. Buttrick's *Homiletic: Moves and Structures*, described as the major book on homiletic theory of the twentieth century.[1] Specifically, we are asking how Anabaptist preaching will be informed by considering Buttrick's thinking regarding how people hear sermons.

The chapter develops three theological categories that demonstrate a compatibility, if not full agreement, between Buttrick and Anabaptists. First, Buttrick claims that congregations hear sermons as a social unit and not primarily as individuals. The concept of a social consciousness of a congregation is fundamental to Buttrick's approach.[2] Anabaptist emphasis on the primacy of the covenant community, the church, in God's salvific purpose resonates with this emphasis.

Second, Buttrick understands the essence of Jesus' Good News message as "conversion to the radical kingdom of God,"[3] a message consistent with Anabaptist focus on the reign of God as announced by Jesus.

Third, Buttrick emphasizes fashioning sermons that "do" what the text "does" through structural analysis rather than distilling a theological truth from the text.[4] The emphasis on doing resonates with the Anabaptist priority of *orthopraxy* over *orthodoxy.*

Buttrick also stands in tension with Anabaptists at certain points, and readers are well advised to be aware of these differences. Anabaptists would challenge Buttrick's notion of the church. On the one hand, Buttrick is critical of what he views as the Anabaptist sectarian tendency to withdraw from social engagement in culture. On the other, Buttrick is pessimistic about the church because of its history of privilege and power.[5] According to Anabaptists, Buttrick's dilemma is resolved with a New Testament understanding of the church as a people apart, *in* but not *of* the world.

Buttrick's view of the authority of Scripture will also raise some Anabaptist eyebrows. In his attempt to avoid bibliolatry, Buttrick questions the articulation that the Scriptures are the final authority in matters of faith and practice. Instead, he posits a prior theological understanding as the norm for reading and interpreting the Bible. Anabaptists might be reassured to discover that Buttrick describes his theological canon as the "being-saved community before [located in the presence of] Christ crucified."[6]

In sum, David Buttrick will help us focus on how the covenant community functions as a hearer, listening to the voice of the preacher who proclaims the good news of God's inbreaking reign.

PREACHING AS COMMUNICATION IN METAPHOR

"Do you see what I'm saying?" we ask.

"Yes," comes the response, "I get the picture."

Hearing is seeing word pictures. The postmodern world has witnessed a turn from printed word to oral-aural event.[7] Although mass-media have precipitated this word revolution, communication by spoken word has experienced a renaissance. In this oral-aural word culture, preaching the Word has the promise of a world-transforming event.[8]

Preaching uses word-pictures to name the world of faith. Preaching is the work of metaphor. Using images, preaching brings God's Word into the view of the congregation. Preaching constructs "God's world" in the congregation's consciousness.

Buttrick refers to these descriptors as a "phenomenology of language." "Language," he says, "constitutes our world by *naming*, and confers identity in the world by *story*."[9] Through preaching we rename the world. We claim the world for God. We are transformed by preaching which brings our stories into God's story.

We begin by recognizing the power of language. With words we name the world. What is unnamed may not exist *for us*. Language constitutes the world-in-consciousness. It is a social world, a world in which we live together. Although God alone creates the world with a word, words name the world of our social consciousness.[10]

Our identity as humans is shaped by stories, another kind of language. Stories give identity to individuals and to communities. The role of preaching is to transform identity by transforming individual stories into the story of God's world of faith.

As Anabaptists, we confess that Jesus gives focus to God's story. As we see Jesus living, teaching, dying, rising, we gain an image of God's purpose in the world. Preaching pictures God's rule for us by metaphorically drawing Jesus.

How does this preaching with metaphors to create a social consciousness really work? Imagine the congregation gathered for worship. Picture the community's social consciousness as a giant screen. Community life shapes the screen, determines the dominant hues and brightness. The worship experience with symbols, songs, Scriptures, and signs of baptism and Eucharist makes the screen come alive as a kaleidoscope of shared experience.

Imagine that the sermon itself offers the preacher the opportunity to develop images upon the screen of congregational social consciousness. What will form in this social consciousness? Abstract ideas, propositions, and principles may flit and flicker but likely will not form in the congregation's mind's eye. What is needed is the language of metaphor.[11] The preacher who will be heard by the congregation will employ word-images that will shape the congregation's identity by incorporating their stories into the story of Christ.

HOMILETIC MOVES:
FORMING THE SERMON IN HUMAN CONSCIOUSNESS

What follows is one approach to preaching to empower the congregation to hear the message. The aim is to develop images with theological congruity within the social consciousness of a Christian congregation. Buttrick's homiletic theory, based on moves and structures, describes how to preach in a way that will "form in the social consciousness" of the hearers.[12] Buttrick suggests that a congregation will be able to follow the logic of a series of word-images created on the screen of social consciousness. Labeled "moves," these image sets are not simply scenes from a flannel-board Sunday school story. Each move is a self-contained, separate, complex image. The preacher will enable the congregation to recognize when a new image-move is being placed on the screen and when that move is complete. Together, the full set of moves operates like pieces of a conversation and will be viewed as a growing series by the hearers. A sermon involves a sequence of images arranged in a structural design.

Developing a move

Let's begin by considering a single move. A move is a language module, a piece of a conversation. Each module involves a concept of simple meaning. The simple meaning is developed into a move of about three to four minutes in length. The preacher attempts to form each concept as an image in the social consciousness of the big screen. The preacher is not so much talking to people as forming a conceptual meaning in their mind's eye.

The move is the development of a simple meaning within a complex set. This complex set is made up of three subsets. The move begins with the first subset, theological definition. At the heart of the move, the primary subset is the theological content. The move is stated simply. It conveys a single meaning. As an example of the theological content of a move, Buttrick offers the following simple sentence: "We are all sinners."[13]

To develop this move on the big screen of the congregational social consciousness the preacher begins by stating the theological content as a simple sentence. To clarify that a new move is being opened on the screen, the preacher repeats the move with variations. This signals to the hearers that a new idea is being pursued. So, the opening lines of the move might be stated as follows: "We are sinners. We might resist the label, but it's true. We are all sinners. All of us—sinners."

Buttrick argues for repetition of the theological content sentence on the basis that a single sentence carries little weight in forming social consciousness. Although one can switch topics regularly in one-on-one conversations, a gathered audience demands a process of several sentences. We are asking a community to focus; we are waiting for an idea to form. In communication before a congregation, the block of three sentences functions as one. Although the repetition seems awkward, it is a necessary adjustment for work on the big screen. Failure to start with a clear focus allows the congregational consciousness to drift.

Note that the move is stated directly, not obliquely. An indirect approach is distracting, irritating the audience with potential misdirection. The preacher is not concerned that the scaffolding of the sermonic structure may be obvious. In fact, it is helpful for the hearers to have clear direction as they begin focus on a move.

In addition to focus, the statement of the theological content of the move must show the logic by which one goes from one move to the next. If the two moves stand in contrast to one another, the opening statement of the second move must establish the perspective or viewpoint of that move. It must set the mood of the move. Unless a clear boundary is developed between moves, the sermon will not develop a structure in consciousness. "The opening statement of a move is all-important."[14]

So far, all we have on the screen is a simple idea, not much different from a traditional sermonic point. Needed in a world that hears by seeing images is a metaphor or image. This is the second subset of a move.

An image is a metaphor. The image itself may be a simple word picture, an allusion to a piece of art, a contemporary marketing slogan. Although an image may involve a story or what could pass for a traditional illustration, the image subset is not simply equated with an illustration. With an image we are using a symbol to bring into view the theological content. Just as worship is formed around the symbols of the Lord's Supper and baptism, so preaching forms in the consciousness of the hearers when symbols are explored. Because our aim is to develop an image in social consciousness, we bypass traditional rationalistic developments of logic. We do not simply explain meanings, we explore symbols.

The purpose of metaphors is that they help the congregation to see what we as preachers mean. Because illustrations combine narrative, emotion, visual images, and use of the senses, they communicate on many levels at one time.[15] In juxtaposition with established ideas, images open the hearers to a completely new set of meanings.

As preachers, we are always looking for good examples and illustrations. For the sake of discussion, Buttrick distinguishes between examples and illustrations as follows: Examples come from the everyday life of the preacher and the congregation. Illustrations are brought to the congregation from beyond the sphere of shared experience.[16]

Examples have a clear purpose. They establish truth by themselves being true to life. Examples form analogies, demonstrating the way in which God acts. Examples can help us explore situations in our lives. They help us study what's going on in our lives by bringing to consciousness a specific life experience. Buttrick suggests the example of watching TV news reports of starving children. Examples should be specific without overwhelming the hearers with detail.

Illustrations also form analogies, but come from outside the realm of shared experience. Because they are imported, illustrations present special challenges. The preacher must be careful not to overwhelm a move with an extended anecdote. The story may be so memorable that the theological content of the move is wiped out. While a long illustration may seem effective, a disciplined illustration will usually function with greater force in forming meaning in consciousness. Along the same vein, a strong illustration must be matched to a major matter within a move to avoid throwing the sermon out of balance.[17]

Several basic rules govern the use of images, examples, and illustrations. First and foremost, there must be one and only one image per move. Let's return briefly to the image of the big screen. The purpose of the image is to paint on the screen of social consciousness a vivid visual image which contains within it the simple statement of theological content. Double images will do to social consciousness what double exposures do to prints. Although there may be fascinating and pleasant accidents, as a rule the double exposure does not give clear communication of the idea. The rule of one image per move should not be misunderstood as demanding an illustration in every move. The danger is that such a strategy will cause all the moves to look alike because they are designed around the statement-illustration-closure form.[18] A system of moves with a variety of images will better form in the congregation's social consciousness.

Second, use of personal anecdotes presents special problems. Again, instead of focusing consciousness, the anecdote may instead call attention to the preacher's character.

Third, quotations should be used sparingly. Contemporary language and brief quotes work best.

Fourth, humor should be used by design, for a reason that corresponds to the move (e.g., celebration), and never to attract attention to the wit of the speaker.[19]

Care is needed to see that the illustration remains united to the content. Interrupting the connection with introductory material makes it likely that the content will separate from the illustration. The transition from the illustration to the content is also critical. A thoughtful connection helps blend image and meaning into a single understanding in congregational consciousness.[20]

Images are important for move development. The rhetorical logic of a move may develop the theological content through elaboration, oppositions, exceptions, personal development, and exploration of theological concerns. Images associate biblical insights to lived experience. Images also disassociate, pointing to the tension between Christian symbols and the fashionable worldly strategies. Images bring into view God's mysterious purposes. The rhetorical tools available for move development include analogy, metaphor, analysis, explanation, illustration, example, testimony, dialectic, antithesis, and opposition.[21]

The third subset of a single move is the lived experience. Rather than attaching a series of practical applications at the conclusion of a sermon, Buttrick's move theory invites the preacher and the congregation to explore the implications of the theological content immediately within the move itself. The third subset is intricately related to the second. Most often, the image itself will invite the congregation to consider how the content implicates congregational behavior.

Examples, coming from the shared experience of the congregation, by definition invite exploration of the lived experience. There are dangers that threaten to prevent the lived experience from reaching the big screen of social consciousness. The gravest of these is the failure to fully analyze the contemporary experience and to fall back to an overused and superficial application. In some Anabaptist circles, the tendency is to offer pietistic solutions to most problems. The spiritual answer is usually intimacy with Jesus, more prayer, and faithful Bible reading. Usually neglected is an approach which considers social justice. Others are threatened by the opposite extreme. Within the larger ecclesiastical culture, the tendency to give a therapeutic solution, most commonly involving popular psychology, is common. Perhaps the most challenging part of the move is the analysis of the lived experience. The preacher's quest must be to determine how the truth of the gospel probes to the depth of genuine experience rather than settling for a stock illustration.[22]

The body of the move involves three subsets that are developed simultaneously. Their purpose is the formation of a theological idea in the social consciousness of the congregation. The idea is stated in a simple sentence. The idea takes form in the big screen as it is linked to an image. The image offers opportunity for bringing out the symbol, for associating it with images of lived experience, and/or for disassociation by considering the challenges to the concept or the confrontation it suggests with the world. The move development is usually incomplete without some reflection on how the idea connects to the audience's lived experience.

In order for the move to form on the big screen both variety and unity are essential, Buttrick argues. By variety, he means that the move's developmental structure must avoid following the same rhetorical structure as the other sermonic moves. The result is not only boredom but such an overlap of moves that there will be confusion for the hearers. Successive moves will run together in the social consciousness, rather than forming as distinct ideas. Altered use of bringing out, associating, and disassociating images offers help in pursuing variety.

Lack of unity within a move is another prime factor in preventing a move from forming in congregational consciousness. Moves must make a single, simple statement. Compound moves will fragment on the big screen. A compound move might split in consciousness to two weak moves, neither of which will form enough to be remembered. A split focus between the biblical world and the contemporary experience is an example of a fragmented move. In an oral sermon, only one idea can form per move. It must form a single understanding in social consciousness. Attention to unity is critical.[23]

One more element is crucial for the formation of a single move on the big screen of social consciousness. The move must have clear closure. Closure is achieved by returning to the opening statement. This ensures that understanding will form in communal consciousness. Failure to close a move will allow it to run together with the move that follows.

The final sentence of a move should be simple. It ought to be a terse, closing sentence. Often it will be the inverse of the opening sentences of the move. In the illustration used above, this would mean that the move would close as follows: "We are all sinners. All of us—sinners. We might resist the label, but it's true. We are sinners."

Closure frames the field of meaning in consciousness. Each move should be a closed module in thought, a section of a single conversation. Moves must begin and conclude with precision. Within the move, development must be careful and unique. The result is the formation of an understanding in consciousness.[24]

Joining moves

Like human conversation, a sermon which forms in social consciousness will shift, by logical association, from one idea to the next. Just as a flowing conversation moves uninterrupted by transitional statements, so a move sermon follows a logic that avoids transitional statements. Instead, the individual moves are developed sequentially in oral form. The movement of a move sermon happens not within a move but between moves. The big screen of congregational consciousness is able to handle a series of moves, usually between four and six, allowing the screen to project each individual move while keeping in consciousness the entire sequence.

The problem of joining a series of moves is *"to keep moves distinctly separate and yet logically connected."*[25] Each move should form as a single unit, with a strong opening and a strong concluding statement of the theological understanding of that move. The move is a module in a theological conversation. The transitions will be intentionally abrupt to avoid confusion of move boundaries.

Although we have already looked at the development of a single move, we actually will begin a move sermon by writing out in order the theological content statements that anchor each move. These statements will reveal, if properly constructed, a sequential conversational logic. Buttrick offers the following example:

Be honest: We are all sinners,
but we have been forgiven by Jesus Christ,

so we can now live new lives.
Well, don't you want to tell your neighbors?
By the spreading of the gospel, God redeems the world.[26]

The logic of the text will shape the logical sequence of the sermon, so that the sermon "does" what the text "is doing." Although the textual sequence may inform the preacher, it is more important to *do* with the sermon what the text *does*, than it is to follow the text's sequence.[27] For instance, a text may celebrate God's mercy or it may announce God's judgment. The preacher's logical strategy may indicate beginning at a different point than the text does, but it is important the sermon aim should coincide with that of the text itself.

Moves are linked by the logic that follows a sequence like modules of a conversation. Each move has integrity established by its structure. The point-of-view and mood of each move, if distinctive, reinforce the boundaries between moves. Point-of-view and mood are related to distance, focus, perspective, and emotional tone. In the sequence listed above, for instance, the contrast in mood between the first two moves might well be a transition from grief to celebration.

Conjoining moves depends on clear statements of the individual moves, a natural sequential logic, and sharply defined structure based on the opening and concluding statements.[28]

CONCLUSION

The method just outlined shapes sermons that will be heard. We have suggested that sermons that are heard are those which form in the social consciousness by following clues from ordinary conversation. Modules of understanding in a conversation correspond to sermon moves. Each move forms in consciousness if it imitates conversation by stating the theological content, associating the content with an image, and exploring the lived experience as developed in the move. The moves are joined in a logical sequence that acts like a conversation. The result is a series of murals that form on the screen of congregational consciousness. Each congregational conversation, each sermon, helps hearers explore their identity within the story of God at work in the world.

Anabaptist preachers will be particularly informed by the notion that the congregation's theological identity is being formed by experiencing the sermon. The preacher, in announcing the good news of God's rule, is creating a "faith-world in human consciousness," a "being-saved-in-the-world" community.[29]

A SAMPLE MOVE

One of the criticisms leveled against Buttrick's approach is its apparent complexity. Perhaps a sample move can better illustrate the approach. What follows is the final move of 14-minute homily on "Tender Mercies" from the biblical text of Jeremiah 9:23-24.[30] The last full move of the homily is produced in the left column with a running commentary in the right column.

FINAL MOVES. God's tender mercy embraces even a stranger as member of the clan. God's tender mercies are explosive. Biblical loving kindness radicalizes traditional family values. Tender mercy, God's way, treats strangers like they were members of the family. We see into the heart of God whenever God produces steadfast covenant love among us.

COMMENT. *The opening words of the move do double duty. One, they state the theological content. Two, through repetition these words mark a new beginning, a fresh move. Earlier the sermon has equated the Hebrew* hesed *with "tender mercies," "loving kindness," and "steadfast covenant love."*

How does God *do* tender mercies in the earth? We could contrast biblical characters. We could compare Ruth's love of Naomi with Jonah's mission to Nineveh. Ruth, who is herself a foreigner, uses covenant-love-tender-mercies language to embrace Naomi. "Your God," she says, "is my God." "Your people are my people." Jonah, on the other hand, is God's prophet, an insider. When God calls for

With the second paragraph the move is developed with biblical material. The development explores the biblical basis for the theological assertion that tender mercy embraces the stranger. The aim here is development of content, not shaping an image. The paragraph explores the content but postpones formation of an image.

evangelism, Jonah runs the other way. Reluctantly, he arrives in Nineveh to preach the world's worst sermon, then pouts when Nineveh repents. Yes, we could do a biblical study of tender mercies with a character contrast.

Instead, let's draw nearer to home. Look at Wilma Doerksen. Wilma's thirteen-year-old daughter, Candace, is kidnapped, then found murdered in the icy Winnipeg winter. Wilma's first words at the news conference are, "We have chosen the word *forgiveness*. This is a deliberate choice."

Later Wilma spoke of her struggle to forgive. When asked if the murderer's execution would satisfy her sense of justice, she fiercely replied, "No. He deserves to die. If ten murderers were shot, and if I could pull the trigger on everyone. . . . That feels delicious."

Horrified by her attitude, Wilma began Victim's Voice, a ministry that brings victims in touch with violent criminals. She herself met a roomful of murderers, hearing their stories. As she listened, she found herself being washed with God's compassion. When she left the room, she realized she had been with ten men and no longer had a desire to harm any of them. God's tender mercy was at work.

The image to be formed in the mind of the hearers comes as an illustration. The story is dynamic, threatening to overpower the move. Its telling is sparse, avoiding unnecessary details. In chapel, I used silent projection of Wilma's testimony on video while I told her story.

The image focuses "tender mercies" on forgiveness. It aims to illustrate that God does a work in Wilma's heart to produce forgiveness. The story is meant to show that God's tender mercies are what God does "in the earth" (Jer 9:24).

The story, while beyond what most of us experience, is contemporary. The story allows us to reflect on the contemporary experiences of our lives, to consider how God may be at work doing tender mercy among us.

When we forgive, God's tender mercies are at work. When we love a stranger as if a family member, God is doing tender mercy. Whenever God produces steadfast love among us, we see into the heart of God. God's tender mercies explode in love. God's tender mercy embraces a stranger as a member of the clan.

The final paragraph has two aims. (1) It acts as a boundary by repeating almost verbatim the sentences of the first paragraph of the move. (2) It aims to pull the hearers into the hesed *of God, to connect them with the God at work in bringing forgiving attitudes into congregational life.*

NOTES

1. McKim, Donald K. *Presbyterian Outlook* 169, no. 30 (Sept. 7-14, 1987): 26.

2. G. Lee Ramsy, Jr., *Care-full Preaching: From Sermon to Caring Community* (Chalice, 2000) applies Buttrick's homiletic theory and argues that preaching forms congregations that function as covenant communities.

3. Thomas G. Long, "Review of *Speaking Parables: A Homiletic Guide*" *Interpretation* 55, no. 4 (October 2001): 430.

4. Richard L. Eslinger, *A New Hearing: Living Options in Homiletic Method* (Nashville: Abingdon, 1987), 139, and David Buttrick, "On Doing Homiletics Today," in *Intersections: Post-Critical Studies in Preaching* (Grand Rapids: Eerdmans, 1994), 98-100.

5. Long, "Review of *Speaking Parables*, 30) criticizes Buttrick's "good Jesus/bad church" dichotomy for misperceiving the church as rich and powerful when it is in fact struggling "with the reality of cultural disestablishment."

6. David Buttrick, *Homiletic: Moves and Structures* (Philadelphia: Fortress, 1987) 240, 246-47. D. W. McCullough, "Review of *Homiletic*," *Christianity Today* 35, no. 1 (January 14, 1991), 38, criticizes Buttrick's inattention to the preacher's character. Donald Macleod, "Review of *Homiletic*," *Interpretation* 43, no. 1 (January 1989: 84), also argues that Buttrick's approach would be strengthened with attention to how the preacher's person influences the sermon's impact and to the role of the preacher's rapport with the hearers of the congregation.

7. Walter J. Ong, *Orality and Literacy: The Technologizing of the Word* (New York: Methuen, 1982) analyzes this shift from orality to literacy and the subsequent transformation of culture, noting that "it takes only a moderate degree of literacy to make a tremendous difference in thought process," 50.

8. Walter J. Ong, *The Presence of the Word* (New Haven: Yale University Press, 1967) describes the phenomenological approach as "word as event."

9. Buttrick, *Homiletic*, 11.

10. David M Greenhaw, "The Formation of Consciousness," in *Preaching as a Theological Task: World, Gospel, Scripture In Honor of David Buttrick* (Louisville: Westminster John Knox Press, 1996), 1-16, explains that Buttrick's notion of forming in social consciousness is central to his phenomenological rhetorical homiletic. The world which we intuitively perceive through a common sense understanding of

what is real is, in actuality, more complex. We must understand that how we view and participate in the objective world depends on a shared experience mediated by a community's perspective. For instance, we are convinced that the platform upon which my computer rests is a "desk" and not a "bundle of word." Greenhaw helpfully criticizes Buttrick for relying overly much on the single sermon to shape consciousness, and failing to recognize that the faith-world of a congregation is "formed in consciousness" through preaching "season after season" and "year after year," 13.

11. For Buttrick, metaphors are images or models that empower congregations to understand theological meaning. "Homiletic thinking," says Buttrick, "is always a thinking of theology toward images" (*Homiletic*, 29).

12. Buttrick's terminology may appear confusing. "Form in consciousness" refers to Buttrick's phenomenology of language, to his notion that words offer shape and meaning to the world in which we live. The "world-in-consciousness" refers to the understanding of reality that is created through language.

13. .Buttrick, *Homiletic,* 28-29.

14. Ibid., 39.

15. Ibid., 128.

16. Ibid., 128.

17. According to Buttrick, "The stronger the illustration, the *more* content will be needed prior to its inclusion." 148.

18. Ibid., 49.

19. Ibid., 135, 140-47.

20. Ibid., 148-49.

21. Ibid., 41-42.

22. Ibid., 32-33.

23. Ibid., 48-50.

24. 53. Thomas Long, *The Witness of Preaching* (Louisville: Westminster/John Knox Press, 1989), 104, questions whether ideas really get formed in consciousness in this way. Long argues persuasively that not every idea happens as Buttrick wants a move to shape them, by stating the idea, developing it, then restating the idea. Buttrick's sermons rarely follow this format slavishly. Even though not all ideas "happen in consciousness" in this manner, the form does offer the preacher a clear rubric to empower the congregation to visualize the message.

25. Buttrick, *Homiletic,* 70.

26. Ibid., 75.

27. Eslinger, *Intersections*, 144.

28. Long, *Witness of Preaching,* 104, questions whether this "string of ideas" is really the best way to conceptualize a sermon. Mechanical employment of the method could reduce sermons to "a series of idea-laden boxcars moving down the track."

29. John Riggs, "Review of *Homiletic, The Journal of Religion* 69, no. 2 (April 1989): 271, argues that Buttrick is unclear as to whether the sermon creates the world in which we live (thus denying a metaphsycial reality) or whether preaching mediates the divine mystery from a metaphysical view. Riggs questions whether Buttrick succeeds in holding these two approaches in creative tension.

30. This sermon was preached in Tabor College chapel, September 11, 2002.

Chapter 11

Let Me Tell You a Story: Narrative Preaching

Renée Sauder

"The Shade Tree" is the name of a gift shop in my hometown of St. Jacobs, Ontario. When The Shade Tree first opened its doors for business I invited my father to accompany me on a walk through the gift shop, not because I like to take my father shopping, but because this shop is located in the large, rambling old house that belonged to Aunt Lena, my father's sister. Since her death a few years earlier, neither of us had been back to Aunt Lena's home. So together we went.

The stately red-topped maple trees that loomed large on the front lawn seemed to welcome us that fall day. Every autumn for as far back as I could remember, when the air became crystal cool and glistening morning frost blanketed the ground, the trees began to drop their leaves. Their silent descent was a signal for the neighborhood children to converge, to gather the handfuls of crimson and gold, and to shape them into imaginative leaf houses.

Dad led the way through the front door of this century-old home. As we walked into each room, now filled with gift paraphernalia, I lingered with him as he remembered something that had happened there. Standing in the kitchen, he told me how he had watched Aunt Lena brew her herbal medicines and teas, teaching him the secrets of healing drawn from the weeds, flowers, and berries gleaned from her garden and along the river. It was Aunt Lena whom Dad would call when he needed treatments for cuts, colds, and flu.

In the once-elegant dining room, we gazed at the tall ceilings and beautiful woodwork, remembering the times our extended family gathered here for special occasions, to celebrate Christmas or my Grandmother's birthday. A massive oak table adorned the spacious room, laden with food offerings each family had brought to share—homemade bread, roasted potatoes, and the pickled bounty from someone's summer garden. Our plates and stomachs would be filled with the goodness of the earth.

We explored the back staircase that had been the *secret* staircase in the imaginations of us cousins. Here we would hide from our parents to prolong our stay. Now we walked through that stairwell like pilgrims in search of memories. Story after story spilled from our remembering, bringing both laughter and tears.

In the literature of both the Old and New Testaments—from the Psalmist, to the prophets, to the writers of the gospel narratives—all of God's people have been commanded to remember. The Psalmist David sang a joyful song of thanksgiving, sung in remembrance and gratitude for God's goodness, faithfulness, and love. "Remember God's wonderful deeds," David sang. "Remember, and tell the coming generations." (Psalm 105:5) The memory of God's goodness and grace would be uttered again and again in the course of Israel's history through the poetry and hymns of thanksgiving to God.

In Deuteronomy, the people of Israel are about to enter Canaan after forty years of wilderness wandering. Moses wanted them to remember their history, to remember the commandments given to them by God, for he knew that the commandments contained the blueprint for their tomorrow. If they forgot the decrees and statutes and ordinances of God, Moses knew his people would be lost and bereft of both direction and identity. So he said to them: "Recite them to your children . . . talk to your children about the wonderful works God has done, how God brought us out of Egypt, and displayed before our eyes, great and awesome signs and wonders" (Deut. 6:7-25). That is the story they were to remember and tell.

The prophets continually felt obliged to call their people to a remembrance of things past, to remind them of who they were, where they came from, to whom they belonged. The prophet Isaiah was concerned that if his people forgot their past, it would make them vulnerable to the idolatries of the present. It was in remembering the past that they would be better prepared for the future, for the new thing God was going to do in their midst.

As Scripture portrays them, David, Moses, and Isaiah knew that life and their hope in a future consisted of miracles remembered, promises trusted, and believing God was truly present in their own lives and the lives of their people. The church likewise is a community in constant need of remembering. Not only is it important that we remember and tell the stories of our biblical faith, we must also take time to look back at the lives we have lived, to remember the happiness we have seen, to ponder the precious moments and people who have graced our lives. We must remember too our hurts, our sadnesses, the mistakes and crippling losses. We must remember intentionally to search through our past so we can discover where our journeys have brought us, who we are, and who we are becoming. At the heart of our Christian faith is the awareness of a personal God who is present and active in our lives.

As Thomas Long suggests in *The Witness of Preaching*, if we believe the gospel is not simply a set of abstract concepts or principles to which we give assent, but a total way of being in the world, then preachers should tell stories in their sermons about human experience, to show how the Christian faith is embodied in the actual circumstances of life.[1] This is what narrative preaching seeks to accomplish.

Briefly stated, a narrative is the telling of a story. In the case of a preaching narrative, that story may be a biblical one or a personal one. A narrative is not about make-believe. It is about an event-in-time. A story is not just a literary device used to provide an interesting illustration. Nor are stories "just decorations for the sermon or windows to let the congregation get some air before we get back to the real sermon" writes homiletician Charles Bugg. "Rather, stories stand on their own and effect changes of their own in our lives."[2]

Narrative preaching is embedded in Jesus' own model of storytelling. When Jesus sought to explain to his listeners the nature or ways of God, he did not present a learned treatise, or expound on God's character by way of a three-point sermon. Rather, Jesus told the story of God, who like a shepherd goes after the one lost sheep, like a woman will not rest until she has found her lost coin, and like a father desperately wants both of his sons to come home (Luke 15:1-32). Jesus used things around him—metaphors, images, people, to illustrate the most profound matters of the kingdom of God. Jesus knew stories have power to involve the hearer experientially.

The stories of Jesus, both those by him and those about him, were told by followers who were part of a storytelling tradition, reaching back to the stories of Israel, that told of the actions and presence of God. In telling and listening to these stories and to the stories of Jesus, early Christians made connections with their own lives that made clear to them how God was present. When the stories were recorded in the Gospels, they were written down so they could be read aloud and re-learned, reheard, and retold. To tell these stories in our preaching is to be part of that incredible storytelling tradition.

We too, live in a series of narratives—our own as well as those of our family, our nation, our church, our faith tradition. The narratives of the Anabaptist-Mennonite tradition are particularly rich in faith and history. These narratives have been passed down to us in word and image in the *Martyrs Mirror* as well as in the melodic ballads of our earliest hymnbook, *The Ausbund*, which carries the martyrs' stories on the wings of song. When successive generations of Anabaptists were forced to become refugees, fleeing homelands in Europe and Russia in search of safer havens in North America, they brought their stories with them. These tales of hardship and miracle begged to be told. Stories are the gift of memory of a faith community. It is this rich legacy of storytelling that inspires the narrative preaching of Anabaptist-Mennonites.

Every person and every human community has a story. What makes narrative preaching so effective is finding the intersections between our own lives and the lives of the characters in the biblical narrative. Thus the experience of walking with my father through Aunt Lena's house was enlightened by the connections that emerged with the stories of Israel. Our purposeful remembering in the house that day was indelibly connected to the remembering that Scripture portrays Moses and David as undertaking. There was an entirely different meaning to my experience with my father because of the biblical stories with which it was associated. This intersection between the biblical story and our own is no accident. It is where authentic revelation takes place in a profound way.

But story per se is an inadequate kind of preaching unless it is bigger than our own little narratives. The story we preach must be God's story.

The biblical text must be the central concern of our preaching. If we take seriously the Scripture passage from which we preach, the way in which we express the biblical narrative has the power to transform lives. This requires imagination, which Charles Bugg describes as "the power to see the story, to move inside its characters, to experience the emotions, as well as hear the words. Imagination gives height, depth, breadth, and length to words that are flat on a page."[3]

One might think imagination is accomplished when the preacher puts himself or herself in the shoes of a biblical character and tells the story as that character would, typically in the present-tense. This can indeed be an effective form of narrative preaching, but it is not the only form. For example, I have filled years of sermons with retelling of stories recorded in both Old and New Testaments. The stories themselves have given my sermons shape, movement, and content.

On Palm Sunday, I told the familiar story of the sheer excitement and expectancy of the crowd lining the Jerusalem streets. Setting the story in the context of the misery of their nation's peace-starved past and their tenacious hold on the prophetic hope that God would send someone to return their nation to its original glory, I sought to capture the crowd's conflicting moods. On the one hand was the crowd's delirious enthusiasm, as they caught a faint glimmer of hope on the horizon of their nation's tormented past. But as they watched Jesus ride toward them on a small donkey, the burden of the poor, their shouts of hosanna turned to lumps in their throats and their hopes and dreams began to fade. With tears stinging their eyes, they wondered how they could have been so wrong. How could someone like this defeat the enemy?

In retelling this story from the perspective of the conflicting moods of the crowd, I wanted my listeners to recognize themselves as people who despaired of their own hopes, as people who also feel discouraged and helpless when God doesn't live up to their expectations. Amid a post-September 11 world at war and hungry for retribution, I wanted them to experience in this story, one of the great reversals of human history, a revelation of the folly of humanity's notion of power. Most of all, I wanted to enable them to change their perspectives and worldview of how things should or ought to be and invite them to consider what will indeed bring true and lasting peace.

"The climax of the retelling of a biblical story is always a disclosure of the active God to whom we are invited to respond in faith" writes

Wayne Robinson in his book, *Journeys Toward Narrative Preaching*. "Congregational engagement depends upon their identification with the human drama described. It also depends on the naturalness with which the sermon's conclusions grow from the retold tale."[4]

At other times, non-biblical stories can be effectively used. These are stories that come from human experience and show, once again, how our lives intersect in meaningful ways with the biblical story. A few years ago, the overarching theme of our Lenten series was *Welcome Home*. During this series, the congregation was invited to discover anew the divine images of welcome and homecoming. On this particular Sunday, the Scripture texts from Genesis 15:1-18 and Luke 13:31-35 provided an intimate image of a God, who offers comfort, safety, and protection.

I began by describing each of these stories: God takes Abram by the hand, leading him out under the canopy of the night sky, showing him the stars, promising Abram countless descendants. In Luke, the writer tells the story of Jesus, standing on the slopes of the Mount of Olives some distance from Jerusalem, looking across the Kidron Valley at the great city and speaking these words of lament: "Jerusalem, Jerusalem, the city that kills the prophets and stones those who are sent to it!" And then Luke quotes Jesus as speaking these comforting words: "How often have I wanted to gather your children together as a hen gathers her brood under her wings, and you were not willing!" (Luke 13:34)

I was struck with God's incredible compassion and great devotion as revealed in these narratives. Compassion, devotion, comfort, security, protection, commitment—all were words I associated not only with these stories but also with what it means to be "at home."

My sermon went on to describe all the homes I've known: My childhood home. The love and acceptance I experienced as a child and youth in my church home. Following the death of my mother and my father's remarriage, our family moved into a new home. I lived in a house that didn't feel like home, yet it was the only place I had to call home. There I would discover that you have to accept some things to find home and you must begin to build new memories and dreams. During a two year stint in a voluntary service assignment, away from family and all things familiar, I learned that in a household of strangers, home is each other, wherever we are and with whomever we may be.

My first pastorate took me to yet another home—the Kansas prairie, a land rich in grass and wind and sky. The seeming emptiness of this wind-filled expanse made me homesick for the familiar treed land-scape of southern Ontario. A caring parishioner took me out into the Kansas countryside one gorgeous fall day, showing me the brilliant pinks, oranges, and blues of the prairie grasses that filled the fields and roadside ditches. My narrow-minded view of what makes a place beautiful began to change. I learned that home is geography, the physical place where we find ourselves and discover what is beautiful in it.

In the case of this sermon, the biblical text was used as a reference point rather than as the hub from which the sermon was formed. Some might criticize this as making the biblical text peripheral or preaching a non-biblical sermon. But I think it is possible to maintain the centrality of the biblical story by interweaving the biblical and non-biblical story in such a way that they form a seamless narrative from beginning to end.

There was affirmative response to this sermon. Some said it enabled them to look at their own home situation with fresh perspective, helping them see all-too-familiar things in a new way. Others said it helped them come to terms with some life situations, opening up new possibilities for the future as they came to an acceptance and understanding of their past. Such comments made me aware of how narrative preaching can create community. You connect with people, even bind with them in special ways, when you share your own story, especially if there is a piece of their own life experience in the story you share.

In an Ephiphany sermon, Barbara Brown Taylor suggests the effect that listening to stories has on people. She writes that "It is always a good idea to watch other people who have listened to the story—just pay attention to how the story affects them over time. Does it make them more or less human? Does it open them up or shut them down? Does it increase their capacity for joy?"[5] These are the ways that stories can take hold of us and move us.

The preacher's own life story is an indispensable resource for preaching. But we must use caution. We do not want to make ourselves look like the hero or like a person who has all of life neatly resolved and packaged. Nor do we want to manipulate the congregation's emotions and make them feel sorry for us. Thomas Boomershine offers wise counsel when he advises preachers to be careful that the connections we make to the sacred story are appropriate. "The most typical problem" he says, "is reading our experience back into the story in ways that are incongruent with the biblical story."[6]

I am glad for the power of stories, images, and illustrations in preaching. At the same time, I agree with Charles Bugg when he says, "I do not believe that a diet of strictly narrative preaching will be satisfying for most congregations. They want to hear words of explanation or interpretation from their preacher. They deserve more than just a story or a succession of stories."[7] There needs to be a balance between explanation (analytical, deductive, logical speaking) and story.

As Thomas Long reminds us, "The biblical writers themselves do not always tell stories, because the communication of some aspects of faith is best done in a poetic or didactic or proverbial voice and not always through narrative."[8]

I personally work with a number of preaching styles. I unpack biblical passages by using the historical-critical method. I preach topical sermons where I attempt to bring insight to a particular subject or issue. There are times when in my preaching I need to explain concepts and beliefs and talk about practical ethics. So a narrative form is not necessarily the best means to accomplish the tasks of preaching.

But I am always amazed, that when I use these techniques by themselves, I find few are affected by my preaching. I have learned that long after the rest of the sermon has been forgotten, what people can still recall are the stories told. It is the stories that people remember, connect with, and take home. It is the stories and images that they refer back to when I visit with them. Narrative has the special power to move the heart and touch the human soul.

If, for example, I say from the pulpit, "The church is a spiritual house made up of living stones, built on the foundation of Christ, the cornerstone of our faith," (a reference to 1 Peter 2:4-8) my listeners may hear it, they may even like the metaphors. But it may remain, nonetheless, remote from their experience.

If, on the other hand, I share stories of persons who have been living stones in my life, those who have been evidence of God's presence, my listeners will be able to participate in that sermon in relation to their own life experience. They will be able to reflect on those dear ones whose lives and influence continue to live and endure and shape them.

I would tell them a story about Leah, who in the summer following my mother's death, when I was sixteen, extended to me her hand of friendship. Leah was expecting her third child when she asked if I would come work for her on their farm. I agreed.

Thus began a daily ritual of going out to the farm to do whatever cleaning she had waiting for me. Wherever I was, whether scrubbing floors or out in the corn patch weeding or folding laundry, Leah would pull up a chair or grab a pail and sit beside me. While she nursed her infant daughter, she would engage me in conversation. We talked about life and relationships, vocational choices, questions of faith. She became a caring mentor.

I would come to understand years later, that in her wisdom, she had thrown me a lifeline. She had seen an adolescent adrift in the abyss of grief and extended to me the gifts of love and support. She continues to be a *living stone*, a constant reminder of God's faithful presence in my life.

Non-narrative passages of the Bible, as cited in the above example, pose a particular challenge for narrative preachers. Eugene Lowry speaks to this challenge well when he writes, "The preacher can and ought to move behind the text, finding the lived moment which prompted any given pericope."[9] I would add that the preacher must also move ahead of the text to find the lived moment in the here and now that will put flesh on and breathe life into what may appear to be a dull and lifeless text.

It is so easy for preachers to turn Scriptures into objects of investigation rather than as subjects, intended to engage us. For those of us tempted to approach sermon preparation through the cognitive faculties of reason and logic, we must always hold out the impact that sermons can have, must have, on our hearts and on our souls.

Narrative preaching is not a recent innovation nor is it a passing homiletical trend. I am commited to it as being one of the ways to faithfully and powerfully carry out the task of communicating the good news.

NOTES

1. Thomas Long, *The Witness of Preaching* (Louisville: Westminister/John Knox Press, 1989), 37.

2. Charles B. Bugg, *Preaching From The Inside Out* (Nashville: Broadman Press, 1992), 124.

3. Ibid., 71.

4. Wayne Robinson, *Journeys Toward Narrative Preaching* (New York: The Pilgrim Press, 1990), 8-9.

5. Barbara Brown Taylor, *Home By Another Way* (Boston: Cowley Publications, 1999), 28.

6. Thomas Boomershine, *Story Journey:An Invitation to the Gospel as Storytelling* (Nashville: Abingdon Press, 1991), 21.

7. Bugg, 124.

8. Long, 40.

9. Eugene L. Lowry, *Living The Lectionary: Preaching Through The Revised Common Lectionary* (Nashville: Abingdon Press, 1992), 20.

Chapter 12

Acting the Word: Preaching in the Context of Worship

Rebecca Slough

*T*he evening was late. I was tired. We stopped for a short visit with my elderly uncle, a recently retired pastor whom I had not seen in over a year. Our conversation covered vast expanses as usual, then came the zinger. "What are you teaching about preaching there at the seminary? I went to a service to honor my good friend R.E., and he only got ten minutes to preach! There were so many preliminaries—songs, prayers, readings. . . . Is that what you're teaching folks these days? That sermons should only be ten minutes long?"

It was late. I was tired. But I was alert enough to know that many assumptions and values were tied up with these questions. The issues underlying my uncle's concerns included the following: (1) the nature and purpose of preaching; (2) the nature and purpose of congregational worship; (3) the relationship between the action of preaching and other actions of worship; (4) patterns of worship that have developed in the Mennonite church and other Protestant denominations; (5) Mennonite preferences for certain patterns; and (6) the question of whether Scripture can only be interpreted through preaching. Given this range of issues (and these are by no means the only ones at play), my brief response did not allay his fears. To thoroughly discuss his question would have taken time and energy I didn't have.

Recent decades have seen many changes in Protestant worship. Worship patterns emerged with different emphases and values. Some parts of the Protestant church adapted a form of nineteenth-century camp meeting worship with a "contemporary style" wedding the flow of preaching, music, and prayer to high-tech sophistication. Other parts of the church organized worship to address spiritual seekers, modifying the evangelistic worship structure of the late nineteenth and early twentieth centuries. These services use musical idioms of popular culture along with low-key leadership style. Some Protestant congregations dug back into the church's history, reclaiming earlier practices of communion, Scripture reading, confession, prayer, and congregational song. Other congregations blended "traditional" worship patterns with contemporary music, using various art mediums, and a casual leadership style.

Each pattern carries particular assumptions about the natures of God, humanity, the divine and human relationship, the church, faith formation, and discipleship. Rarely are all these held in tension when exploring the relationship between worship and preaching.

THE NATURE OF PREACHING

Preaching connects people with God by interpreting God's redemptive work in history and in their own lives. By its nature preaching brings people into relationship with God's Word—revealed in Jesus and in Scripture. As the preaching event unfolds, the Holy Spirit does its work in those who hear and in those who preach. The purpose of preaching is to stir the soul to claim (and reclaim) the gospel of salvation in Jesus Christ. Its outcome is to motivate believers to live as redeemed and faithful witnesses of God's kingdom on earth. Preaching functions to continue the saving work of God in the church and in the world.

The terms *preaching* and *teaching* are used interchangeably in biblical texts (particularly Mark and Acts)[1] and describe the activity of interpreting Scriptures. Christian preaching has deep roots in the synagogue tradition. Rabbis interpreted the writings of the Torah, and preaching/teaching was exposition on specific texts. Eventually rabbis began using the writings of the prophets to interpret the writings of the law. Today some pastors distinguish between preaching and teaching, assuming that preaching is more formal, elevated, and authoritative while teaching is more informal, low-key, and less forceful. Scripture does not justify this distinction.

The New Testament indicates two kinds of audiences for Jesus' and the apostles' preaching: (1) public proclamations to non-believers, and (2) teaching of the believing Christian community. Especially the Gospels and Acts give evidence of the content and style of the church's public preaching. Less evident is what preaching/teaching within the community sounded like. Surely there was exposition of the law and prophets in light of Jesus' life, death, and resurrection. The structure of the Epistles offers a view of how the apostles preached and taught using Old Testament texts as well as new texts created by Christian communities (e.g. Phil. 2:6-11). Paul's writings demonstrate how he used the particular contexts of the first century congregations to preach and teach salvation and the style of life it entails. The *Didache* describes preaching and teaching (here note the distinction) as central to common worship, but exactly how they were carried out is not detailed. Justin Martyr's *Apology* describes reading the writings of the prophets and the memoirs of the apostles "for as long as time permits"[2] followed by instruction.

In his book outlining the history of preaching, Hughes Oliphant Old identifies five types of preaching that have persisted from biblical times to the present.[3] The characteristics of one type overlap with other types on occasions. In some instances, a single sermon may exhibit two or more types. These descriptions do not define exclusive categories, but do serve to demonstrate specific types of preaching.

Expository preaching interprets specific passages of Scripture with direct life applications.

Evangelistic preaching is directed to nonbelievers, proclaiming the gospel of salvation, and seeking to persuade the listener to repent and accept salvation in Jesus Christ.

Catechetical preaching offers instruction for Christian living, making moral judgments, living ethically; often thematically focused.

Festive preaching involves proclamations for special services or seasonal celebrations that focus on the theological significance of the event for Christian faith.

Prophetic preaching entails a Word from God directed explicitly to the immediate concerns, decisions, or circumstances of the hearers.

These different types of preaching may be used in any style of worship service. A particular worship pattern does not constrain the type of preaching. However, over time the worship pattern may shape types of preaching in certain directions.

THE NATURE OF WORSHIP

Worship is action. The English word *worship* is used to translate several Hebrew and Greek words that have a number of meanings: to bow down, to serve, to honor, and to respect. Each term has Hebrew word roots that we reduce to the single word *worship*. Greek words follow similar patterns of meaning.[4] They are verbs. Christian worship is shaped by actions. To use *worship* or *service* primarily as nouns severely limits our understanding.

The Hebrew and Greek meanings orient human actions toward something or someone. Bowing down, serving, honoring, and respecting require a relationship. In Christian worship this relationship is between the congregation and God with Jesus as the mediator. By the power of the Holy Spirit, the actions of worship engage God with the congregation and individuals comprising it. Worship is a series of actions that sustain the congregation's dynamic and ongoing relationship with God. A number of years ago several Mennonite scholars worked to describe worship as an action of covenant renewal between God and God's people.[5] While their work sadly had little impact on ways congregations ordered their worship practices, their study rightly focused on the relational dynamic of the actions of Christian worship.

What are these actions? The most detailed list includes gathering, praising, adoring, thanking, confessing sin, proclaiming Scriptures (including the reading of Scripture and interpretation of Scriptures), affirming faith, offering, petitioning, interceding, testifying, blessing, and sending. All these actions have deep roots in Scripture and have provided the means for God and God's people to communicate with and to engage each other. It makes no difference whether a congregation prefers a "liturgical," "free," or "contemporary" style of worship, these basic actions are present.

Many theologians claim that the actions of worship create a "conversation" or a meaningful communication between God and the congregation.[6] God's Spirit gathers the congregation into a Body. The Body acknowledges with praise and gratitude who God is and what God has done in the past, but also what God is doing in the immediate present. Some actions of worship focus the congregation's response toward God. Other actions focus its response to the world. Preaching, or proclamation, is always God's initiative toward the congregation. Whether in hearing the Scriptures read or the Scriptures preached it is the congregation that receives God's creative, empowering, or admonishing word. Praise, thanksgiving, offering, prayer, affirmation, confession, or testimony—all are appropriate congregational responses to God's Word received through the reading of Scripture and its interpretation.

CONGREGATIONAL WORSHIP PATTERNS

Over generations some worship actions have been grouped to form coherent sequences of communication. Gathering actions frequently move into praising actions. In some worship patterns praise moves into confession. Seeing clearly who God is through their praise, worshipers recognize their sinfulness and limitation. Scripture reading often leads directly to preaching. In so-called liturgical traditions, the sequences of action are codified in ways that make sound theological coherence. In so-called free church traditions, the sequences may be of shorter duration and may be moved to different places in the service of worship from week to week. Nearly all Mennonite congregations follow some type of consistent pattern of action and are "liturgical" to the extent that the *overall* action pattern changes little, even as theme or content of preaching and worship change every week.

The ordering or reordering of worship actions tends to occur when particular issues or problems emerge in the congregation's response to God. Perhaps the fitting action being called forth from the congregation is obscured by other actions of little consequence. Perhaps the sequence of actions is too complicated to follow. Perhaps new believers need clearer patterns to follow as they learn how to worship in Christian community. For many good reasons, ordering worship actions is essential for building up the church. [7]

Several patterns have emerged in the Christian church and have endured for generations. Even so-called contemporary patterns have their roots in earlier structures.

SYNAGOGUE PATTERN

Some time before the Babylonian exile, men in Jewish communities would gather daily and on the Sabbath to hear a rabbi (teacher) interpret parts of the law. Often there was great discussion about the meaning of the passages. An informal cycle of readings (perhaps a type of lectionary) developed.[8] Prayers became associated with this interpretive activity, and eventually singing emerged as part of the synagogue service. Later interpretations of various prophets' writings were introduced, frequently set in relationship with readings from the law, which led to the practice of using Scripture to interpret Scripture. (Jesus' interpretation of Isaiah in Luke 4 demonstrates this practice.) The synagogue pattern sustained the Jews during the Babylonian exile and persisted alongside temple worship until 70 A.D. Most scholars of Christian worship agree that the first-century churches of Jewish Christians followed the structure of synagogue worship.

SERVICE OF THE WORD

As the church continued to grow and develop its own distinctive worship patterns, the synagogue service remained the basic structure, but with more thoroughly Christian hymns, prayers, and teaching. Eating at the Lord's table continued as a central worship action and developed its own prayer pattern called the *eucharistic* or thanksgiving prayer. Over the course of several centuries the Christian church developed a pattern of worship comprised of two equally important parts: the service of the word and the service of the table.

The service of the word was increasingly regulated. Informal cycles of readings developed by the fourth century into set lectionaries with Old Testament, Gospel, and Epistle readings continuing the practice of Scripture interpreting Scripture. Christian leaders realized the necessity of hearing in worship Jesus' saving story through the Gospels, showing how his story fulfilled the Old Testament law and prophets, while witnessing the church's appropriation of his story through the epistles.

Preaching in the context of the service of the word provided interpretation of biblical texts. The unchanging structure of worship actions did not limit the time or the skill of the preacher. Believers during these centuries (second to sixth) could hear outstanding preachers, steeped in piety, grounded in biblical knowledge, and skilled at public speaking.[9]

Nor did a long sermon require skimping on other worship actions. Worship in the early church was not tyrannized by the one-hour time limit.

However, preaching in the context of the service of the word was not always strong. The collapse of the Roman Empire, social and political turmoil, war, and a host of other problems took their toll on preaching during the Middle Ages. Brilliant itinerate preachers, like Bonaventure and Francis, kept the gospel alive during these centuries. But they more often preached outside the church's walls than inside them. By the late renaissance, cultural, political, and religious currents were converging to pave the way for the Reformation.

Luther renewed the theology and practices of the service of the word and of the table, holding them both as sacramental signs of Christ's promised presence. The Anabaptists, following Zwingli, dropped the service of the table as a regular part of weekly congregational worship. This left a stripped down service of the word comprised of prayer, reading Scripture and preaching. Zwingli created an order for worship that focused on hearing Scripture texts and preaching (usually expository); he rejected congregational singing. The Anabaptists allowed singing and ordered worship only in the broadest possible sense.

For all intents and purposes, the Anabaptists and their free church heirs retained the service of the word pattern with some accretions and variations. Celebration of the Lord's Table did not figure significantly into the regular pattern of congregational worship on Sundays then or now. As with the early church, there is clearer evidence of the content of public preaching among the Anabaptists than of the preaching directed to the community.

FRONTIER WORSHIP PATTERN

The basic actions of the service of the word (gathering, praising, confessing, proclaiming Scripture, preaching, and praying) persisted in most free church Protestant traditions, albeit with variations in style and theological accents. Developments in North America in the nineteenth and early twentieth centuries have directly influenced some current worship practices.

During the beginning years of the nineteenth century in "the west" (i.e., Ohio, Kentucky, Indiana, Illinois, Missouri) camp meetings were started to attend to the spiritual needs of settlers who had little or no congregational affiliation. Circuit riders would come to an area and gather settlers in the region for a period of preaching and worship. Three to four times a year large gatherings of believers of various denominational backgrounds assembled for days of worship, preaching, spiritual guidance, and communion. James White calls the camp meeting pattern frontier worship,[10] whose pragmatic approach to ordering worship has persisted into the twenty-first century.

This pattern consisted of long periods of congregational singing, perhaps an hour or two in length, followed by long periods of evangelistic preaching intended to convert the growing number of pioneers who were unsaved. Preaching, often done by ministers of various denominational persuasions, concluded with calls for repentance or conversions that led into periods of prayer. Singing, preaching, and praying could extend through the entire day. The Lord's Supper was celebrated at the meeting's close, often in denominational groups. Some of the preaching was evangelistic. Some was expository, instructing frontier people in what the Bible said and its relevance for their lives. The frontier pattern can be seen in the worship of the African-American church, in the structure of many revival meetings, in the contemporary worship style of evangelical, charismatic, and Pentecostal types, and the ministries of televangelists.

The frontier worship pattern also shaped the urban evangelistic services of the late nineteenth and twentieth centuries. Evangelistic preaching followed lengthy song services and concluded with invitations to make a commitment to Christ. Preaching played a public function, outlining and heralding the New Testament's good news to nonbelievers. Its presence can be felt in modified form in contemporary seeker services.

RENEWING LITURGICAL PATTERNS

The worship reforms of Vatican II sent shock waves throughout many Protestant denominations in several directions. Roman Catholics and Protestants reclaimed the Bible as a fundamental resource for shaping their worship, not just a resource for personal devotion. The creation of a common ecumenical lectionary, used in many congregations including some Mennonite ones, allows for more Scripture to be heard during worship. The set of readings appointed for each week frequently creates opportunities for Scriptures in one part of the Bible to interpret those in another part. Biblical themes and images arising from weekly lections allow preachers and worship leaders to coordinate music, prayers, and Scripture readings more effectively. Scripture is interpreted through a variety of worship actions and not solely through hearing a passage read and preached, though these remain most prominent. The individual actions of worship were clarified in ways that helped worshipers feel a sense of progression and momentum as their service to God unfolded. These actions can be grouped into larger units: Gathering, hearing the word, sharing at table, and sending out. Preaching in liturgical contexts may be relatively short (7-10 minutes) or significantly longer (20 minutes or more).

In congregations following this "liturgical" pattern, preaching and communion hold equal importance. Both are recognized as moments in which Christ's presence is known fully in the congregation. Where communion is celebrated only monthly or seasonally, the time for preaching expands on the noncommunion Sunday.

Robert Webber proposes a blended pattern of worship that uses the structure of the liturgical pattern of gathering, word, table, sending, but draws on the sensibilities of contemporary culture and its mediums, particularly music and the arts.[11] Preaching in this blended worship pattern can be a substantial part of the service (that includes the hearing of Scripture as well as the interpretation of it), but does not dominate other worship actions.

MENNONITE PATTERNS

Mennonites traditionally have shared the basic worship actions with all other Protestant groups. Congregational singing (which served a variety of functions), preaching, and prayer were the predominant actions of congregational worship. It would be safe to say that historically Mennonite worship patterns were not shaped by an overall theological understanding of worship. Certainly the themes of hymns, sermons, and prayers were intensely theological, but the ways the actions of worship were grouped into coherent patterns was not discernibly so.

Hymnal: A Worship Book takes the basic elements of Christian, and therefore ultimately Mennonite, worship and places them in a action sequence that is coherent theologically. Within this framework, preaching sits squarely in the middle of the structure. It recognizes that the congregation gathers and acknowledges who God is before receiving the word for the day. Deviating from the pattern proposed is not a problem (unless a gathering action occurs somewhere toward the end of the service and would make no sense). Since the mid-part of the previous century, Mennonites have felt great freedom to move these actions around to suit various thematic purposes. A lack of structural clarity in worship patterns led to developing thematic threads to provide a sense of coherence for worship. The primary value of the *Worship Book* outline is that each worship action is seen to have its own communicative character and interaction structure. This encourages an understanding of worship as action that uses theological themes as a way of responding to God.

SUMMARY

Within worship patterns there are all kinds of worship styles—traditional, contemporary, evangelistic, charismatic, formal, informal, and so forth Over time all the basic actions of worship will appear in each pattern. The fundamental purpose of preaching remains the same regardless of the worship pattern employed—to proclaim the gospel of Jesus Christ testified to by the Scriptures and to interpret that gospel in ways that strengthen faith and build up the church. Preachers may exposit, evangelize, instruct, celebrate, or prophesy in all worship patterns and styles. No single approach to preaching or worship can be demonstrated in biblical sources or in the church's history.

All of the patterns or structures of worship described in this section are found currently in the Mennonite Church across North America. They are expressed in a wide range of styles because the racial and demographic profile of the Mennonite Church began changing radically over a generation ago. With increasing commitment to being a missional church, we can only expect that multiple structures and styles will continue to emerge in the church's preaching and worship.

What remains constant is this: worship is an engagement between God and God's people that God begins and ends. God speaks through the reading and the interpretation of Scripture. The Holy Spirit unites the members of the Body and joins them to Christ who is known in their midst. By the Spirit's power the congregation responds to what God has spoken and done in creation, in Jesus Christ, in Scripture, and in the church through its praise, prayer, confession of sin and of faith, offering, testifying, and blessing. When God's Word coming into the congregation is squeezed out by other worship actions or when protracted preaching silences the congregation, the relationship between God and God's people is severely distorted.

PREACHING IN WORSHIP

Worship and preaching arise out of a congregation's experience of salvation in Christ. The shapes of its praise, confession, offering, and prayer are conditioned by the social and cultural context in which it experiences its collective redemption. The interplay between the congregation's response to God present in the *now* of its existence and God's Word spoken into the *now* of its need must be discerned. The congregation's response to a sermon should be allowed within the service of worship while the Body is still assembled and not presumed to occur after the service is completed. Offering, confessions, affirmations of faith, prayer, or testimony are appropriate congregational responses to God's word. These actions must be done in styles and forms that allow the congregation to act with integrity and to speak with authenticity in its location.

Theoretically, there is no reason why the purposes of worship and those of preaching must be in conflict. Nothing outlined in this essay would suggest that turf battles should ensue as a result of the congregation's need for responding to God gracious gift of salvation and the preacher's calling to preach God's word. Yet if my uncle's comments are any indication, competition seems to be felt in some congregations. I hazard a few possibilities for why this may be so.

Most white, middle-class, North American Mennonite congregations are committed to the sixty-minute worship service. In some instances the service may "go over" and press to seventy or seventy-five minutes, but sixty minutes is the ideal length, given the other activities of Sunday morning. Where congregations have been given more time to praise, confess, or pray in their own voices, preaching may seem to get the squeeze.

This tension is basically unknown in African-American, Latino, Asian, or charismatic churches because these congregations do not presume to limit worship to an hour. There is time for everything to be done properly. Assumptions about what sustains congregational life differ in these two approaches to worship and time. Values about the level of personal attention during worship and the engagement of the heart and mind through the worship actions play themselves out differently in this tension over time.

While setting strict time limits on worship and preaching creates numerous problems, other legitimate congregational activities are accomplished on Sunday morning that constrain worship. To avoid unnecessary competition between the preacher and the worship leaders, a careful assessment of how the hour of worship is actually spent is essential. Does the service routinely start on time? A good many do not. Many congregations give far too much time to announcements or the "sharing of joys and concerns." Congregations risk becoming therapeutic communities, more like support groups than congregations.

These practices have dubious merit within a theological understanding of worship. How long is the children's story on average? What fundamental purpose does it serve within the structure of the congregation's hearing of God's word? When the interaction between God and the congregation must fit within an hour, then everything planned must have clear intention and focus. The specific actions of the congregation must have a rationale and a reasonable chance of being successfully accomplished. The sermon's purpose and primary theme must be clear. The pastor-preacher should be prepared to get to the point at a pace that is congenial with the message that is to be spoken.

To coordinate the congregation's reception of God's Word and its response requires close communication among the pastor-preacher, the worship leader(s), the musicians, and the sound technician(s). Each leader must have high respect for other leaders, recognizing that each significantly aids the congregation's engagement with God. Competition arises out of mistrust and a lack of understanding of the ministry all leaders provide in the service of congregational worship.

Generally pastor-preachers spend more time preparing sermons than they spend preparing worship. Their identities as spiritual leaders are connected with preaching rather than with their gifts in worship leading. Some pastor-preachers simply have little interest in what happens in worship beyond their sermon and may even abandon the planning of worship entirely.[12] This is the environment in which turf issues arise. Pastor-preachers want whatever time necessary to preach, and worship leaders want whatever time necessary for worship to unfold hospitably and with decorum appropriate to the congregation. Without clear understandings of the vital interrelationship of worship and preaching, it is easy for leaders to feel competitive.

Many people have a low view of preaching, in part because they have endured too many poor sermons. If the sermon, as a moment of God's address to the congregation, is rambling, unfocused, confused, uninspired, or out of touch with real life issues, then people think God must be dead or on holiday. If preaching is claimed as the high point of worship and takes up the majority of worship time, then when the sermon fails to convince, convict, or inspire, the congregation's service of worship can seem meaningless. Congregational singing and prayer have salvaged meaning in many services when the sermon faltered.

The ministry of preaching demands pastor-preacher discipline. The purpose and direction of sermons must be clear to the preacher so that God's Word to the congregation can be understood. The ministry of preaching also requires humility. Hymns, prayers, and other worship actions serve to interpret Scriptures along with the sermon. While pastor-preachers are the primary mediums God uses to make the message heard, they are not the only mediums that communicate the living word for the congregation. Far too many sermons and patterns of worship action are so muddled that many believers, even those of great maturity, do not know what they are doing when the Body worships.

To assume that a sermon always needs to be a certain length (whether ten or forty-five minutes) puts the Holy Spirit in a straitjacket. God's message to a congregation may require a long time to unfold on occasions. Other times it may be completed in five to ten minutes. Some Scriptures demand long expositions, while other texts yield short pithy interpretations. At times the congregation's response may be hushed silence and at others fervent prayer. If congregations and pastor-preachers were to let the Holy Spirit—rather than individual egos and tightly or loosely planned programs—truly lead worship, there would be time for everything, and with more variety then we currently enjoy.

CONCLUSION

Actions of worship inherited from our Jewish and Christian forebears sustain and deepen the congregation's relationship with God. Proclaiming Scripture, preaching, and extending the communion covenant are God's gracious actions toward the congregation. Praise, prayer, offering, and confessing are the congregation's humble responses to God steadfast love. Regardless of worship patterns or styles, this is the rhythm of initiation and response that the Holy Spirit maintains between God and God's people.

God's power to act is not limited to these actions, nor is the individual believer limited by the responses of the congregation. God works with each human soul apart from the congregation in a multitude of ways. Each soul is free to respond to God regardless of whether a congregation is present or not. But when the Holy Spirit gathers the body of Christ, these actions of worship are what the Body does in common to receive God's living word and to serve, honor, and revere its God.

NOTES

1. Hughes Oliphant Old, *The Reading and Preaching of the Scripture in the Worship of the Christian Church* (Grand Rapids: William B. Eerdmans, 1998), 118, 126, 165-166.

2. Quoted in Old, 266.

3. Old, 8-18.

4. David Peterson, *Engaging with God: A Biblical Theology of Worship* (Grand Rapids: William B. Eerdmans), 1992, 55-74.

5. See Alvin Beachy, *Worship as Celebration of Covenant and Incarnation*, Newton, Kan.: Faith and Life Press, 1968.

6. In *Life as Worship: Prayer and Praise in Jesus' Name* (Grand Rapids: William B. Eerdmans Publishing Company, 1982), Theodore Jennings writes that "In these [many mainline and "conservative"] churches the most important "liturgical reform" that can be imagined is the careful and complete distinction between those words addressed to God and those addressed to the congregation," 44.

7. This is not to say that ordering worship limits or controls how God may be encountered or that God's Spirit is bound by the patterns we create. It is to say that for human beings *to act together*, patterns and lines of action need to be clear and can be clear without stifling the Sprit's movement.

8. A lectionary is a table of scripture readings appointed to each Sunday of the year as well as weekdays. Old, citing John Bright, pursues to the line of thought that claims Ezra codified the first Jewish "lectionary" at the time of the exile's return so that the Torah could be read systematically (99-100).

9. Notable examples are Origen, John Chrysostom, Basil of Caesarea, Gregory of Nazianzus, Clement of Alexandria, and Augustine.

10. James White, *Protestant Worship: Traditions in Transition* (Louisville: Westminster/John Knox Press, 1989), 171-191.

11. Robert Webber, *Planning Blended Worship: The Creative Mixture of Old and New* (Nashville: Abingdon Press, 1998), 20-21, 26-29. Contrary to much popular usage, blended worship is not just about using a wide variety of musical styles in worship. It goes much deeper in its intent, which is to integrate older worship patterns with contemporary expressions and embodiment.

12. After leading worship workshops and seminars for a number of years, I am distressed that the division of ministry in congregations is so strong. Pastor-Preachers by and large do not attend worship workshops. Worship leaders, by and large, do not attend preaching seminars. Ignorance abounds on both sides of the divide as to the purposes and functions of the other ministry.

Chapter 13

The Ethics of Persuasion in Preaching

Dennis Hollinger

*P*reaching is not only a proclamation of God's Word. It is invariably an attempt to change the thinking, sentiments, and actions of the hearers. As such, preaching is generally an act of persuasion, and persuasion carries with it some ethical risks.

In preaching we of course offer information, but always with a particular end in view—the transformation of people by work of the Holy Spirit. At one level this may seem to set preaching apart from other communication genres, but many forms of communication try to persuade audiences in ways similar to preaching, though without the transcendent element. Not all communication is persuasive in nature, and in contemporary preaching there is often a stress on a dialogical or communal nature of preaching. But even in dialogical style there is hope that the Word takes root and evokes change.

Persuasion is "a conscious attempt by one individual to change the attitudes, beliefs, or the behavior of another individual or group of individuals through the transmission of some message."[1] Because of the intent to change and influence thinking and action, it is quite possible for a communicator, such as a preacher, to employ means, design ends, or use content in ethically questionable ways. Ethical analyses of persuasive preaching are somewhat scant,[2] but the Christian commitment to moral character and actions compels us to engage the subject and evaluate our own rhetorical devices—and sometimes vices.

Communication ethics has generally attempted to make judgments on the basis of either the ends sought in the communication process or the means used. The first approach, consequentialist ethics (i.e. utilitarianism), runs the risk of achieving good ends by questionable means. The second approach, assessing communication methods in light of ethical principles, often fails to do justice to the full dimensions of the communication process. All forms of communication, including preaching, entail three primary elements: the sender, the message, and the receiver. An ethic of persuasion in preaching needs to do justice to each of these elements. I want to suggest that one of the best ways to analyze ethics in persuasive preaching is through the len of integrity, as it relates to sender, message, and receiver. Such an approach will examine results of attempts to persuade and assess methods on the basis of principles, but it will attempt to look at persuasion in preaching from within a larger framework of biblical and Christian worldview commitments.

While the word *integrity* occurs a number of times in English Bible translations, the term clearly embodies a number of other biblical concepts and principles as well. We tend to think of integrity as honesty, but it literally means the state of being whole and complete, coming from the mathematical word integer—a whole number. Integrity, as a Christian vision of what God calls us to be and to do, embodies notions such as authenticity, veracity (or truthfulness), and wholeness.[3] Stephen Carter, law professor at Yale, sees integrity as involving three steps: " (1) *discerning* what is right and what is wrong; (2) *acting* on what you have discerned, even at personal cost; and (3) *saying openly* that you are acting on your understanding of right from wrong."[4] As such, says Carter, it is first among the virtues and akin to what Jesus called "the pure in heart" (Matt. 5:8). Integrity has rich possibilities as a criterion for judging our persuasion in preaching. In each dimension of communication—the sender, the message, and the receiver—integrity needs to be guarded.

INTEGRITY AND THE SENDER (THE PREACHER)

In the ancient world the philosophers understood character or ethos (akin to what we are calling integrity) to be a fundamental part of rhetoric. These classical thinkers believed that oral communication invariably involves persuasion, and they typically emphasized "the role of the moral character of the source as important, and even essential for successful communication."[5] Aristotle, one of the first to give a comprehensive articulation of rhetoric, stressed the place of perceived personal character in speech:

> The character (ethos) of the speaker is a cause of persuasion when the speech is so uttered as to make him worthy of belief; for as a rule we trust men (sic) of probity more, and more quickly, about things in general, while on points outside the realm of exact knowledge, where opinion is divided, we trust them absolutely. . . . It is not true, as some writers on the art maintain, that the probity of the speaker contributes nothing to his persuasiveness; on the contrary, we might almost affirm that his character (ethos) is the most potent of all the means to persuasion."[6]

Aristotle believed that perceived moral character in rhetoric was not only important for the sake of ethics, but was essential to the act of persuasion itself. He understood every form of rhetoric to include *logos* (the logical appeal), *pathos* (the emotional appeal), and *ethos* (the appeal of character).

Several centuries later, Quintilian (A.D. 35-95), the great Roman teacher of rhetoric, contended that a speaker needs two essential qualities: speech skill and moral character. He wrote, "My aim . . . is the education of the perfect orator. The first essential for such an one is that he should be a good man [sic], and consequently we demand of him not merely the possession of exceptional gifts of speech, but of all the excellencies of character as well."[7] These ancient writers clearly understood that the integrity and character of a speaker were essential in persuading people to follow their ideas.

It is no surprise, therefore, that when we come to the New Testament, the biblical writers insist on moral character for the preachers and leaders of the early church. Jesus articulated the role of moral character in life and speech for all of his followers: "The good person out of the good treasure of the heart produces good, and the evil person out of evil treasure produces evil; for it is out of the abundance of the heart that the mouth speaks" (Luke 6:45). Yet integrity and moral character were especially emphasized for those in leadership roles, not because they were intrinsically more important than the laity, but because by its very nature the leadership (including the preachers) was so visible in modeling the way of Christ. Thus, the apostle Paul wrote,

> Those who are taught the Word must share in all good things with their teacher. Do not be deceived; God is not mocked, for you reap whatever you sow. If you sow to your own flesh, you will reap corruption from the flesh; but if you sow to the Spirit, you will reap eternal life from the Spirit. (Gal. 6:6-8).

Integrity is at the heart of the various ministerial standards in the New Testament:

> Whoever aspires to the office of bishop [overseer] desires a noble task. Now a bishop must be above reproach, married only once, temperate, sensible, respectable, hospitable, an apt teacher, not a drunkard, not violent but gentle, not quarrelsome, and not a lover of money. He must manage his own household well, keeping his children submissive and respectful in every way—for if someone does not know how to manage his own household, how can he take care of God's church? (I Tim. 3:1-5).

It was expected that the leaders of the church be trustworthy in handling the truth of the gospel (1 Cor. 4:2, 2 Cor. 4:2), "rightly explain the Word of truth" (2 Tim. 2:15b), and have a "firm grasp of the Word that is trustworthy in accordance with the teaching [apostolic teaching]" (Titus 1:9).

Each of these texts teach that church leaders must be one with the message they espouse. Integrity as the sense of authenticity, trustworthiness and wholeness of moral character is essential to the proclamation of the gospel. While the gospel and the Word have power in their own right that transcends the worthiness of the messenger, God has chosen to use finite, fallen humans to be the vehicles of divine truth. That truth and its implications for life are more readily understood and accepted when conveyed through people whose inner character and outward actions are "at one" with the message they proclaim.

Integrity not only commends the message of the sender but also prevents other potential abuses in the persuasion process. "Communicators need to realize that multiple objectives and motives constantly operate within every communicative act. They ought not be deluded into thinking they are moved by only one motive, although at any given moment a dominant motive may be operating."[8] Hence preachers must be aware that even our most righteous and sincere attempts at persuading a congregation to follow biblical teachings are still bound up with some questionable motives and self-aggrandizement. We never purely preach the Word. Recognizing our own proclivities is important for an even deeper commitment to and nurturing of personal character and integrity, which comes not through our own native efforts, but through the discernment of Holy Scripture, the empowerment of the Holy Spirit, and the influence and accountability of Christian *koinonia*. The development of integrity acts as an internal mechanism of control to shield the preacher from potential misuses that reside within his or her power as a persuasive communicator.

What are potential pitfalls of the messenger? Raymond McLaughlin notes that some ethical issues are centered in personal preparation, including procrastination or avoidance of sermon preparation, failure to prepare adequately, and using other people's material without giving credit. Other problems stem from personal ethical practices, such as "preaching for personal glory, power, prestige, or money. . . . preaching what one fails to practice. . . . [and] acting as an authority in a field where one isn't an authority."[9] Similarly, J. Vernon Jensen notes that communicators sometimes "manipulate their claims about themselves to create a higher credibility than is deserved."[10] This may not only entail such strident practices as padding one's resume but can be an exaggeration of personal credibility by sounding like an authority on a given issue through voice tone or appealing definitively to the original biblical languages when one's knowledge is rather scant.

Personal integrity of the preacher can also be diminished by an excessive "pandering to an audience's emotional attachment to them. When a communicator is held in awe, the temptation to draw on that reservoir of prestige and good will rather than on reason and substantial material is great."[11] This is particularly a temptation for those who are well-known and highly revered. They are no longer one with their message, for they are attempting to persuade on the basis of popularity, personal charisma, or past achievements.

Personal character and integrity of the sender (the preacher) must always be the starting point for an ethic of persuasion in preaching. Integrity ensures a trust in the speaker by the audience, for "principles of fidelity and veracity derive from this recognition of the central role trust plays in healthy communication."[12] Nonetheless, character and integrity of the preacher alone are not sufficient. Because we are fallen and struggle with multiple motives in the preaching moment, we must be aware of the potential abuses that can come relative to the other dimension of the communication process. In recent years character ethics has become the rage in moral philosophy and Christian ethics, and it is an important corrective to an ethic that focuses only on behavior. But a full-orbed ethic must incorporate both character and action, ethos and method.

Thus we must explore the potential ways in which integrity can be assailed in both the message and the receiver, even given the highest commitments to personal integrity on the part of the sender.

INTEGRITY AND THE MESSAGE

In every act of communication there is a message that the sender seeks to convey to a receiver. The message may range from cognitive information to affective sentiments, and the sender may disclose it in multiple ways, but every form of communication involves some message. In a technological world where the medium sometimes becomes the message, or in a postmodern world in which cognitive meaning seems to give way to image and emotion, it is particularly important to recognize that a message is nonetheless a part of every communicative act. And it is possible in conveying that message to denigrate its integrity.

It may at first seem somewhat odd to speak of integrity of the message as an element of ethics. We tend to think of the authenticity, truthfulness, or wholeness of the Christian message as theology and a matter of orthodoxy. But if the gospel and the teaching of the Bible are rooted in transcendence and essential to becoming what God intends us to be and do as human beings, then this is not just a matter of orthodoxy, but ethics as well. To distort the integrity of the message in preaching is just as unethical as loss of integrity in the sender and the receiver.

A message that has integrity and is truthful or trustworthy generally incorporates two things: it is accurate and complete. Jensen helps us understand this with the following scenario:

> In answering her parents' question about where she had been the
> night before, a daughter might mention two places but omit a

third. Her reply was accurate but incomplete. . . . A statement can be completely true, but not truly complete. If the daughter had named two places she had not been, her statement would have been inaccurate. Sins of omission and commission, of concealment and falsification, are both at the core of lying. In the first instance we *keep* people in the dark, and in the second, we *put* them in the dark.[13]

Of course in our communication we are never "complete" in terms of all that might be conveyed regarding a subject or an incident. In some cases we are ethically right not to convey all. As Dietrich Bonhoffer wrote from a German prison, "Truthfulness does not mean uncovering everything that exists. . . . Many things in human life ought to remain covered."[14] The crucial issue is whether we have intentionally distorted the message to an audience in such a way that they are misled. (Here I will not deal with the ethical dilemma Bonhoeffer himself faced in hiding information from a tyrannical government, on the grounds that there were overriding warrants to do so).

In preaching there are various ways in which we can distort the integrity of the message. Certainly one way is through exaggeration of the gospel or the claims of biblical texts. For example, if a preacher states, "When you come to faith in Christ, your personal problems will be over," they have clearly distorted both the claims of the gospel and what we know to be true in human experience. Or if we contend that to "turn the other cheek with our enemies will invariably lead to a cessation of international conflict," we have said far more than Jesus himself did, more than what the whole of Scripture claims, and far more than what history itself yields. An exaggeration of biblical truth yields loss of integrity and is unethical.

Conversely, we may distort the integrity of the biblical message by understating its claims and its impact. This is particularly a temptation in a secular, pluralistic world in which the claims of the gospel often run contrary to the cultural mood. We might, for example, play down the supernatural element of prayer, miracles, or events in Scripture by giving a purely naturalistic explanation or minimizing the divine elements in an act or event.

When faced with the feeding of the 5,000 and the 4,000 (Mark 6:30-44; Matt. 15:29-39) many moderns are tempted to turn these miracles into a parable on personal sharing of one's goods or justice. But if there are no clear hermeneutical reasons to support such an interpretation of what actually happened, we may well be engaging in a loss of integrity for the sake of cultural conformity, even if one application of the story centers on sharing or justice. As Christians in the modern and postmodern world we are prone to the understatement distortions of biblical texts that don't fit the cultural ethos or that we find personally difficult to implement in our lives.

A third way in which the integrity of the message might be distorted is through using supporting data that are simply not true or at best misleading. In preaching we use a wide range of supporting data, such as illustrations (stories), statistics, and current events. We employ these as points of contact, for clarity, or to influence parishioners' beliefs, sentiments, and actions relative to a biblical text or theme. However, a number of ethical issues surround our use of such data.

One issue has to do with illustrations and stories from our own personal experiences. The dilemma we face is that these stories are often the most personal and powerful in supporting or conveying the message, but they involve other human beings and issues of confidentiality. Thus many have suggested that it is ethically legitimate to change contexts, characters, or even issues of the story to maintain confidentiality. Some preachers at times combine two stories or incidents into one to protect the persons involved.

But is this tampering with reality ethical? Here we face a complex ethical issue with competing claims or principles. My own practice has been to always protect the confidentiality of persons involved and thus to change or combine elements of stories and conversations. The ethical test is whether there is an essential congruence of the story as told with the spirit of the events that transpired, and a oneness of the story with the meaning being conveyed in the message.

Another ethical issue involved in our use of supporting data is use of statistics. We are increasingly aware that statistics can lie, distort reality, or convey half-truths. Even among professional social scientists or natural scientists there is often a high degree of variation in conclusions reached about what statistics say, depending on starting assumptions, methodology, or the group sampled. "Statistics can have a strong appeal because of their precision and scientific aura and their ability to support a claim in a clear and compelling fashion."[15] It is precisely their persuasive nature that compels us to evaluate seriously their use in preaching.

Few preachers of course have the statistics expertise to weigh the merits of one set of data against another, but our commitment to integrity should motivate us to ask whether the data (as best we understand them) merely support our ideology, cause, or biases, or do indeed reflect reality. Knowingly using bad data to support supernatural truth is hardly worthy of the truth we commend.

A final way in which the integrity of the message can be distorted is employing media not commensurate with the message. Traditionally preaching employed just one medium—oral communication. Today we can use music, videos, TV, radio, drama, the Internet, projection of images and of the text itself. Some preachers have been opposed to using new technologies solely on grounds that preaching by its very nature must be traditional oral communication. But there is minimal biblical support for such an assertion. It's hard to imagine the apostle Paul using only classical rhetoric if he were living in our cyberspace world. But what are we to make of all the new technological possibilities at our disposal?

If we employ our theme of integrity, then the test quite simply is this: Does the medium distort the integrity of the message? The principle itself is far more easily stated than its application, but there is the possibility that over-reliance on image, video, music, and cyberspace in our preaching can distort the biblical message. Not only do the various mediums themselves have this potential, but a failure to find balance of content and image in use of media might oversimplify, merely entertain, or fail to capture the heart of the gospel and the Word. I personally use various media in my own preaching and teaching but continually ask, "Is it one [integrity] with the message I seek to convey?"

INTEGRITY AND THE RECEIVER (CONGREGATION)

There is no true communication unless someone receives and responds to a message transmitted by a sender. And just as there are ethical issues related to the sender and the message, so there are ethical issues pertinent to those on the receiving end. Here too integrity must be maintained.

In the communication process the receivers or audience clearly have an ethical responsibility to respect the sender and weigh the evidence of the message for themselves. But my focus here is not so much on the audience's own ethical responsibility as the speaker's guarding of the receivers' integrity. This particularly becomes an issue today in that non-mediated, natural communication has tended to give way to an artificiality in which communication "has substantially shifted from its human axis." Thus as Antonio Pasquali insightfully points out, there is a "growing apartheid between interlocutors; an easy introduction of noise into messages; and the curbing of all direct and immediate responses, preventing lineal message from developing into dialogue."[16] Pasquali may overstate his case, but clearly it becomes harder in contemporary modes of communication to guard the human element and the integrity of the audience.

One reason ethical issues arise in regard to audience integrity is the

> power differential [which] often exists between senders and receivers in the communicative act. . . . When the sender of the messages holds considerably more power than the receiver in a given context, the highly ethical communicator must be careful not to use that advantage to the detriment of the audience.[17]

In preaching for persuasion this is no less a problem, for the preacher has power by virtue of position, knowledge, and sometimes charisma. How might a preacher with such power violate the integrity of his or her parishioners?

Most violations of receiver integrity come through some sort of manipulation of the audience. In an era of mass media where consumer choice is heralded, there is a tendency to overlook such manipulations, for "the moral burden . . . is then put on audiences, whereas the media go scot-free: they are only offering choices."[18] But in the Christian worldview, every human in the audience is a person of dignity and value, having been made in the image of God. Thus the messenger, medium, and message must guard that dignity and value—the integrity of the person.

When mass media communication became technicized in the twentieth century, one of the first forms of audience manipulation was the subliminal cue in advertising:

> The process whereby the name or picture of a product is flashed on motion picture or television screen so rapidly that it cannot be seen by the conscious eye. The message is registered in the fringes of the viewer's attention and . . . may thus motivate him (sic) to buy.[19]

This is but one form of hidden persuasion employing varying techniques.

> Whether they be subliminal cues, mass hypnosis, constant repetition, loaded language, the subtle use of social pressures, or the appeal to irrelevant loves, hates, and fears, they all seek the same kind of response from the listener or viewer. They attempt to make him (sic) buy, vote, or believe in a certain way by short-circuiting his conscious thought processes and planting suggestions or exerting pressures on the periphery of his consciousness which are intended to produce automatic, non-reflective behavior.[20]

Similar kinds of abuses can occur in persuasive preaching. A prominent form of audience manipulation in preaching has been misuse of emotionalism. Throughout much of the twentieth century, reason was heralded as the ethical mode of communication and appeals to emotion were repudiated. In fact one communication scholar, Arthur Kruger, argued that reliance on pathos appeals was inherently unethical. But Josina Makau has rightly contended that "nearly all the works of poets, novelists, composers, and artists rely heavily upon emotional appeals. Acceptance of Kruger's views preclude even the possibility of writing an ethical poem."[21] An ethical approach to persuasion in preaching does not eliminate emotion, but rather seeks a balance between affective and rational appeals.

Nonetheless, there can be a play on an audience's emotions to the point that their own integrity is threatened. Overly dramatic appeals to fear, emotionally charged language, and stories that sweep the congregation away by sentimentality can all lead to emotional abuse of the hearer. Raymond McLaughlin tells the following story illustrating an emotionalism that leads to loss of congregational integrity:

> A popular preacher nearly hypnotized an audience with his extended emotional sermon. His message had little solid content. It presented no biblical exposition, sparse evidence and reasoning, and consisted of an almost unbroken chain of emotional stories. The preacher closed his message with a dramatic, kneeling portrayal of the death of his "dear old alcoholic daddy," in his arms, without Christ. Two women were sobbing uncontrollably. . . . The invitation of this preacher got "results." But were these results intelligent, responsible, lasting, and ethical?"[22]

Emotions and affections are significant parts of our humanness, and preaching without emotion hardly does justice to our created nature. But appealing only to emotion or playing with an audience's emotions are manipulative and produce results that contradict Christian moral commitments and the dignity of human beings.

A second form of audience manipulation is crowd pressure. Preachers can employ tactics that rob the audience of the freedom to make their own spiritual decisions. One of my most memorable experiences of such abuse occurred while I was working in a Christian youth camp one summer. A well-known preacher gave an emotionally charged evangelistic message, then had the audience "bow their heads and close their eyes." He invited people to raise their hands as an indication of their decision for Christ. I was sitting at the back of the tabernacle that night and didn't totally follow the preacher's instructions of eyes shut. After several seconds he began to say, "Yes, I see that hand," repeated over and over. But there were no hands raised. After several minutes of this tactic, hands did begin to go up, but I suspect in part as a result of the crowd pressure manipulation, accomplished through a lie.

A third form of audience manipulation involves the misuse of personal charisma. Various individuals, including many powerful preachers, have a personal charisma that has a powerful impact on those who meet and listen to them. Sociologists have always had a hard time describing the exact nature of personal charisma or predicting its occurrence, but the results are striking. By virtue of certain personal qualities (demeanor, appearance, voice, and so forth) one is able to persuade and influence people.

The point here is not that we must repudiate all forms of personal charisma, for that would cause loss of integrity to the sender. Rather, in preaching it is important for preachers with charisma to not allow their charismatic qualities to carry the freight of the message. Solid preparation, careful exposition, clear arguments, fitting stories, must not give way to the power of personal charisma but rather be coupled with the preacher's personal qualities in conveying the message.

When preachers communicate to a congregation, they must always see men and women, boys and girls, older and younger, in all their diversity, who are made in the image of God. They need to see in the audience people with great spiritual, physical, emotional and social needs, waiting for a biblical message that can touch their deepest longings.

They need to see parishioners who have been given to their care by God to love and to nourish. It is with such awareness and divine calling that we are able to guard the integrity of the receiver.

CONCLUSION

Preaching is and must be a form of persuasion. Grounded in the Word, motivated by the love of Christ, and empowered by the Holy Spirit, we seek to influence the thinking, affections, and actions of those who hear. But preaching for persuasion must be ethical and the results must not contravene the gospel itself and the larger understandings of a biblical worldview.

Ethical persuasive preaching is best accomplished when we guard the integrity of the entire communicative process. The integrity of the sender, the message, and the receiver should be protected for preaching to be not only ethical but biblical. For biblical preaching not only proclaims the Word, but proclaims it in a way that fits the very teaching and spirit of that Word.

NOTES

1. Erwin P. Bettinghaus, *Persuasive Communication*, 2nd. ed. (New York: Holt, Rinehart and Winston, 1973), 10.

2. There is a paucity of work on the ethics of preaching and persuasion in preaching. The only significant work I found was Raymond W. McLaughlin, *The Ethics of Persuasive Preaching* (Grand Rapids: Baker, 1979), and he too is "disappointed to find so little written on the subject in homiletical literature," 9.

3. See for example J. Daniel Hess, *Integrity: Let Your Yea Be Yea* (Scottdale, Pa.: Herald Press, 1978).

4. Stephen L. Carter, *Integrity* (New York: Basic Books, 1996), 7.

5. Kenneth Andersen, "A History of Communication Ethics," in Karen Joy Greenberg (ed.), *Conversations on Communication Ethics* (Norwood, N.J.: Ablex Publishing, 1991), 7.

6. Lane Cooper, transl., *The Rhetoric of Aristotle* (New York: Appleton, 1932), 8-9.

7. H. E. Butler, transl., *The Institutio Oratoria of Quintilian* (Cambridge, Mass.: Harvard University Press, 1953), 19.

8. J. Vernon Jensen, *Ethical Issues in the Communication Process* (Mahwah, N.J.: Lawrence Erlbaum Associates, 1997), 39.

9. McLaughlin, 24.

10. Jensen, 43.

11. Ibid.

12. Josina Makau, "The Principles of Fidelity and Veracity: Guidelines for Ethical Communication," in Greenberg, 115.

13. Jensen, 89.

14. Dietrich Bonhoeffer, *Letters and Papers from Prison*, trans. and ed. E. Bethge (New York: Macmillan, 1972), 158.

15. Jensen, p. 127. For further discussion on this issue see C. Crossen, *Tainted Truth: The Manipulation of Facts in America* (New York: Simon & Schuster, 1994) and D. Huff, *How to Lie with Statistics* (New York: Norton, 1993).

16. Antonio Pasquali, "The Moral Dimension of Communicating," in Elifford Christians and Michael Traber, eds., *Communication Ethics and Universal Values* (Thousand Oaks, CA: Sage Publications, 1997), 31.

17. Jensen, 163.

18. Michael Traber, "Conclusion: An Ethics of Communication Worthy of Human Beings," in Christians and Traber, p. 329.

19. Franklyn Haiman, "Democratic Ethics and the Hidden Persuaders," in Richard L. Johannesen, ed., *Ethics and Persuasion: Selected Readings* (New York: Random House, 1967), p. 58.

20. Ibid., p. 59.

21. Makau, pp. 112-113.

22. McLaughlin, p. 159.

Chapter 14

Preaching Grace to Hardworking People

Ervin R. Stutzman

"*T*wo men went up to the temple to pray, one a Pharisee and the other a tax collector" (Luke 18:10). With these words, Jesus began a story to religious people who considered themselves righteous and regarded others with contempt. As the scene unfolds, the Pharisee declares his moral superiority over the tax collector, vainly disguising his recitation of good deeds with a veil of thanksgiving to God. In contrast, the tax collector beats his breast and begs God for mercy. Jesus ended the brief story with a punch line, turning the tables on his listeners' moral sensibilities by blessing the tax collector: "I tell you, this man went down to his home justified rather than the other; for all who exalt themselves will be humbled, but all who humble themselves will be exalted" (Luke 18:14).

In this parable as in many others, Jesus displayed his fondness for upsetting the status quo by telling stories that set his listeners' teeth on edge. Just as a picture may be worth a thousand words, parables can pack the punch of a dozen sermons.

Perhaps the most arresting aspect of the parables that depict God's generosity is the seeming inability of hardworking people to appreciate God's grace. In the parable of the vineyard workers, those who labored all day resented the generous pay to those who came to work later on

(Matt. 20:1-16). In the parable of the prodigal, the older son rejected his father's invitation to celebrate the return of his wasteful brother (Luke 15:11-32). We hear the same truth in Jesus' conversation with the Pharisees—hardworking, religious people find it difficult to receive God's grace. It was to a Pharisee, a member of the Jewish ruling council, that Jesus spoke about the need to be born again (John 3:8). We have no record that he ever gave such an imperative to the tax collectors and other sinners whose homes he frequented on occasion.

Herein lies a deep irony. The very people who seem to care the most about following God's commands—concerned to cross every "t" and dot every "i"—may overlook the most basic laws of God (Matt. 23:23). People who readily notice the sins of others may be the most blind to their own sins (John 9:40-1). People who care the most deeply about God's holiness may offend God's holiness in flagrant ways (Matt. 23:27-28).

These traits, I suggest, are sometimes found among contemporary Anabaptists, including myself and the people with whom I associate. They are amply demonstrated in worship services each Sunday morning, including the preaching. I suspect that if we as Anabaptists were to put ourselves into the parable from Luke 18:9-14, we would most resemble the Pharisee.[1] Like the Pharisee, we are grateful to God that we are not like some of the sinners we could name. We too practice spiritual disciplines. We too tithe of our income. We too neglect to ask God for forgiveness at times because we don't perceive our need for it. And like other hardworking people, we would prefer to earn God's favor rather than receive it as a gift.

Consequently, I believe that if we were to experience God's grace more deeply, we would preach much more freely about God's initiative through Christ. We would more readily emphasize the power of the Holy Spirit. Our sermons would be transformed. Our churches would gain new vitality. And new people would come to faith.

To develop this thesis, below I examine briefly the concept of grace, then look at the ways Anabaptist concepts of grace have influenced our preaching. I then speak of my own experience of Mennonite preaching and give a number of suggestions for preaching to hardworking— and sometimes grace resistant—people.

THE CONCEPT OF GRACE

In his popular book, *What's So Amazing About Grace?* Philip Yancey cites the claim that grace is the sole theological concept that sets Christianity apart from all other world religions. Yet he asserts that grace is often elusive in Christian communities. He claims that in his four-year sojourn at a Bible college he experienced as much "ungrace" as anywhere else in his life.[2] He even suggests that grace may be hardest to find in those churches who have the word in their church name.

Christians commonly understand grace to be God's gracious initiative in Jesus Christ. The Scriptures, particularly the New Testament, consistently present God's initiative in salvation. God knew from the beginning that humankind would need grace and redemption. That is why Jesus is called "the Lamb who was slain from the creation of the world" (Rev. 13:9). God's plan for salvation by grace is an expression of his love for all people.

Tom Finger, an Anabaptist theologian, explored the concept of grace in various faith traditions. Based on this study, he asserts that "believers churches often expect a higher degree of sanctification than Lutherans or Reformed."[3] That is, they expect an experience of grace to transform a believer's life over time. From an eschatological point of view, believers see human sinfulness as belonging to the Old Age, while Christian perfection or maturity are hallmarks of the New Age in Christ. Grace introduces this possibility into the human condition. Further, Finger avers, while believers churches may see Christian discipleship as a condition to obtain salvation, Jesus' calls to discipleship may also be seen as "acts of grace " (212). "As Jesus' own mission was empowered by the Spirit, so the Spirit energizes and communicates this call and the caller's own presence" (210).

Grace lies at the heart of Christian faith. Most Christian communions believe eternal salvation comes only through God's grace. Why then do Christian sermons (and the Christian schools that train preachers) often fail to communicate God's grace? Why are hardworking people often "grace resistant?" Why is there so much "ungrace" in the church? After reviewing Anabaptist Mennonite concepts of grace, I will attempt to address these questions.

ANABAPTIST-MENNONITE CONCEPTS OF GRACE

Early Anabaptists, along with other reformers in the sixteenth century, confessed their need for the grace of God. Menno Simons, a prominent Dutch Anabaptist, wrote: "Mark, beloved reader, that we do not believe nor teach that we are to be saved by our merits and works, as the envious accuse us of without truth; but that we are to be saved solely by grace, through Jesus Christ."[4] Yet this confession was made in the context of his assertion that Christ intercedes for those who "turn from evil, follow that which is good" and "sincerely desire, with Paul, that they [might] attain the perfection which is in Christ."[5] In Menno Simons' writing, as with most other Anabaptist literature, the gracious initiative of God is rarely discussed without an equal (or greater) emphasis on the need for human response.

Hans Denck, also an early Anabaptist, wrote that "no one can truly know [Christ] unless he follow him in life, and no one may follow him unless he has first known him."[6] This oft-quoted maxim reveals the core of early Anabaptist teaching. Clustered around this core were concepts of repentance, faith, duty, obedience, and good works.

How then did the Anabaptist concept of grace, as manifested in discipleship, influence early Anabaptist preaching? There are few primary sources, since many Anabaptists worshiped in caves and woods to escape persecution. However, historians John Oyer and Keith Graber Miller argue that "what is most distinctive about Anabaptist worship (in contrast to surrounding Catholic or Protestant groups) is related to preaching."[7] "Nearly every Anabaptist sermon included something about repenting of one's sins and the grace of God in Jesus to forgive" (8). "The preaching style tended to be admonition style." "Sin, repentance, and admonition to live a good Christian life were fundamental Anabaptist themes" (4) Elias Schad, a detractor who stole his way into a secret meeting, "makes reference to the Anabaptists' pharisaic piety, the notion that they were the best of all Christians" (4). Oyer and Graber suggest that while Anabaptists may have said this about themselves early on, it soon became more common for others to say it. "Early Anabaptist sermons often included stories about the results of being good to inspire others also to be like Jesus" (8).

There was also a certain democratization occurring among the Anabaptists, in that they took quite literally Paul's counsel in 1 Corinthians 14:29-31. They invited not only appointed ministers to speak but anyone who had a word of exhortation. All were free to respond to these sermons, a practice that came to be known as *zeugnis* or witness, an opportunity for listeners to pass judgment on the biblical veracity of the exhortation or to offer other commentary.[8] It may have been a practice born out of necessity, Oyer and Graber suggested, since strong literate leaders were scarce in days of persecution. It seems clear that the early Anabaptist way of life was accompanied by a particular kind of preaching, accented by an emphasis on repentance, obedience, and admonition to bring all of one's life into conformity with the way of Christ.

Historian Harold Bender drew upon the legacy of the Anabaptists as a way to inspire his generation of Mennonites with a new vision and identity. While presiding over the American Society of Church History in 1943, Bender argued that the central tenet of Christianity for Anabaptists was discipleship. Anabaptists believed that the reformers, "whatever their profession may have been, did not secure among the people true repentance, regeneration, and Christian living as a result of their preaching."[9] To Anabaptists, discipleship "meant the transformation of the entire way of life of the individual believer and of society so that it should be fashioned after the teaching and example of Christ" (105). That was the goal of Anabaptist preaching. "The focus of the Christian life was to be not so much *the inward experience of grace* as it was for Luther, but *the outward application of that grace* to all human conduct and the consequent Christianization of all human relationships" (106, emphasis added).

A second major element in Anabaptism, according to Bender, was a new concept of the church. "Voluntary church membership based upon true conversion and involving a commitment to holy living and discipleship was the absolutely essential heart of this concept" (108). This principle led to a rejection of infant baptism as practiced by the state churches. While an infant "might conceivably passively experience the grace of God," Bender wrote, "they could not respond in pledging their lives to Christ" (108). Anabaptist belief in discipleship had corollary doctrines about disciplined church membership and nonconformity to the world. They set up a "line of demarcation" between the Christian community and worldly society, willing to suffer persecution rather than compromising their beliefs" (109).

A third element of the Anabaptist vision as articulated by Bender was the ethic of love and nonresistance. For Anabaptists it meant "complete abandonment of all warfare, strife, and violence, and the taking of human life" (110). Bender argued that this practice stood in stark contrast to Lutheranism, which avowed that a compromise must be made by a Christian in a sinful world order, for instance in making war, "and for this his only recourse is to seek forgiveness by the grace of God" (112). Bender clearly believed that such a view of grace was inferior to an understanding of grace as enablement to follow Christ—"to practice what he taught, believing that where He walked we can by His grace follow in his steps" (112).

The essence of Bender's speech was printed in a booklet and marketed as *The Anabaptist Vision*. Bender's biographer called it "the most influential Mennonite speech of the twentieth century."[10] Many of Bender's students and other readers of the *Anabaptist Vision* became apologists for Anabaptist-Mennonite theology and practice. Revisionist historians have since questioned some tenets of Bender's thesis, believing that he attributed too much historical continuity to diverse groups of Anabaptists.

However, Stephen Dintaman, a contemporary Anabaptist theologian, finds fault with Bender's vision and those influenced by it on a different score. He believes that Bender's vision, particularly as interpreted over the past fifty years, was short on grace. This has left the church with a profound spiritual poverty. Dintaman argues that while theologians who followed Harold Bender "greatly deepened and expanded the concept of discipleship," they gave "only passing, non-passionate attention to the work of Christ and the work of the Spirit in the inner transformation of the person."[11]

The result was that students and church leaders learned "some of the behavioral aspects of the Christian faith without learning equally well that discipleship is only meaningful and possible because it is an answer to who God is and what God is doing in the world, and without necessarily experiencing what it means to have a vital and life-changing personal friendship with the crucified and risen Jesus" (205). "The challenge before us now," Dintaman asserts, "is to experience and name these transcendent works of grace in ways that are authentic and empowering for our times" (208).

With Dintaman, I believe an Anabaptist focus on discipleship, coupled with an Arminian belief that the human will is fundamentally free, may fool preachers (and perhaps their hearers) into thinking that anyone's life can readily be transformed by a simple change of mind. Since the admonitions in our sermons are generally aimed at those who are in "fundamental control of their lives," as Dintaman asserts, there is little good news for persons trapped in addictions. This rings true with my own experience of preaching, first in an Amish Mennonite context, then in different Mennonite congregations.

MY OWN EXPERIENCE OF MENNONITE PREACHING

From my childhood, I was taught that salvation comes to us by God's grace through faith in Jesus Christ. But what I remember most clearly is the warning that humans must respond with repentance and obedience to receive God's salvation. Obedience to church rules was an essential part of that obedience. Further, to continue in sin by participating in questionable activities was to cheapen God's grace. Although one could not *earn* eternal salvation, one could readily *forfeit* it by loose living. One could only be assured of salvation by walking daily with Christ.

The churches that nurtured my early spiritual life emphasized nonconformity to the world. We didn't work on Sunday. We didn't participate in worldly entertainment like fairs, rodeos, bowling alleys, movies, and pool halls. We didn't cuss, swear, or use many bywords. We were warned from the pulpit that Christ might return at any moment and catch us involved in sin. While we confessed belief in God's unmerited favor, we also worked hard to earn God's merited favor. Our emphasis on discipleship impelled us to put our faith to work. (Or was it our work ethos that led us to emphasize discipleship in the first place?)

In my youthful perceptions, I saw grace as the first leg of a relay race. God started the race, so to speak, by offering free grace through redemption and salvation. Then the baton was passed to us. We were called to complete the race by working for Christ in the world.

Again, I understood grace as God's willingness to compensate for human shortcomings. By "topping off" our human merit, God enabled us to meet the highest standards for salvation. The more goodness we were able to supply toward the merit needed for salvation, the less God needed to contribute as compensation for our lack. By this method of accounting, we sometimes reckoned that it took less of God's grace to save us Mennonites than it took to save our Protestant and Catholic neighbors who sometimes smoked, drank, and "carried on."[12] Now I'm convinced that we Mennonites need as much of God's grace to save us as anyone else.

Mennonite sermons are often filled with moral admonitions—"shoulds" and "oughts" intended to define the narrow way and keep us walking in it. These exhortations emphasize the importance of duty, obedience, and self sacrifice. The specific applications depend on the preacher and the congregation. Some call for piety or holiness in response to God's call. Others urge members to engage in witness, service, or social action. Thus, Mennonites may have a sense of self-righteousness based on perceived superiority to other Christians on a variety of attributes, whether it be holy living, peace and justice ministry, Christian service, social responsibility, or even perceived humility.

As I reflect on my overall experience of the Mennonite church, I'm convinced that while we sincerely believe in God's grace, we often live with profound ungrace. As we wrestle with the tension between God's initiative and our human response, we readily emphasize the latter to the point that it tends to obscure the former. In this sense, we are like the Pharisees portrayed in the New Testament as trusting that they were righteous and therefore justified in treating others with contempt.

I will speak more personally. Because I have so much in common with the Pharisees as depicted in their encounters with Jesus, I sometimes call myself a "recovering Pharisee." I use the language of addiction and recovery quite deliberately. Even though I deeply value God's grace, I readily "fall off the wagon" and return to thought and behavior patterns ingrained from my youth. When I sit down to prepare sermons, my first impulse is to deliver moral admonition that is short on God's grace.

When I admit my addiction to self-righteousness, I find myself in good company. Paul, the great apostle, was also a "recovering Pharisee." In his list of reasons for "confidence in the flesh," he described himself as "a Hebrew born of Hebrews; as to the law, a Pharisee; as to zeal, a persecutor of the church, as to righteousness under the law, blameless" (Phil. 3:5b-6). Yet in his letter to a young pastor, Paul testified that "the grace of our Lord" had overflowed in his behalf, appointing him to God's service although he had once been a blasphemer, a persecutor, and a man of violence. He went on to designate himself as the foremost of sinners (1 Tim. 1:12-17). Perhaps these two Scripture passages refer to different stages in Paul's spiritual journey. As I read Paul's writings, I get the sense that his spiritual transformation from proud Pharisee to humble recipient of God's grace was marked by struggle, pain, and occasional setbacks.

If my sermon notes adequately reflect my spiritual state, I have concrete evidence of struggle, pain, and setback in my own spiritual journey. As I leaf through my sermons from days gone by, I find at times a paucity of grace. At the time I prepared and preached them, I would not have viewed them that way but my standards for "auditing" have changed. I'm seeing grace through new eyes.

I have not fully resolved the mystery of God's initiative and human response, the interplay between God's sovereignty and human free will. Along with other preachers, I often wrestle with the implications for preaching, particularly in postmodern times with its rampant pluralism, decreasing biblical literacy, ambiguous concepts of sin, and low view of church authority. How can a preacher best convey a sense of God's grace to hardworking people?

PREACHING GRACE TO HARDWORKING PEOPLE

All good sermons convey movement. The first and most important movement is that of God's grace through the preacher in the preparation process. I've adopted the adage that "If the sermon hasn't moved me, it won't move anyone else." In other words, if I've not been touched by the grace of God, it will be difficult to communicate grace to my hearers. Coming to the point of tears during sermon preparation is often a clue to me that God is at work in the process, preparing me for the task.

I try to cultivate a sense of willingness, not just willfulness, in the preparation process. Willingness stands for openness and self-surrender to God, gently awaiting God's revelation. It invites me to be aware of my own inner struggles with a readiness to receive God's help. Willfulness stands for ego strength and commitment motivated by concerns for self—self-actualization, self-aggrandizement, self-expression, and self-confidence.[13]

Over the past several years, I've become more aware of God's grace in my life by keeping a daily "gratitude journal." Each day, I jot down something for which I'm grateful. This exercise keeps me keenly aware of God's goodness.

Also, I try to be alert to God's initiative or movement in other people's lives. The more keenly I am aware of God's movement in their lives, the more alert I am to the message God may be wanting to speak to them now. I am often moved by the "holy coincidences" I witness in people's lives. Even the ordinary events of life can yield profound evidence of God's initiative and generosity when viewed with the attitude of the apostle Paul as expressed to the Philippians. He wrote: "I am confident of this, that the one who began a good work among you will bring it to completion by the day of Jesus Christ" (Phil. 1:6). Here the focus is on God's initiative and God's ability to finish what he has started. This is *grace* at work, as Paul notes in the very next verse.

Prayer for the potential hearers can also be a vital part of sermon preparation. Consider the concept of leading people to "the throne of grace" (Heb. 4:16). Thrones are not usually associated with grace, sympathy, or understanding. Rather, they are associated with justice, authority, and power. Yet Jesus shows mercy in the face of judgment. As a minister of the gospel, I find myself praying with this image in my mind quite often. I come to Jesus boldly and with confidence that he will show mercy and grace in my time of need. I often pray, "Lord Jesus Christ, have mercy on me, a sinner." And I bring others to the throne of grace with me. When I pray this way while preparing sermons, they are more likely to be filled with grace.

Grace-filled sermons demonstrate a sensitivity to context. The parable that Jesus told about the Pharisee and the tax collector was developed for a specific context and for specific hearers. Jesus intended that parable to communicate in a particular way in that context. This may be called the rhetorical dimension in preaching—the preparation of the sermon for a specific audience and for specific ends. This requires a great deal of awareness on the part of the preacher, since the meaning of the sermon lies as much in the hearer as in the speaker. Too many times in our sermons, people hear something different than what we intended to say.

For example, women often hear exhortation differently than men. A sermonic style designed to shake men out of complacency may have the effect of "beating up" on women. Since women often feel responsibility to make things turn out right in the family, they often feel guilty when they are unable to accomplish it. So when preachers aim a truth at men, the men may miss the point altogether, whereas the women, sometimes innocent bystanders, may feel the full weight of the accusation.

Even the stories we tell in sermons will be heard differently depending on the listeners' experience. Yet stories of grace, both from the Scriptures and contemporary life, often touch people at a deeper level than simple exhortation. That was the purpose of Jesus' parables. As preachers, we do well to tell stories of our own struggles at times, as I have done in this chapter. Admitting our vulnerabilities and faults can be a powerful experience of grace for those who struggle with self-condemnation or self-righteousness. The most important thing is that our stories communicate a sense of God's mercy, love, or empowerment in action.

Again, we do well to remember that our hearers may be unbelievers or members at different stages of conversion.[14] Each stage of conversion, including initial trust in God, is brought about by God's grace. Even the call to discipleship, as noted by Tom Finger above, constitutes an act of grace. Yet how people perceive that call depends in part on our preaching. Do we depict Christ's call as a personal invitation to a rich feast, or as an obligation such as military conscription? The former is more likely to be experienced as a blessing, whereas the latter may feel like a curse.

This provides a clue as to why people often experience ungrace in the church, and particularly in our preaching. People may experience ungrace when we consistently emphasize duty over privilege, rules over relationship, sacrifice over abundance, and human responsibility over God's initiative. Although both of the ideas in the above pairs must be emphasized at times, the emphasis, order, and movement of these ideas in the sermon makes a great deal of difference in how people hear it. Anabaptist sermons built on an understanding of discipleship that emphasizes the outward application of grace at the expense of an inner experience of grace will likely develop a congregational atmosphere of ungrace. The church will be spiritually impoverished even though its members may believe themselves righteous and view others with contempt.

My comments about discipleship in this chapter may have convinced the reader I hesitate to preach about Christ's call to discipleship. Quite the contrary! I am deeply committed to discipleship. To symbolize my commitment, I have on my desk a piece of worship art in the form of a disciple's cross. The symbol consists of a small cross underneath the arms of a larger cross. Balthasar Hubmaier, an early Anabaptist, describes its meaning this way:

> Where Christ is and dwells, there he brings the cross with him on
> his back from which he gives every Christian his own small cross

to carry and to follow after him. We are to expect this small cross, and if it comes accept it with joy and patience, and not pick and choose our own chips and bits of wood in false spirituality.[15]

The disciple's cross helps to put my preaching in perspective. Human response always stands under and is dwarfed by God's initiative. At least in a minimal sense, the preacher should refer to both God's initiative and human response in every sermon. However, the movement in the sermon should leave people with a sense of God's grace in their lives, rather than an obligation to do something in response to the sermon. Wilson asserts: "Only an exceptional preacher or an unusual sermon can end by detailing our responsibilities and what we must do, and in so doing also end with a powerful sense of what God is doing."[16] It is the latter which brings a sense of hope and empowerment to the hearers.

As a "recovering Pharisee," I've learned to ask myself a few questions as I prepare my sermons to help my listeners experience God's grace. The answers to these questions help to shape my sermons in grace-filled ways. In regard to the Scripture text(s) I might ask, What is the evidence of God's initiative in or behind this text? What are the signs of God's mercy and forgiveness in response to human shortcoming? What difference does God's presence and activity make? What offer is God extending? How are people empowered to do God's will?

In regard to the congregation or situation where I will preach, I might ask, Where has God been at work in this congregation? What dreams and visions could be accomplished by God's enablement? What fears could be addressed by an assurance of God's presence and power? What needs could be met by bringing them to the throne of grace? What burdens could be lifted by God's comfort? What hope could be engendered by a reference to God's action in the world?

I have also found it helpful to tell stories of God's grace in my sermons. Particularly the younger generation responds more readily to stories of grace than to moral admonition. The Bible is filled with such stories. God promised Abram and Sarai that they would be the father and mother of a people too numerous to count. God rescued Moses and his people from the hand of Pharaoh. God redeemed Hannah from barrenness so she became the esteemed mother of Samuel, a great prophet in Israel. God's angel delivered Peter from prison.

The daily newspaper, too, is full of stories that point to clues of God's goodness. Notable achievements, deeds of kindness, narrow rescues, and heroic acts all carry the seeds of grace for humankind. Preaching grace does not imply that I ignore God's judgment. The Bible and the daily newspaper offer poignant reminders of judgment, divine as well as human. My aim in preaching is to balance judgment with grace, yielding hope. In today's harsh world hope can be hard to find.

Let me not leave the impression that the hearers' experience of grace depends solely on the preacher. Such a conclusion would run counter to the central thesis of this chapter, which emphasizes God's action. I firmly believe preaching is God's event. The sermon is not simply words *about* God's grace. The preaching event, properly conceived, is *an act of* God's grace. The apostle Peter wrote, "Whoever speaks must do so as one speaking the very words of God. . . so that God may be glorified in all things through Jesus Christ" (1 Pet. 4:11). What a great privilege and responsibility for preachers! It is indeed *God's message* we are called to share. The gospel is God's idea, not ours. When we preach in God's name, God can do wonderful things beyond our own ability.

So, even when our best prepared sermons seem to go awry or fall to the ground as we preach, God can redeem them.[17] When God's Spirit is at work in the preaching event the hearers' response does not depend entirely on us. Therefore, the sermon that seemed to go so wrong may be the very one that makes the biggest positive difference in a listener's life. The phrases we crafted may at times be heard in different ways than we intended, resulting in an even better end. And for a hardworking preacher like me, that is grace.

NOTES

1. See Kathleen Kern, *We are the Pharisees* (Scottdale, Pa.: Herald Press, 1995). She asserts that most Christians throughout history have had Pharisaical tendencies.

2. Philip Yancey, *What's So Amazing about Grace?* (Grand Rapids: Zondervan Publishing House), 15.

3. Tom Finger, *Christian Theology: A Eschatalogical Approach, vol. 2* (Scottdale, Pa.: Herald Press), 206.

4. Cited in J. C. Wenger, *Introduction to Theology* (Scottdale, Pa.: Herald Press, 1954), 288.

5. Wenger, 288.

6. Cited in Finger, 214.

7. John Oyer and Keith Graber Miller, "Worshipping with the Early Anabaptists," *Gospel Herald* 90, no. 34 (September 2, 1997): 8.

8. A similar form of *zeugnis* is still practiced among the Old Order Amish, direct descendants of the Anabaptists.

9. Harold S. Bender, "The Anabaptist Vision," in *Refocusing a Vision*, ed. John D. Roth (Goshen: Mennonite Historical Society, 1995), 103.

10. Albert Keim, "The Anabaptist Vision: Reassurance and a Rallying Point for the Church," *Gospel Herald* (April 19, 1994), 1.

11. Stephen F. Dintaman, "The Spiritual Poverty of the Anabaptist Vision," *Conrad Grebel Review* 10 (Spring 1992): 205.

12. Actually, Mennonites did get involved in those activities at times, but they generally took pains to avoid been caught in them by fellow church members.

13. I've borrowed the terms *willingness* and *willfulness* and these general definitions from Gerald May, *Will and Spirit: A Contemplative Psychology* (New York: Harper & Row, 1982).

14. Some writers speak of specific stages of conversion, moving to a point of complete union with God. Wesleyans and other "holiness advocates" speak of a "second work of grace," the believer's movement toward Christian perfection. I prefer to think of many works of grace, each moving the believer toward greater maturity and love for God and neighbor.

15. Balthasar Hubmaier, *Balthasar Hubmaier: Theologian of Anabaptism*, trans. and eds., H. Wayne Pipkin and John H. Yoder (Scottdale, Pa.: Herald Press, 1989), 364.

16. Paul Scott Wilson, *The Practice of Preaching* (Nashville: Abingdon Press, 1995), 110.

17. As a professor of preaching, I do not offer this as an excuse for neglect of thoughtful preparation or abuse of pulpit privilege!

Study Guide

*T*he purpose of these questions is to help the reader grasp the meaning and significance of each essay.

The short set of questions at the end of this study guide draw from the essays in the whole book. They are written to help the reader integrate the insights from various parts of the books into a fuller understanding of the whole.

Chapter 1: David Greiser
WHAT EXACTLY IS MENNONITE PREACHING?

1. In his historical survey of Anabaptist/Mennonite preaching, Greiser lifts out the role of the "hermeneutical community" as an enduring value. What does he mean by "hermeneutical community?" What are some of the forms in which this value has been practiced in Mennonite congregations through the centuries?

2. Greiser describes how, over the years, Anabaptist-Mennonite preaching has been influenced by surrounding Protestant models. In addition, however, he also identifies distinctly Anabaptist themes at various points throughout his overview. What are these unique themes? How unique or distinctly Anabaptist/Mennonite are they? Would you add other important preaching themes from your study or experience?

3. Greiser lists four "noteworthy" characteristics of Anabaptist preaching. Which of the following is not included in this list?

    a. Preaching has been biblical with wide-ranging attention to the whole Bible.

    b. Preaching has tended to be evangelistic in focus.

    c. Preaching has been done in a communal voice.

d. Preaching has been important and prominent in worship.

e. Preaching has emerged from within the congregation.

f. Preaching has a strong ethical component.

4. Greiser summarizes his review of Anabaptist-related preaching by suggesting that the "Anabaptist tradition deserves to be a conversation partner with the thinking and writing in the broader homiletical world." What is your response to this suggestion? What can the Anabaptist tradition add to the discussion with other preaching traditions? What impulses from other traditions could Anabaptist preaching benefit from?

Chapter 2: Michael A. King
WEAVING ENCHANTMENT

1. King is "convinced" that Brian McLaren is correct in his observation that Western Culture is moving to "the other side" of the modern era. King wants to "teach and preach" this new reality with authority and conviction; Sunday school member William provides a skeptical counter-point. With whom do you identify most closely in this exchange? Why?

2. According to King, preaching is done with an authority not found in speaking or conversing. Where does the preacher gain this authority? How is this authority tested? Does Anabaptism offer a perspective on this question? Does authority in the pulpit have primarily an objective or subjective basis?

3. King suggests that "weaving enchantment" is the key to preaching in a postmodern age. He notes that storytelling—an ancient art form—has gained fresh attention in the new era. In what other ways do premodernity and postmodernity share similar features?

4. Discuss King's distinction between "understanding seeking faith" (modernity) and "faith seeking understanding" (postmodernity). How helpful is this attempt to frame these different modes of theology?

5. Drawing on Brueggeman, King proposes that a.) reality is scripted; b.) as Brueggeman puts it, "The preacher traffics in a fiction that makes true"; and c.) the right script for the preacher to use in "making true" is provided by the Bible. If Brueggeman as cited by King is correct, how might this shape preaching? Does it give preaching more or less power than if it were not true? What are dangers of this view?

5. What do you make of King's proposed hermeneutic for preaching that combines exegesis and eisegesis? What does exegesis offer the preacher studying the biblical text? What potential does eisegesis bring to the hermeneutical task? What are the pitfalls for preaching in each method? What is your assessment of the "demon possession" example he describes?

6. King raises the possibility that postmodernity may open the door to a "golden age" for the church's proclamation and experience Jesus Christ. Do you share his hopefulness? Why or why not?

Chapter 3: Nancy Heisey
PREMODERN TEXT TO POSTMODERN EARS

1. Which is *not* a characteristic of postmodernity described by Heisey?

    a. reality is viewed as more complex and less mechanical;

    b. religious meaning has ceased to be understood;

    c. human beings are not defined by rationality;

    d. the link between cause and effect has become more unpredictable.

2. Why does the postmodern perspective offer "a more hopeful way to bring the Bible into conversation with the life of the church?"

3. What is the "dance" between three "worlds" that Heisey recommends? Why does she believe this method of biblical interpretation offers a better model than "throwing a bridge" across the gap between the world today and the world of the Bible?

4. Circle One, "The world before the text": Identify several life issues that your congregational members face. To what extent are the members of your faith community partners in the dance of interpretation? How do you respond to the call to converse with the Bible when it offers a picture that seems unjust or ungodly?

5. Circle Two, "The world of the text": Four skills were necessary for early Christian students of the Bible:

    a. textual criticism;

    b. reading the text out loud;

    c. interpretation, or exegesis;

    d. judgment.

Which receives most attention today? Which is short-changed?

6. Heisey suggests a plan of ten steps for getting into the world of the text. Are there other steps that commend themselves?

7. Why does Heisey believe it is important to consider the relationship between English versions and the original languages? And why is it best to begin with a personal encounter with the text rather than reference materials?

8. Circle Three, "The world behind the text": What are some the benefits and limitations of this historical-critical study for sermon preparation? What is meant by the Anabaptist "Christocentist" approach to biblical interpretation?

9. Heisey's dance-between-worlds metaphor is interactive rather than strictly sequential. Yet she seems to place an emphasis on the "world before the text." How does this priority affect the process of biblical interpretation?

Chapter 4: Mary Schertz
PREACHING AND THE BIBLE

1. By Schertz's definition, what is the heart of the preaching matter?

2. Schertz discusses what she believes people mean by "biblical preaching." What is your own definition? Schertz suggests that sermon length is "a central and crucial issue to biblical preaching." To what extent do you agree? Explain.

3. Schertz identifies four important goals achieved through canonical rambling:
   a. A range of biblical voices was heard, highlighting the various ways God has spoken.
   b. The Bible hung together in the "big picture" despite the diversity and contradictions. Its basic themes emerged.
   c. The lives of the faith community were to be in continuity with the biblical pattern.
   d. What factors does Schertz see as "shrinking" the dimensions of the relationship of church members with the biblical text?

4. What do you make of Schertz's claim that "We are in serious trouble in many respects both with the issues of biblical preaching and indeed the issues of living by the word of God at all?"

5. Why does simple "reading the text" become so important in Schertz's call to revive biblical preaching?

6. As Schertz suggests to her students, make a list of ten biblical texts "without which you cannot live." Share it with a group of others who also have a list. Talk about the texts you selected and why.

Chapter 5: Dawn Wilhelm
GOD'S WORD IN THE WORLD

1. Which of the following is *not* part of Wilhelm's definition of Anabaptist prophetic preaching?

_____ divinely inspired speech enlivened by the Holy Spirit;

_____ preaching that focuses on social justice topics;

_____ envisions past, present, and future concerns of God's reign;

_____ speech that is amid the gathered community.

2. To what extent do you agree with Wilhelm's definition of prophetic preaching? To what extent are you persuaded by her willingness to honor the "full range of prophetic expression"? What, if anything, gives you pause?

3. What are ways in which Anabaptist religious views and practices have stood in contrast to the dominant and political order? In what ways have Anabaptists realized this "historical formation and theological disposition" for the prophetic witness? How does this fit together with the convention of living as "the quiet in the land," still characteristic of many traditional Anabaptist groups?

4. Why does Wilhelm say "the passion of Christ is not only at the heart of the gospel, it is also essential to the prophetic impulse?"

5. Why is the "language of lament" crucial to prophetic voice in preaching, according to Wilhelm?

6. Why are the "promises of God" an essential element of prophetic preaching? How did Jesus refer to the promises of God as a source of recollection and anticipation for his hearers?

7. Which of the following are two homiletic concerns identified by Wilhelm that help point the way to new possibilities of God in prophetic preaching?

   a. understanding God's blueprint and timing for the consummation of history;

   b. provoking creative responses by the listeners;

   c. providing accurate cultural analysis and consciousness raising;

d. evoking alternative ways of imagining God's purposes at work in the church and world.

Chapter 6. David Stevens
THE FIRST COVENANT IN THE TWENTY-FIRST CENTURY

1. Stevens lifts out three challenges for preaching from the Old Testament:

   a. Hearing and proclaiming the text in its "own voice." What does he mean by this phrase?

   b. The legitimacy of a non-Christian Scripture for Christian preaching. Can we preach it in its Jewishness or should it be viewed as preparation for Jesus Christ?

   c. The bridge to the OT is even longer for us than to the NT. Why does this make the contemporary task of preaching more difficult?

2. Stevens cites "internal reasons" for preaching from the OT:

   a. Its theological pluralism. What value does that have for the preacher today?

   b. Its integration of theology and life, vertical and horizontal relationships. To what extent is this possible in a secular society?

   c. Its brutal honesty about life. What advantages does this have for preaching to present audiences?

   d. Its breadth of emotional color of the religious life. How might this emotional color affect today's sermon?

   e. Its powerful voice of self-criticism. How can preaching reflect self-criticism?

   f. Its picture of a passionate God of lavish grace and uncompromising demand. Does the New Testament offer a different vision of God? Explain.

Chapter 7: June Alliman Yoder
COLLABORATIVE PREACHING IN THE
COMMUNITY OF INTERPRETERS

1. After citing snippets of evidence about early Anabaptist worship, Yoder concludes, "It seems safe to say that for some sixteenth-century

Anabaptists, preaching was an interpretation of the Scripture that was followed by a response by one or more of the other gathered believers." What is your experience of such feedback?

2. Which of the following is *not* named as a factor that influenced change from "witness and discussion" to "monologue" preaching?

    a. Preaching has become ministerial "turf" to be protected.

    b. The notion that "doing your own work" is more respectable.

    c. Preachers move around more than they used to.

    d. The preacher has become the paid expert; others are relieved of the task.

    e. A concern for efficiency.

3. Yoder claims, "If we think of preaching as more conversational and dialogical, we will be reaching toward a more thorough understanding of what it can mean to be a priesthood of all believers as well as what it can mean to do public address well." What are the benefits of thinking of preaching as "more conversational and dialogical?"

4. Which of the following describes Yoder's preferred partnership between the Holy Spirit and the preacher?

    a. The partnership is a relationship that recognizes that neither the Holy Spirit nor the preacher can get the job done alone.

    b. The Spirit is in charge of the preaching event and the preacher deserves neither blame nor praise.

    c. The Holy Spirit is called on to fill in when the preacher feels inadequate.

5. Yoder is wary about electronic media making sermon preparation "easy?" What is the difference between "looking for fresh ingredients to make the sermon good, and looking for the thaw-n-serve dinner that makes sermon preparation easy?"

6. Yoder names a number of collaborative partners in the preaching task. Rank these according to the area in which you most want to grow.

    _____ Holy Spirit

    _____ Scripture text

    _____ Expert knowledge and opinions

    _____ Congregational analysis

    _____ Conversation with people in the church

    _____ The worship setting

7. What does Yoder mean by "Collaborative preaching . . . is not so much a style of preaching, as it is a way of viewing preaching"?

Chapter 8: Mark R. Wenger
THEOLOGICAL PREACHING IN AN AGE OF DOCTRINE LITE

1. To what extent do you agree with Wenger's diagnosis of the erosion of theological preaching in the Western Christian church? What do you make of his assertion that theological preaching "is not easy preaching?

2. Discuss the definitions offered for *theology, doctrine,* and *dogma.* Are these synonyms varying in "scale and scope," as Wenger proposes, or are there more basic distinctions between them? How do these terms ring in the ears of the typical contemporary preacher and listener?

3. In what ways, according to Wenger, do theology and doctrine function like a map? How helpful is this analogy to you? What other analogies might you offer to explain the place of doctrine and theology in preaching?

4. Which of the following, offered by Paul S. Wilson, is *not* one of the methodological helps from systematic theology for preaching theologically?

    a. Identify as clearly as possible your own theological method or approach.

    b. Choose one major systematic theologian to work with consistently.

    c. Keep God in the center of the sermon rather than at the periphery.

    d. Test the logical consequences of any doctrinal position taken.

5. Wenger speaks of "ancient and always new" and "new ways of looking at old pathways to God." To what extent is the preacher a discoverer and reframer of theology, and to what extent a creator or designer?

6. According to Wenger, why should the preacher never set out "to preach without careful attention to the biblical text," especially for sermons with an explicit theological focus?

7. In what sense is "preaching theologically" the same as "doing local theology?" To what extent may such preaching also be conceived as having universal import?

8. Wenger suggests several "case studies from contemporary experience" that lend themselves to doctrinal/theological preaching. What other situations of contemporary human experience can be used in the same manner and for what particular theological point?

9. Why does Wenger stress the connection between theological preaching and theological living?

Chapter 9: Nathan Showalter
PREACHING IN MULTICULTURAL CONTEXTS

1. "Preaching in a multicultural context is about sharing God's message in the heart language of our hearers." Why has that been an important objective in the Christian faith tradition?

2. Take a moment to analyze the cultural fabric of your congregation. What cultures are represented? What other cultures are represented within a five-mile radius of the church building?

3. Into how many languages has the Bible or portions thereof been translated? Do you agree with Showalter's assessment that the "next Christendom" will be largely influenced by the southern hemisphere? Why or why not?

4. "Preaching to a multicultural audience is done in the context of the new song the Spirit gives to people of various tribes and nations. . . . The sermon is always set in the context of the new song, the sign that God's Spirit is translating the message into the heart languages of the people." Do you find Showalter's metaphor of "new song" helpful in understanding preaching in multicultural settings? Explain.

5. What are techniques Showalter suggests for bringing the multicultural dimension of the Scripture to the fore in an illuminating way?

6. "When preaching in a multicultural context we will affirm the cultures of our audience, while still offering an encounter with the God who creates and renews culture." Evaluate this assertion.

7. "The preacher in a multicultural context is always a storyteller." Showalter advocates telling Jesus' parables so that audiences experience a "dynamic equivalent" of the first century story. Try to create examples for: The Good Samaritan, The Workers in the Vineyard, The Lost Coin.

8. In the postmodern context, what are the shifts preachers must make, according to Leonard Sweet, if they want to communicate with the "natives" in this new culture?

From *rational* to _____.

From *representative* to _____.

From *word-driven* to _____.

From *individualistic* to _____.

Chapter 10: Lynn Yost
Preaching for a Hearing

1. Jost contends that David Buttrick and Anabaptist preaching share a compatibility. Which of the following is *not* one of them?

a. Orthopraxy takes priority over orthodoxy.

b. Scripture is the final authority in matters of faith and practice.

c. The heart of Jesus' Good News message focuses on the kingdom of God.

d. It is important for sermons to function within a social or community unit.

2. "Preaching is the work of metaphor. Preaching uses images to bring God's Word into the view of the congregation." As a simple exercise in metaphor, complete the following sentence with a variety of images: "When you are part of the church of Jesus Christ, you are part of _____.

3. According to Buttrick, cited by Jost, "Language constitutes our world by _____ , and confers identity in the world by _____."

4. A "move" is Buttrick's way of speaking of single language module involving a concept of simple meaning. A move is made up of three subsets:

- theological definition, a simple statement of meaning;
- the use of metaphor, examples and illustrations;
- the lived experience.

Why is it important for a "move" to begin with repetition? What is the purpose of the metaphorical aspect of a "move?" How is the lived experience different from a series of practical applications?

6. "The moves are joined together in a logical sequence that acts like a conversation. The result is a series of murals that form on the screen of congregational consciousness." How might this view affect specific aspects of preaching?

7. Which of the following, according to Jost, does not help a move reach the big screen of social consciousness?

a. two ideas are combined for synergy and variety;

b. a clear closure to the move;

c. the use of image and symbol;

d. reflection on how the ideas connect to audience's lived experience.

8. Movement in a sermon is an important rhetorical principle. Where does movement occur in the model recommended by Buttrick and Jost?

Chapter 11: Renee Sauder
NARRATIVE PREACHING

1. Why does Sauder make such a point about "remembering" as an act of faith? What connection does this have with narrative preaching?

2. Narrative preaching, says Sauder, is especially effective because we find "intersections between our own life and the lives of the characters in the biblical story." Think of a favorite Bible story. What makes it meaningful to you?

3. Name some of the benefits and limitations of narrative preaching. For what tasks is narrative preaching best suited? For what task is it least well suited?

4. Which of the following is cited by Sauder as sources for narrative preaching?
   a. Stories of people in the Old Testament and New Testament;
   b. the preacher's own life story;
   c. fables or collections of mythological tales;
   d. non-biblical stories from life;
   e. Jesus' own example with parable
   f. composite stories drawn from several places.

5. How much imagination can be inserted into the storytelling of a Bible story and still retain the integrity of the account?

Chapter 12: Rebecca Slough
ACTING THE WORD

1. The New Testament identifies two kinds of audience for preaching done by Jesus and the apostles:
   a. public proclamation to non-believers, and
   b. teaching internal to the believing Christian community.

What percentage of your own preaching or that of others fits into each category? What are the differences between them?

2. Hughes Oliphant Old names five enduring types of preaching:
   expository;

evangelistic;

catechetical;

festive;

prophetic.

Which type, if any, tends to dominate in Anabaptist circles? In contrast, which type generally receives the least attention and use? What does that say about the chief concerns of Anabaptist preaching?

3. These basic actions of worship are present regardless of the style of worship:

- gathering;
- praising;
- adoring;
- thanking;
- confessing sin;
- proclaiming Scripture;
- affirming faith;

- offering;
- petitioning;
- interceding;
- testifying;
- blessing;
- sending.

Reflect on the worship in your congregation. Which three of the above actions get the most attention? The least?

4. Summarize the main features of the following patterns of worship:

a. synagogue pattern;

b. service of the Word;

c. frontier worship pattern;

d. renewed "liturgical" pattern.

Which pattern holds sway in your congregation? What attempts, if any, have you made to blend them?

7. What are some of the reasons for the perceived tension between purposes of worship and those of preaching? What might be the remedies to reintegrate preaching and worship?

Chapter 13: Dennis Hollinger:
THE ETHICS OF PERSUASION IN PREACHING

1. Preaching as an act of persuasion carries ethical risks. Communication ethics has usually attempted to make judgments based on the following:

a. the ends sought, also called _____, or;

b. the means used.

Hollinger suggests that one of the best ways to analyze ethics in preaching is through the lens of _____.

2. According to Stephen Carter, cited by Hollinger, which of the following are the three steps necessary for integrity:
- discerning what is right and what is wrong;
- acting on what you have decided, even at personal cost;
- weighing the situation and its unique circumstances;
- saying openly that you are acting on your understanding of right from wrong.

3. *Integrity and the Preacher:* Why does Hollinger stress that "personal character and integrity of the preaching must always be the starting point for an ethic of persuasion in preaching?" What relative merit do competence and character carry in assessing effectiveness of preaching?

4. *Integrity and the Message:* "A message that has integrity and is truthful or trustworthy generally means two things: it is accurate and complete." Which of the following practices does Hollinger suggest may distort the message?
   a. borrowing from the sacred texts of other religions;
   b. telling personal stories where confidentiality or facts are breached;
   c. using statistics loosely;
   d. composing fables and fictional illustrations;
   e. understating the radical or counter-cultural elements of the gospel story;
   f. employing "God and country" political rhetoric;
   g. employing media not fitting the message;
   h. citing misleading data and supporting material;
   i. exaggerating the gospel or claims of biblical texts;
   j. drawing attention to oneself as a model believer.

5. What additional message distortions have you witnessed?

6. *Integrity and the Receiver:* "In the Christian worldview every human being in the audience is a person of dignity and value, having been made in the image of God. Thus, the messenger, medium and message must guard that dignity and value—the integrity of the person." Discuss the dangers of emotionalism, crowd pressure, personal charisma, or other forms of audience manipulation by a preacher.

Chapter 14: Ervin Stutzman:
PREACHING GRACE TO HARDWORKING PEOPLE

1. What is Stutzman's thesis? Try to state it in a sentence or two.

2. In early Anabaptist writing "the gracious initiative of God is rarely discussed without an equal (or greater) emphasis on the need for human response." What kind of preaching resulted? What were its emphases? To what extent are these emphases still present today?

3. Stutzman contends that contemporary Mennonite theology may fool preachers into overestimating human initiative and undervaluing God's transforming grace. What evidence does he cite? To what extent does this ring true to your own observations?

4. What are the specific suggestions Stutzman offers to enhance the place of God's grace in Anabaptist preaching?

5. The sermon is not simply words about God. The preaching event, properly conceived, is an act of God's grace.

> "People may experience ungrace when we consistently emphasize
> duty over _____,
> rules over _____,
> sacrifice over _____, and
> human responsibility over _____."

6. Take a sermon you recently preached or heard. Evaluate the emphasis it gave to grace and judgment, divine generosity and human responsibility. What was the balance between these elements?

GENERAL QUESTIONS

1. What thematic threads run through all of the essays in the book? How do these threads give insight regarding Anabaptist preaching?

2. Pick two or three of the essays and put their authors into an imaginary conversation with each other. What new insights emerge?

3. Which of the essays, if any, produced an "aha" moment, a sense of clarity or a sense of urgency for you? Write a brief paragraph about it.

4. Which of the essays seem to probe the most uniquely Anabaptist theology or habits of preaching?

5. What unique aspect of Anabaptist or Mennonite preaching is not discussed in any of these essays? Explain.

6. Which of the essays , if any, produced a sense of dismay or disagreement? Explain.

7. If you are a preacher, to what extent do you consider yourself an Anabaptist preacher? In what ways do you resist the label?

8. Imagine a dialogue between the authors of this text and preachers from a tradition other than Anabaptism. What are the points of agreement? Disagreement?

9. If you are a preacher, analyze a recent sermon using the criteria set forth by one or more of the essays in the book. What new insights emerge for you?

10. In what ways, if any, will your preaching be changed by your experience of reading this book? In what new ways do you view a sermon?

The Index

Ordination, 109
Origen, 49
Orthopraxy, 148
Oyer, John S., 20

P

Parables and preaching, 85, 88-89,
    141, 143, 200-201, 210
Pasquali, Antonio, 195
Pathos in speaking, 186-197
Pentecost, 137, 138
Performance, preaching as, 50
Peterson, Eugene, 132
Pietism, Anabaptist, 21-22
Points of attachment, 61, 62
Postmodernism, 33, 44, 48, 122, 144,
    208
    Postmodern preaching and the
    Old Testament, 95, 103
Prayer and preaching, 54, 100, 208-209
    personal devotions, 66
Preaching
    biblical, 61
    catechetical, 122, 173
    dialogue preaching, 109-110
    and doctrine, 96
    evangelistic, 18, 173, 178
    expository, 173
    festive preaching, 173
    from manuscript, 18
    Holy Spirit in, 113-114, 119,
        129, 186
    humility and, 18
    imagination in, 89
    as lament, 86, 87
    monologue preaching, 110, 111
    pastoral preaching, 83
    from Paul, 131
    politics and, 100
    promises of God and, 87-88
    and Protestants, 19
    Psalms and, 86, 98

Puritan plain style, 123
professionalism in, 110, 111
from Proverbs, 100
role of the congregation, 11
and seminary education, 72
and social justice, 76-77, 99
synagogue preaching, 172, 176
Priesthood of believers, 109
Prophetic preaching, 85-90
    defined, 77, 173
    in community, 81

Q

Quintilian, 188
Quotations, use in sermons, 153

R

Radical Reformation, 49
Redaction criticism, 64
Rhetoric, 188-189
    defined, 188
    Paul's use of, 194
    rhetorical strategy, 17
Robinson, Wayne, 166
Rose, Lucy Atkinson, 117
Roundtable preaching, 117

S

Schneiders, Sandra M., 55
"Scripted reality," 37, 45
Seminary education for preachers, 24
Sermons
    collections of, 21-22, 100
    delivery of, 25, 62
    illustrations in, 61
    length of, 62-63
    narrative, 67
    preparation of, 63, 99, 109-119
    topical, 67, 73, 74

The Contributors

Nancy R. Heisey, Harrisonburg, Virginia, is joined in her commitment to love God and neighbor by her husband, Paul Longacre. They have two adult daughters and two beautiful granddaughters. Nancy grew up as a Brethren in Christ missionary kid among Navajo people. She is a graduate of Messiah College, Eastern Mennonite Seminary, and Temple University. Heisey teaches New Testament and church history at Eastern Mennonite University and is current chair of the Bible and Religion Department. Heisey is President of Mennonite World Conference, a global family of Mennonite and Brethren in Christ churches.

Dennis Hollinger, Camp Hill, Pennsylvania, is Vice Provost and College Pastor as well as Professor of Christian Ethics at Messiah College. Before coming to Messiah in 1997, he served as pastor of the Washington Community Fellowship in Washington, D.C. For eleven years he was a full-time seminary professor and over the years has done short-term international seminary teaching in India, Russia, and Ukraine. Hollinger is the author of over fifty articles and two books, most recently *Choosing the Good: Christian Ethics in a Complex World* (Baker Academic, 2002). He has a Ph.D. from Drew University in Religion and Society and an M.Div. from Trinity Evangelical Divinity School. Hollinger is coeditor for the Eerdmans' series, Critical Issues in Bioethics, is a Fellow with the Center for Bioethics and Human Dignity, and sits on the Health Care Ethics Committee at Holy Spirit Hospital. Hollinger and his wife, Mary Ann, have two daughters.

Franklyn "Lynn" Jost, Hillsboro, Kansas, graduated with a B.A. from Tabor College, an M.Div. from Mennonite Brethren Biblical Seminary, and an M.A. and Ph.D. in homiletics and Hebrew Bible from

Vanderbilt University. He was pastor of the Hesston Mennonite Brethren Church from 1982-1990, has taught biblical and religious studies at Tabor College since 1990, and is currently the chair of the humanities division. He was chair of the North American Board of Faith and Life and its task force that produced the 1999 Canadian and US Mennonite Brethren Confession of Faith and currently chairs the US BFL. Lynn and his wife, Donna, are parents of a daughter and a son.

Renée Sauder, Kitchener, Ontario, graduated with an M.Div. from Associated Mennonite Biblical Seminary in Elkhart, Indiana, and went on to serve as a pastor of the Bethel College Mennonite Church, North Newton, Kansas; and Erb Street Mennonite, Church, Waterloo, Ontario. The stories of these faith communities have inspired her sermons and nurtured her love of preaching over the last twenty years.

Mary H. Schertz, Elkhart, Indiana, is professor of New Testament at Associated Mennonite Biblical Seminary in Elkhart. She received her Ph.D. from Vanderbilt University and has been happily occupied teaching Greek and New Testament for the past fifteen years. She co-authored *Seeing the Text: Exegesis for Students of Greek and Hebrew* (Abingdon, 2001) with Perry B. Yoder. She is a member of Assembly Mennonite Church in Goshen.

Nathan D. Showalter, Mount Joy, Pennsylvania, enjoys preaching as a pastor, bishop, and church planter, serving most recently as overseer and director of leadership development with Lancaster (Pa.) Mennonite Conference. He has preached in multicultural congregations in North America and Asia, and for eight years was senior pastor of Taipei (Taiwan) International Church. He has helped start more than a dozen new congregations, including a Filipino congregation in Taiwan. Showalter also worked as a communications specialist with World Vision International, collaborating with World Vision staff on six continents. A graduate of Eastern Mennonite University (B.A.), Fuller Theological Seminary (M.A.), Lancaster Theological Seminary (M.Div.), and Harvard University (Th.D.), he is author of "The End of a Crusade: The Student Volunteer for Foreign Missions and the Great War" (1990). Showalter's wife Christina was born in China and their son Eli born in Hong Kong.

Rebecca Slough, Elkhart, Indiana, is Associate Professor of Worship and the Arts at Associated Mennonite Biblical Seminary. She holds an M.Div. from AMBS, an M.A. in liturgical studies from the University of Notre Dame, and a Ph.D. from the Graduate Theological Union.